IT'S JUST ME!

STORIES OF A LIFE IN A CHANGING WORLD

It's Just Me!

Stories Of A Life In A Changing World

Konrad Brinck

TAMARIND TREE BOOKS
Toronto

Inquiries should be addressed to:

Tamarind Tree Books Inc.,
14 Ferncastle Crescent,
Brampton, Ontario. L47 3P2, Canada.

or

Konrad Brinck,
30 Parkside Drive,
Brampton, Ontario, L6Y 2G9, Canada.

Library and Archives Canada Cataloguing in Publication

Brinck, Konrad, 1946-, author
It's just me : stories of a life in a changing world / Konrad Brinck.

ISBN 978-0-9938199-2-6 (pbk.)

1. Brinck, Konrad, 1946-. 2. Germans--Ontario--Toronto--Biography. 3. Sales personnel--Ontario--Toronto--Biography. 4. Toronto (Ont.)--Biography. I. Title.

FC3097.9.G3B75 2014 971.3'54100431 C2014-906615-5

This book is manufactured under Sustainable Forestry Initiative® (SFI®) Certified Sourcing.

To the four women in my life:
my wife Jackie and our daughter Toni who made my life worth writing about and granddaughters Ivy and Kenley, without whom there would have been no need to write it.

Contents

FOREWORD		XI
A FEW MORE WORDS...		XIII
INTRODUCTION		XV
Chapter 1 :	The Beginning	17
Chapter 2 :	Mother	20
Chapter 3 :	Father	24
Chapter 4 :	Uncles & Aunts	
	Aunt Hanna	30
	Uncle Fritz	32
	Aunt Herta	34
	Uncle Karl	35
Chapter 5 :	My Two Uncle Willies	
	Uncle Willie in Potsdam	38
	Uncle Willie in Ebstorf	42
Chapter 6 :	Growing Up Amongst The Ruins	46
Chapter 7 :	A Childhood Christmas In Berlin	51
Chapter 8 :	Home, Sweet Home	58
	Our Neighbours	60
Chapter 9 :	My 10th Birthday	70
Chapter 10 :	Pranks	74
Chapter 11 :	Recycling, Berlin Style	78
Chapter 12 :	My School Years	
	Karl Weise Public School - 1953-1959	80
	Ernst Abbe High School - 1959-1962	84
Chapter 13 :	A Boy And His Dog	88
Chapter 14 :	Television	93
Chapter 15 :	My Sporting Life	
	Soccer, Rowing & Boxing	97
	Baseball, Hockey, Skiing & Golf	101
Chapter 16 :	What Was He Thinking?	106
Chapter 17 :	Who Were They?	112
Chapter 18 :	The Berlin Wall	
	Caged Inside The City	116
	Symbol Of Freedom & Resistance	119

Contents

Chapter 19 :	The Apprenticeship	124
Chapter 20 :	Rosie	127
Chapter 21 :	Leaving The Nest	131
Chapter 22 :	Fun And Turmoil In Berlin	136
Chapter 23 :	A New Challenge!	141
Chapter 24 :	Welcome To Canada	145
Chapter 25 :	Jobs, Jobs, Jobs!	152
Chapter 26 :	Love At First Sight	159
Chapter 27 :	A Tale Of Two Friendships	163
Chapter 28 :	Life With A Girlfriend	166
Chapter 29 :	Love, Lust And Happiness	
	The Commute	170
	Learning To Live Together	171
Chapter 30 :	The Party	175
Chapter 31 :	Road To The Altar	
	The Proposal	179
	Planning The Wedding	180
	The Wedding	183
Chapter 32 :	Hospital Horror	186
Chapter 33 :	Two Different Worlds	
	Germany	191
	South Africa	194
Chapter 34 :	Planning A Career In Sales	205
Chapter 35 :	Commercial Union Assurance Company	208
Chapter 36 :	Olivetti: 1971-1978	213
	The DeFillippo Incident	219
Chapter 37 :	Pitney Bowes: 1978-1983	222
Chapter 38 :	O/E Canon: 1983-2001	
	The Early Years 1983-1986	227
	The Management Years 1986- 1990	230
	The Turbulent Road To Retirement 1990-2001	231
Chapter 39 :	The Penis Trilogy	
	The Unwanted Erection	238
	No Toy For A Pussy	240
	The Sperm Test	241
Chapter 40 :	Camping, A Return To Nature	244
	Sharky And The Bear	246
	Other Adventures	248

Contents

Chapter 41 :	The Blue Monster	255
	Shake, Rattle And Roll That Tire Down The Road!	257
	The Death Of The Blue Monster	263
Chapter 42 :	The In-Laws Are Coming!	268
Chapter 43 :	What The Heck, Let's Buy That House!	275
	Moving Day	277
Chapter 44 :	Joy And Happiness	280
Chapter 45 :	Mom Versus Granny	285
Chapter 46 :	Toni's Big Adventure	288
Chapter 47 :	Memories Of A European Family Vacation	
	Linguistic Adventures	292
	Guess Who Was Watching Us	294
	Epilogue	298
Chapter 48 :	Death And Dying In Berlin	300
Chapter 49 :	A Perfect Neighbourhood	320
Chapter 50 :	The VV's	329
Chapter 51 :	Toni's Big Announcement	334
Chapter 52 :	Journey Into The Unknown	338
Chapter 53 :	The Final Chapter?	342

Foreword

"It's Just Me!" is a most understated title, implying by the "just" that this is a conventional tale of an average person. It's anything but!

The people within this book are survivors of war, imprisonment, racism ... the outrageous tragedies that occur when evil is allowed to flourish. It's a coming-of-age book in an era that put ordinary people into extraordinary circumstances.

Perhaps they are "ordinary" in the sense that they were simply trying to lead regular lives, but they are heroes in the way they responded, protested, and tried to be decent human beings amid the vestiges of despicable misuses of power.

Not only does Konrad Brinck present vivid characters, he does so with a humorous voice that provides an almost innocent view of horrific events. Except with the hindsight of history, the majority of us have this view — we are simply trying to live our lives with love and optimism.

Sprinkled throughout the book, therefore, are many hilarious events, the kind that we all might experience. Those funny memories stay with us because even years later, we can laugh at our antics or marvel at how truly innocent or silly we were. We can relate to the follies of youth! If you don't have too many memories like that, borrow Konrad's. His are priceless.

Themes of regret, growing up, marriage, relationships and growing old are all wrapped in touching or humorous anecdotes.

You will also thoroughly enjoy this book's insights, optimism, portrayals of love, passion and conviction. As Konrad grows from a boy to a man, he gives us an overview of a world that is often frightening and cruel, but where love, generosity and understanding can prevail.

Catherine Astolfo
Arthur Ellis Award-Winning Author
January, 2015

A Few More Words...

Konrad Brinck's memoir grabs the reader's attention right from page one with just the word, "Dora!" Who is she?

This hard-to-put-down book about Konrad's boyhood in post-war Germany and his struggles and triumphs as an immigrant in Canada reads like a war story at times; like a painful comment on racism at other points; and in some places like the humorous goings-on in an adventure movie - riveting all the way through!

Konrad's enduring love for his mother and their quest for a normal life in the bizarre and treacherous post-Reich world is brought to life for the reader in most personal ways. Things like the compulsory sterilization of a member of his family, the helplessness of people forced into serving rulers whose principles they did not share and the post-war revenge against Germans for atrocities committed by the Nazis that devastated German families. The Communists, adding a further blow, then expropriated their properties.

Yet Konrad describes his family's resilience and their post-war life in an apartment surrounded by bombed-out buildings and neighbours who are fascinating, funny, sometimes weird and surprisingly normal.

Konrad displays a beautifully flowing use of language and humour as the story sweeps the reader from continent to continent. But, he also asks tough questions like: "How could six million people have been slaughtered and nobody knew? Who and where were these Germans today? Where were the people that ordered, executed, assisted, knew, collaborated, promoted and justified these murderous crimes? Was everybody living in denial during and after the Third Reich?"

He struggles to reconcile what he knew about the good people with whom he grew up and the unknown faces of a murderous regime in such lines as: "I often looked down from our balcony and watched people walking by thinking, 'Were any of them involved?' When I walked the streets I looked at people and wondered how many had participated in the slaughter? How many people does it take to kill millions? It can't just be a handful, there must be thousands of them walking around with blood on their hands."

Konrad's immigrant experiences in Toronto were also tainted by the realization that racism exists everywhere. When he does fall in love and marries a beautiful, non-white, South African woman he is further exposed to the heartbreaks inflicted by an apartheid regime deeply rooted in the principles of Aryan supremacy. But he and his wife build a life in Canada with their attractive and talented daughter, her serendipitous gift to them of grandchildren and his sense of humour about painful personal mishaps, parenting adventures and the power games of the business world.

Konrad's intuitive and perceptive nature, combined with his gift of story-telling, makes this a must-read memoir.

Vicki Bismilla
Educator / Author
January, 2015

Introduction

The idea to write my memoirs came to me during a recent trip to Germany.

I was amazed how little I knew about my mother's and father's families and the world they grew up in. I felt sad that so much of their lives remains untold and would be lost forever.

I believed that I should preserve some of my family history, a history that shaped many of my values and personality traits and made me the person I am today. I am recording this for my daughter Toni and her children, Ivy and Kenley, but hope that others can also enjoy the stories and thoughts in this book.

The events written about are true but may have been altered to protect the privacy of certain people. Some stories have been slightly embellished to make them more entertaining, while others are compilations of many events.

When I started this project, I wondered how I could make an ordinary life like mine sound exciting.

I found out that my perception of my life was totally wrong. I became more aware of the fact that I had, and still have, an exciting and rewarding life with lots of stories to tell.

I was blessed with great parents, a loving wife and a daughter to be proud of. I am thankful to have two grandchildren that keep giving my wife and me so much joy in our retirement years.

Digging into my memories has brought back many episodes I had almost forgotten about. This trip down memory lane has made me get in touch with relatives and old friends to research and verify the anecdotes I was writing about and made us reminisce about the good times we had. It made me realize how many good decisions I've made over the years and how few mistakes there are to regret. I am happy to have made many friends over the years. I don't know who said 'I don't regret any of the chances I took in my life but only the ones I didn't take.' But I wholeheartedly agree with him.

I hope you enjoy the stories of my family and myself travelling through time and laugh or shed a tear as you follow on the journey that was and is my life.

I would like to thank the two women in my life, my wife Jackie and my daughter Toni, who worked many hours helping me to put this book together with their superior knowledge of the English language.

I dedicate this book to them and my granddaughters. They were and continue to be my inspiration and without them my life would have been empty.

Konrad Brinck
Brampton, ON
January, 2015

Chapter 1

The Beginning

I have never met Dora and don't know what she looked like, but she is the main reason for me being born into this world.

Nobody in our family ever talked about Dora. I became aware of her existence only after my father's death, when my mother confided in me about her not-always picture-perfect marriage to my father.

I have often thought of my father sitting in a cold and dark barrack, barely lit by the midnight sun in northern Norway where he was stationed during WWII. He wrote regularly to my mother and she was always looking forward to his loving words and shared his desire to be back in each other's arms again.

When she received another letter in the summer of 1944, expressing these sentiments and declaring his undying love for her, there was only one problem. It wasn't addressed to her, but to a woman named Dora. My mother had no idea who Dora was, but it became clear to her that she was my father's mistress and that she had received the letter meant for Dora.

The approaching British planes, the twilight of the midnight sun, the rush to take up positions at the anti-aircraft guns or quickly trying to get his letters into the army post box, who knows what caused this momentary lapse in attention. Anybody could have switched the letters with the envelopes by mistake.

Just a dumb mistake! But it surely changed everybody's life.

My mother must have been in shock when she read that my father had the same feelings for this other woman that he had expressed for her. She waited for him to return home from the front to end their marriage and start a new life without him.

Could she perhaps find a way to forgive him? Would he show any remorse and want to continue a life together?

My mother had to wait for almost a year to confront my father. The mixed feelings and uncertainty took a big toll on her life. The long nights, sitting in the bomb shelter in Berlin while bombs rained over the city, gave her lots of time to contemplate her future if she and her husband should survive this war.

My father didn't return until June of 1945, after having been a POW for a short time. He feared the scene and confrontation that was waiting for him. He had a whole year to prepare for it and must have gone over it in his mind again and again.

Dora let him know that she received the letter addressed to my mother, and, according to my father, stopped the affair immediately. She was shocked to learn that there was a Mrs Brinck waiting for his return.

There is one thing I inherited from my father, his persuasive nature along with the gift of the gab.

I have no idea what he said to my mother and how much begging he had to do but he succeeded in making her forgive him for his indiscretion. My mother was a very forgiving and loving person but she insisted on one thing to continue her life with him, a child.

My parents had long given up on the idea of having another child after their first son, Harry, born in 1932 with a heart defect, lived only for 5 weeks, after doctors failed to save him.

A second child was stillborn in 1936, and my parents gave up hope of ever experiencing the joys of parenthood. They agreed to live a life as a couple, devoted to each other and find happiness outside the confines of parenthood to avoid further heartbreaks.

My parents - happy times.

Dora changed all that. They agreed to try one more time to have a child to cement a marriage that was in trouble.

My mother soon got pregnant and I was born in July of 1946. I certainly kept my part of the bargain by keeping them together for the rest of their lives.

I hope to have given them what they were looking for, happiness!

I would like to thank Dora but I don't think she is still alive or ever knew that her affair with a young German soldier ended up in making a family happy, thus, making her responsible for the existence of a pretty terrific human being.

Me!

Chapter 2

Mother

They say that mothers have a special bond with their sons.

I can't disagree!

My mother was no 'Iron Lady' with a Prussian sense of discipline and stern rules. She loved, spoiled, taught, guided and would have sacrificed herself for me. *Mutti* (Mom) lived her life for me.

I was her everything.

Mother was born Hedwig Bertha Louise Kluck on March 22, 1913 as the eighth and last child of Friedrich and Emilia Kluck.

She never really knew her father. He died in WWI during the Battle of Verdun in 1916. Her mother had to bring up her seven surviving children on a widow's pension. They lived in a lower working class tenement on the ground floor in a back building where the sun never shone through the windows of their one bedroom apartment. Her mother made sure that all of them received a good education but higher education was unattainable.

My mother promised herself that her children would not experience a life of poverty and despair.

What a life I had growing up!

I didn't have to clean my room, pick up after myself or do household chores. Anything I wanted, needed or wished for was mine if possible. No daycare or kindergarten for me, Mother was there for me, always. The one thing she didn't teach me was independence.

I was a real Mama's Boy.

She had difficulty giving up control and letting me grow up.

School, however, changed everything!

I had to fight to be able to go to school without her holding my hand and she would still watch me from a distance as my friends Martin, Kalle, Horst and I sauntered off in the morning. Mother would be there, 50 meters behind us to give me the illusion of not being watched. She also made sure I got home in the afternoon. It was only grudgingly that she accepted me becoming a boy who could look after himself. I think she stopped stalking me after the first semester.

My father had a good job, and we were better off than most families in our neighbourhood. There was always enough money to buy me good clothes, toys and treats. All I had to do was ask for them and she would get them, even if she had to sacrifice her own needs.

I became very popular amongst the kids in my age group. I had the best toys and enough of them to share with others and Mom always had some goodies to give them when they came up to play with me in our apartment.

My mother would do my homework so that I would have more time to play. She was able to copy my handwriting perfectly. She would go over my lessons with me to make sure I knew and understood the subject and then she would do all the writing.

As I grew older, I noticed that my mother had this need to help others and sacrifice herself in the process. She needed to be needed, wanted and loved. This compulsion to spoil and pamper was not limited to me, she also extended it to relatives, friends and even my dog.

She never asked for anything in return and never preached, but never understood that she needed people more than they needed her. She was not overbearing or controlling, but I believe she enjoyed the satisfaction of having helped others and loved it when people appreciated her assistance.

My best friend Kalle came from a broken home and my mother took him under her wing. He had many meals at our place and, since he was smaller than me, received a lot of my clothes. During our early teen years, he got jobs on weekends or after school, delivering magazines, setting up bowling pins or distributing fliers. He asked me to join him.

I begged my parents for permission to let me work with him and make some money. My mother never understood why I wanted to work because, according to her, I had everything. She was willing to raise my weekly allowance if I needed more money. She was concerned that the neighbours might think I had to work out of necessity.

My mother cared a lot about others and the phrase *'what will the neighbours think'* was often heard around our house.

When I started High School, my mother went back to work again over the objections of my father who believed he should be the only breadwinner in the family.

I broke my mother's heart the first time I left home. After my apprenticeship, I left to work in West Germany. I had to prove to myself that I could survive without my mother.

I quickly learned that I was ill-prepared for the real world. Laundry, ironing, cooking and good housekeeping were not skills my mother had taught me.

When I returned home eight months later, I gladly accepted her mothering and spoiling. By not having any responsibilities at home, she was giving me a life of pleasure and freedom.

She didn't think I was exploiting her because I could do no wrong. However, if she thought she was being taken advantage of by anybody, her attitude would change.

Mother was never confrontational or carried a grudge, but she would be less friendly and withdrawn until the problem or misunderstanding was ironed out.

She was not shy and would tell people if she was annoyed or bothered by something, but she always tried to avoid hostilities at any cost. My feelings of guilt were unbelievable when I told her in the fall of 1967 that I was immigrating to Canada. She was in denial for a long time. I saw my mother become withdrawn and suffer emotionally over the next nine months as she realized she would lose her only son, after having lost her husband just two years earlier to a brain tumour.

I told her I would spend only two years in Canada and return if things didn't meet my expectations. However, she must have known that I was not going to come home again.

She never showed her sorrow. After I left in July of 1968, she devoted her life to looking after my aunt 'Tante Hanna', joined Caritas, a faith-based provider of health care as a volunteer caregiver and had always more than one iron in the fire to validate her life.

We wrote to each other every week and I called as often as I could. Back in those days, a call to Germany cost a fortune. We saw each other at least once a year, with her coming to Canada or me visiting Germany with my wife Jackie.

It was my marriage in 1970 that made my mother realize that I was not coming back, but the joy she experienced as a grandmother in her last 12 years gave her a new purpose in life. There are many stories to tell about this period in her life. Our frequent visits, vacations and travels with her granddaughter Toni made those years more enjoyable than she could ever have imagined.

In 1985, we celebrated her last Christmas together in Berlin.

She was just a shadow of her former self, having suffered her second heart attack earlier that year. I think we all knew this was the last goodbye when we left for home early in the new year.

Mom had her third heart attack in February of 1986, six weeks after our visit. I was not able to reach Germany in time, to be with her in her last hours. My good friend Annemarie, who was with her in those last minutes, told me later that she called out my name as she took her final breath. It broke my heart!

Chapter 3

Father

I never cried for my father.

When he died at the age of 53, on Easter Monday 1966, I almost felt relief. Little did I know why Papa (Dad) as I called him, was such a changed man from the father I adored in earlier years.

My father was born Kurt Erich Arthur Brinck on August 20, 1912 in Berlin, the second son of Martha and Richard Brinck.

Martha divorced Richard shortly after my father's birth and I don't believe that my father knew or remembered his father at all. He did not talk about him nor did anybody else in the family. All I know is that he died of sclerosis of the liver, giving me some idea why everybody shied away from mentioning him.

I know very little about Papa's childhood in Berlin. He spent a lot of time with his mother's family in the village of Gross Voltz in Pomerania, today Wołcza Wielka, Poland.

His uncle Willie, Martha's brother, owned a small house on a parcel of land and worked for the local duke as a farmhand and later managed the estate. My father told me many stories about his growing up in the country and the fun and adventures he had with his older brother Karl.

As a city boy, I could only imagine the excitement of growing

up with horses to ride, lakes to swim in and forests to explore. He never told me a bad story about his childhood and I thought he and Uncle Karl grew up in Paradise. Only later did I notice that none of those stories ever involved his mother. I never asked him the reason for this omission.

My father and mother met at a dance in early 1931 and they were married in December. Neither one of my parents mentioned the fact that their first child was born just three months later. I was always told they were very much in love and planned the pregnancy to get their families' permissions to get married.

As a true believer in social democracy and personal freedoms, my father hated everything about the Third Reich and militarism, but had no way of avoiding the draft. He spent most of the war in Norway where he learned the language and became very friendly with the Norwegians.

He was even court martialled for collaborating with the Resistance. It was a sympathetic judge and a glowing character reference from his commanding officer that helped his case. The local farmer testified that the ammunition my father gave him in exchange for food was to hunt rabbits and deer. He was sentenced to three weeks 'In The Hole' and a demotion to 'Private', instead of the death penalty sought by the SS prosecutor.

This was just one instance where my father made a decision that wasn't well thought out and without considering the consequences, which was to end up in front of a firing squad. There are lots of stories about my father that should be titled '*It seemed like a good idea at the time*'.

After the war, my father was able to get an apartment fairly quickly since their old one was declared unsafe because of bomb damage. He got a job with a painting contractor and life seemed to get back to normal after my arrival in 1946. Work was there in abundance and there was a whole city to be rebuilt.

In the Potsdam agreement, the Soviets had agreed to grant free access to West Berlin by Land (three freeways), by Sea (three canals) and by Rail (three railway lines). This agreement was, however, soon to be broken.

Nobody expected the Soviets to block all access to West Berlin. Their aim was to force the Allies to abandon Berlin by starving the city and its citizens into submission.

The Berlin Airlift was about to begin in 1948. The only way into West Berlin was by air! Everybody was limited to a ration of 1600 calories a day since all necessities of life, from food to gasoline to coal, had to be flown into the city.

My father lost his job as a painter since no building materials could be brought in.

To supplement our food rations, he left every few days by train for East Germany to trade with farmers for food. He wanted flour, fresh milk and some vegetables and offered items like jewellery, cutlery and other valuables in return. After bartering most of our possessions away, he acquired valuables from friends and neighbours who were promised a share of the food when he returned. In the summer and fall of 1948, he often stayed on farms, sleeping in barns or stables, helping with the harvest in exchange for food to take back home to Berlin.

The biggest threat was being caught by East German or Soviet border guards when crossing the border back to West Berlin, loaded down with suitcases and backpacks stuffed with food. Everything would be confiscated and he would have been charged with smuggling.

They never caught him, but his stories of dodging guards and walking for miles to avoid controls were fascinating and more gripping than stuff I read in books.

My mother always proudly said that my father didn't let us suffer during the blockade and she knew we would get through those trying times.

In 1949, the shortages were over and some normalcy returned to our lives. In 1953, the Berlin Government offered the owner of my father's company the opportunity to become the teacher and department head of the newly opened 'Trade and Vocational

Training Centre'. He accepted under the condition that my father could be his assistant. Gone were the seasonal lay-offs, the uncertainty of the next paycheque. He now had stability and security for the rest of his life.

My father always wanted more out of life, so he worked evenings and weekends renovating the apartments and houses of friends, neighbours and acquaintances. This 'tax-free' money afforded us the things we wanted. We were the first ones on the block to have a car, a television set, a washing machine and other modern conveniences that were becoming available after the war.

I don't think Dad ever told me that he loved me but I knew he did. He tried to spend most of his spare time with me, but there wasn't much left.

In later years, he limited his 'Extra Jobs' to three days a week.

I have fond memories of building kites with him and we would fly them in the park. He would take me tobogganing in winter and picnicking in summer. He loved the outdoors and loved to have fun with me in my younger years. He built me a wonderful model train set and played with me for hours and by himself after I went to bed.

He enjoyed going to the motor-paced cycling races at our local stadium that had a velodrome. He idolized the Belgian cyclist Adolph Verschueren who was the World Champion at that time. We would get there early to get the best seats, meet the athletes and look at the bikes. Whenever the vendors came by, while the races were going on, he would get a beer for himself and I would get candies and pop. He never treated me like a child, it was more like a best friend.

We had fun together. Dad never imposed a curfew, but asked me what time I thought I should be home. He always put a lot of trust in me and I tried not to disappoint him.

My father liked to have his 'Schnapps and a Beer'. He was a happy drunk and the life of the party, but around 1960 his drinking was becoming a problem.

He had constant headaches and our doctor, Dr. Brunner, would tell him they would disappear if he stopped drinking.

By 1964, he was a changed man. He was constantly in a bad mood, trying to pick fights, becoming irritable and anti-social. We almost came to blows a few times and he treated my mother like dirt.

I hated him and urged my mother to leave, but she stayed with him hoping things would get better. I was ready to move out but stayed around because I felt my mother needed some protection although he never became violent. He was just unbearable.

My father didn't feel well the whole Easter weekend. He stayed in bed most of the time, only to get up to get his drink and a little food. When I left to meet some friends in the local pub that evening, he walked into the kitchen shouting that I was never at home. I told him that living with a disgusting creep and drunk like him didn't give me an incentive to stay home. I slammed the door and left.

Those were my last words to him. When I came home, I heard a gurgling sound coming from his bedroom. I will never forget his contorted face, the heavy breathing, the eyes rolled back in his head with just the whites showing. I shook him. There was no response. I yelled for my mother in the other room to come as I ran out to get Dr. Brunner. He was not home. I tried another doctor, no success.

In my absence, my mother had run to Mrs. Schmidt, they had a telephone, and called the fire department. I couldn't have been gone for more than 30 minutes even though it felt like an eternity. When I pulled up to our building, the firemen were carrying my father down the stairs. He was lifeless. Officially, he died on his way to the hospital but I think he was already dead.

The doctor told us to come back the next day to learn about the cause of death. An autopsy was mandatory when somebody died under unexplained circumstances. When we returned, the doctor asked us if my father's behaviour had changed in the last few years and if he had any pain during that time.

We told him about his personality changes, his drinking problem and the pain he experienced the last few years, radiating from his left knee to his hip, to his shoulder and to his neck and the dif-

My Dad with his friends

Uncle Karl & Dad

ficulty he had on Easter Sunday in opening his left eye.

He told us that my father's headaches were not caused by alcohol, but that my father drank to numb the pain. He added that any competent doctor would have noticed that he had the symptoms of a brain tumour, which went undetected and finally killed him. My mother and I were in shock. If we had only known and understood his pain.

I felt guilty about the feelings I had developed towards my father and tried to sue Dr. Brunner for negligence. The doctor in the hospital, however, quickly changed his earlier statement, insisting that my father's drinking habits could have led to the misdiagnosis. He also said that any attempt to remove the tumour could have transformed my father into a vegetable. He assured us that this outcome was most likely the better way.

He didn't understand that my father, in his time of need, had nobody to comfort him and tell him we understood and cared. By not knowing about his health problem, I saw him as a despicable drunk and not the tortured and suffering human being he was.

I did not shed a tear at his funeral, all I felt was an emotional numbness.

Sorry Dad!

Chapter 4

Uncles & Aunts

The Good, the Bad and the Ugly

My mother had three siblings who survived WWII and I learned to love, admire and despise them.

Aunt Hanna

Tante Hanna, as I called my aunt, was the most lovable, loving, pathetic and broken person you could ever meet.

Tante Hanna had childhood epilepsy and was always slower than her brothers and sisters. She didn't finish school, but had outgrown her epilepsy by the time she was 14 years old. Tante Hanna never even had a boyfriend before age 25 and thought she would remain a spinster for the rest of her life. In 1934, she met the man of her dreams and fell in love. She was thinking of starting a family and having children of her own. When they applied for their marriage license at the end of 1936, her life took a turn for the worse, from which she never recovered.

In July of 1933, the German Government had introduced the Law for the Prevention of Hereditarily Diseased Offsprings. This law called for the compulsory sterilization of those afflicted by "congenital feeble-mindedness", depression, epilepsy, schizophrenia, Huntington's Disease, deafness, blindness and other disabilities. Such persons were deemed unworthy to procreate.

Tante Hanna was told she had to be sterilized due to her childhood epilepsy. Both my aunt and her fiancé resisted and tried to sue the Nazi Government.

It was in the middle of the night when the police arrived, arrested her and carted her off to a concentration camp for those with mental disabilities of varying degrees and later transferred her to a forced labour camp. Our family did not hear of her whereabouts for four months. She was released, almost a year later, in the fall of 1937.

By this time, she was a broken woman, a shell of a human being, after being physically and mentally abused. She never talked about her ordeal to anybody. Nobody ever heard from her fiancé again. He disappeared the same night she had been taken away.

After the war, my parents applied for a pension for Tante Hanna under the 'Compensation for Victims of National Socialism'. My parents did not know what to put in the application because my aunt refused to talk about her life in the concentration camp. Was she tortured? Did they perform any medical experiments on her? Since she refused to cooperate, her pension was rejected. She had to live on a small disability pension, based on her poor physical and mental conditions.

She was a loving person and always tried to help my mother even though there was not much she could do on her own.

Her only pleasure was smoking and boy, did she smoke! She developed a bad cough, not the most subtle cough, but a cough that could go on for minutes and produce lots of phlegm. She was not the most pleasant person to be around. She had no teeth and refused to wear dentures. I could not look at her when she was eating or coughing her lungs out, yet, you felt sympathy and warmth towards her. She loved being around me and tried to be my friend and confidant. She was adorable in her helplessness.

In 1966, a letter arrived, notifying her that certain documents had been recovered giving her status as a victim of National Socialism. She received a small increase in her pension and a back payment of several thousand D-Marks.

Tante Hanna had lived in a small and dingy room in the back of a dilapidated tenement, but now had enough money to move into a small, government-subsidized, one-bedroom apartment in a nice neighbourhood. She lived her last ten years with some comfort and dignity and could even afford to buy 'good' cigarettes and didn't have to roll her own any more. That, to her, was heaven.

Tante Hanna died in 1976 of complications from emphysema. She probably died with a cigarette in her mouth!

Uncle Fritz

Onkel Fritz, as I called him, was viewed as an anti-social man and was not liked by his own family. He was different and did not fit the mould of a typical German. He, however, fascinated me!

With a deep, gravelly voice and the figure of a professional wrestler, Onkel Fritz was a free spirit. He did not want to be tied down by a 9 to 5 job and did not accept authority or the rules of society. He married at the age of 19 and had two children, Bruno and Margot, but could not handle the pressure of parenthood and modern life.

In 1926, when his children were two and three years old, respectively, he left to live the life of a vagabond. He crisscrossed half of Europe, jumping trains, walking and hitching the odd ride or working on farms as a day labourer to survive. For more than two years, nobody knew where he was or what he was doing.

His wife, Grete, divorced him when he returned and neither she nor his children ever forgave him. He worked as a farmhand around Berlin and performed odd jobs in the winter months. Every penny that he could spare he gave to his family.

Onkel Fritz didn't believe in amassing a personal fortune or in not sharing wealth and resources, so it was no surprise that he joined the Communist Party of Germany.

In 1934, he was arrested by the Nazis as a subversive and jailed for six months. When he was approached by the Communists to rejoin the Party after the war, he refused. He still prescribed to Marxism, but was disillusioned by Stalinism and the forced discipline of party life.

He opted to live in West Berlin after the war and found one of the few operating farms in landlocked Berlin, a horse stable with some cows and pigs, but no agriculture. It was a permanent job and nobody told him what to do.

He didn't have to punch a time clock. He never took vacations and worked seven days a week. He once told me that he worked for the animals, and they don't take vacations and needed him every day. He had, at last, found something that made him happy.

My mother was the only one in the family close to him and she did understand him. He visited us more often than his daughter Margot, who lived next door to us. I loved sitting with him listening to his stories about his travels. He introduced me to books by Zane Grey and Karl May.

Onkel Fritz worshipped North American Indians and the way they were represented in Karl May novels as the 'Noble Savage' living in harmony with nature.

When he heard that I was immigrating to North America he urged me to visit and research native Indians and find out how they lived today and if the stories about their failure to integrate into the white man's world were true.

The first time I came home to visit, he couldn't wait to question me about the Indians, the country and the wide open living spaces in Canada. I told him about the plight of our native people today and about the deplorable conditions on their reservations.

I also told him that the Indian culture and traditions were still alive. He asked if he could come and visit me if he ever won the lottery. I promised that if I struck it rich, I would send him an airline ticket to come and visit Canada.

His eyes twinkled with delight and he said he just loved the idea that one day he might visit real Indians. However, he died the following year.

His daughter Margot had never visited him and saw his room

next to the stable for the first time after he died. He had seven cats that the farmer promised to find homes for. Besides that, it looked like there was only a pile of junk in his room.

Margot had a hard time finding a junk dealer to clean out his room at no charge, in exchange for keeping anything of value he would find. She signed the contract and felt happy about not having to clean the place.

The dealer called her a few days later and thanked her for the job. The figurines on Onkel Fritz's shelf were 'Meissen Porcelain' and he had sold the collection for 18,000.00DM, about $9,000.00CDN.

Margot was not happy anymore!

Aunt Herta

When Herta came to visit, I always found some excuse to leave. Like me, everybody in our family despised her.

Fortunately, she did not visit very often and I cannot remember ever visiting her. My father could not stand her either, just being around her was a challenge.

Herta was the greatest hypochondriac I have ever known. She had every conceivable ailment. If you had the same medical problem as Herta, she would tell you that hers was ten times worse. She even told Tante Hanna once that her pain and suffering was more excruciating than what Hanna had gone through in her life. If I remember correctly, that was when my father threw her out and we did not see her for a year.

Herta would also compete on who had worse luck, or was mistreated more by officialdom. Everybody in the world was stupid, incompetent, rude or intent on mistreating her.

She complained bitterly that she was turned down many times for a disability pension. It was, of course, the fault of the civil servants and the incompetence of the doctors that kept her from being officially recognized as an invalid. Her husband was the biggest wimp one could find anywhere. He confirmed every little detail and complaint of hers with an agreeable nod or sigh and would throw in the odd, “That’s right Herta, you tell them!”

When my father died in 1965, Herta tried to get closer to us but my mother did not make her feel welcome and we never saw her more than twice a year.

I never heard from Herta again after I left for Canada. My mother never mentioned her, and I never asked about her.

My mother, Tante Hanna, Onkel Fritz and Herta, how could four siblings be so different from each other?

Uncle Karl

My father had one sibling, his brother Karl. Onkel Karl, as I called him, looked nothing like my father. He was 10 inches (25 cm) taller and built like a Roman gladiator.

Their demeanour and personalities were also very different.

My father was a charmer and a talker, Onkel Karl was the silent type with a deep voice, good looks and a broad smile.

My father was impulsive and emotional, Onkel Karl was deliberate and thought about everything more than twice before he acted on anything. There was a warmth about my uncle that made him appear caring, giving and thoughtful. He loved music and played the accordion rather well. He also had a Bavarian zither I could play with when we visited him.

Onkel Karl was the one who introduced me to American music. He was a fan of Nat King Cole and Louis Prima and had bought every record of theirs available in Germany. He was, what you might call today, a ‘Cool Guy’ and I loved him.

There was one problem with Onkel Karl that was hard to overcome, his wife Elfriede. Elfriede was not liked by the rest of my father’s family or by my mother’s family.

She was cold and calculating. It was easy to see that Onkel Karl was under her control. What Elfriede wanted, Elfriede got! If she didn’t get what she wanted, she became moody and unbearable and she did have the smile of a Cheshire cat.

Onkel Karl treated me like the son he never had and made

sure to spend a lot of time with me when our families visited each other. His daughter Inge was 6 years older than me and had no time for me. She was always interested in older men and married somebody 12 years older than her when she was 19. That marriage lasted only a short time.

My dad's mother was the only grandmother I knew. When she was dying, her two sons, Karl and Kurt and their families gathered around the hospital bed. She had been taken to the hospital two weeks earlier and after some exploratory surgery, was told that her cancer was so advanced that she had only weeks to live. That Sunday morning, she had slipped into a coma and we were asked to visit her. She died exactly as visiting hours ended at 4:00 pm that afternoon.

My father agreed to stay behind and complete the paperwork and my uncle went ahead to my grandmother's apartment to start sorting out stuff.

My father signed some papers, arranged for the funeral director to take over and left for his mother's apartment about an hour later. The first thing my uncle said to my father when we arrived was, "I looked everywhere, but couldn't find any money except for a penny jar in the kitchen cupboard."

Three months before her death, my dad had renovated my grandmother's kitchen and she had told him that she kept her money inside a quilt. The quilt was a decorative blanket for her wall unit in the living room. She showed him about eighty 1000.00DM bills, a small fortune in those days, stuffed into the blanket. Grandma had lost all her savings in 1923 during the hyperinflation and didn't trust banks anymore.

Knowing where his mother kept her money, my father told Onkel Karl to follow him into the living room. Elfriede shouted that they had looked everywhere and turned beet red when my father picked up the blanket, reached in and came up with nothing. Onkel Karl stuttered as he said they had looked there already. Elfriede soon found her composure and said she wanted to go home and would search again for the money the next day.

My father was stunned! I had seldom seen my father speechless. He told his brother that he could look after the apartment and keep everything he wanted. My father only wanted a few pictures and a couple of mementos to remember his mother. He said they would meet again at the funeral and asked him to pay for half the expenses. Onkel Karl agreed and also offered to pick up the bill for the memorial dinner my father had arranged to be held after the service. My father declined the offer by telling him that everything should be shared in an equal manner.

My father never spoke with his brother again and I lost an uncle I had adored and trusted. Dad always said that Onkel Karl wasn't a bad guy and that it was Elfriede who turned him into a spineless wimp. He couldn't forgive him for being so weak and allowing her to tear our family apart.

A few months later, we received an invitation to Inge's second wedding but Dad refused to go. From relatives, we heard that Onkel Karl had paid for a lavish reception. As a wedding present, he bought the couple a three-week safari to Kenya and joined them on the trip. Dad always wondered aloud in a sarcastic tone that his brother must have won the lottery after their mother died.

I saw Onkel Karl again at my father's funeral. He seemed emotional and cried his heart out. He promised to keep in touch with me but made no great effort. We met again a month before I left for Canada and he told me he wanted to have a talk with me before I left.

I had to go into the hospital for some minor surgery before I left for Canada. I asked him to come to the hospital to visit me where we could have some time together to talk after so many years. I was in bed for four days and we would have all the time in the world to re-acquaint ourselves.

He seemed enthusiastic and promised to come and clear the air. I was looking forward to hear his side of the story and maybe patch things up between our families.

I never saw him again!

Chapter 5

My Two Uncle Willies

Technically speaking, neither one of my two Uncle Willies was my uncle. Uncle Willie in Ebstorf was my father's cousin and the one in Potsdam was my grandmother's youngest brother. Both of them were named Wilhelm Totzke. It is customary in Germany to address older relatives as uncle or aunt. My father was very close to both of them since he spent part of his childhood with them in Pomerania, now part of Poland.

Their lives were remarkable and I wasn't aware of their stories until I visited them later in my life and they talked about the tumultuous and unbelievable hardships they had to endure.

Here are the stories they told me.

Uncle Willie In Potsdam

When Jackie and I visited Germany in 1975, we visited Uncle Willie, his wife Aunt Minna and their family in Neu Fahrland near Potsdam in East Germany. Uncle Willie had broken his collarbone and was bedridden. On a rainy day, he called us into his bedroom to chat. He was intrigued by Jackie and her African heritage and was eager to find out what life in Africa was like.

He spoke no English and I translated his questions and Jackie's answers all morning. After a while, he asked if we would be interested in hearing his life story after lunch. It turned out to be one of the most fascinating days of our lives.

Uncle Willie enjoyed the schnapps I had brought from West Berlin to make the day more pleasant but made sure that Aunt Minna didn't find out he was enjoying the brandy along with the stories. She did not approve of his drinking during the day.

His timing in telling the story of his life was impeccable. He stopped every couple of minutes for me to translate and used that time to relight or refill his pipe and have a little sip of brandy to wet his throat.

Uncle Willie was born in 1892 and spent his childhood and youth in Pomerania. His first job was as a stable boy on one of Kaiser Wilhelm's estates. He met the Kaiser and had good memories of the days in his employment.

During the First World War, he joined the infantry and fought at the battle of the Marne. He took part in the trench warfare for over two years. The hardship and savagery almost broke him. He talked about fellow soldiers dying next to him in their foxholes, or while advancing or retreating during the constant attacks and counter-attacks.

It was hard for me to find the right words in English to express the horror and the suffering he and every soldier on both sides had to endure, but Jackie understood by his animated gestures and the tears now running down his face. We had a hard time hiding our own tears as we watched him reliving those days.

When he returned from the war he was rehired by the new owner of the estate and through the years of the Weimar Republic he was happy living in Pomerania. He married Minna and his only daughter Ilse was born in 1933.

When Hitler came to power, Uncle Willie noticed that Jews were disappearing from the nearby town of Rummelsburg. Hitler's Brown Shirts also intimidated and terrorized people who refused to join the Nazi Party, and many were incarcerated or vanished. The owner of the estate, who was part of the old German aristocracy and not a Nazi sympathizer, fled to the United States in 1939 after the war broke out. The Nazis confiscated the estate and ran it until the end of the war.

Uncle Willy, due to his age, was only drafted into the army during the final months of the Second World War and was captured by the Russians on the Eastern Front.

He returned from the prisoner of war camp, where he suffered from the cold and lack of food, to his wife and daughter in the early winter of 1945, only to find out that Pomerania was now Polish territory. Germans who did not want to take Polish citizenship were forced to leave. The use of the German language was outlawed and he and his family envisioned a life as second class citizens if they decided to stay.

They, along with thousands of others, were rounded up and told to take only the belongings they could carry and leave Poland. The elderly, children, the sick and the able-bodied had to march for twelve hours a day in the middle of winter to reach the new German border more than 230 km away.

The few hand-drawn carts in this convoy of humanity loaded with personal belongings could only accommodate a few people that had collapsed or were unable to walk. The Soviet and Polish soldiers driving the people towards the border showed no mercy towards those who couldn't find a place on the carts and were unable to continue. They either executed them with single shots to the head or simply bashed their skulls in with the butt of their rifles and left them lying by the side of the road.

The hatred towards Germans exhibited by many Poles and Russians at the end of the war was without limits. This feeling of revenge and payback for the atrocities committed during the Third Reich obviously justified their actions in their minds.

When Uncle Willie described these scenes, we were crying nonstop and had to halt our conversation often to regain our composure.

He arrived in West Berlin and tried to start a new life. Since his experience was in agriculture, the only work he could find was clearing rubble and other jobs to rebuild a city in ruins. Aunt Minna had relatives near Potsdam who owned a small farm. They introduced my uncle to Mrs. Wartenberg, who owned a large estate close-by in the village of Neu Fahrland. She had lost her husband in the war and was looking for a live-in farmhand to assist her and her young son Werner. Uncle Willie and Aunt Minna accepted her offer and moved to East Germany in early 1950.

There were three houses on the Wartenberg property. Mother Wartenberg and her son Wernie, as everybody called him, occupied the main building. The second house belonged to Wernie's sister and her family. The third, and biggest house, was now the home of Uncle Willie, Tante Minna and Ilse.

As Ilse grew up to be a lovely young lady, she and Wernie fell in love with each other. They got married in 1953 and moved into the main building to occupy the quarters on the ground floor. The upstairs was converted into a self contained apartment for Mother Wartenberg to live in.

Everybody seemed to be happy. Then, in 1954, the Communist East German government nationalized all farms and converted them into state owned cooperatives. Uncle Willie and Wernie now lived in state-owned houses and were employees of the East German Government.

At the end of our long day, listening to Uncle Willie's life story, I had to ask him the following question, "Tell me Uncle Willie, you have lived under every imaginable form of government, from the monarchy of Kaiser Wilhelm, to the unruly democracy of the Weimar Republic, to a dictatorship under Hitler, to a western style democracy in West Berlin and Communism in East Germany. Which form of government did you like the best?"

His answer surprised me.

"Konrad," he said, "now, in my old age, I feel secure and know that my family and I are well looked after. I can die in peace knowing my grandchildren will get a good education, they will be guaranteed a job for the rest of their lives and will never starve. I know we are lacking a lot of freedoms and will never live in luxury but peace of mind means a lot after what Minna and I have gone through in our lives. I must say that Communism is maybe the most desirable form of government."

I didn't agree with him, but in a way I understood.

In 1975, when we visited for the first time, there were four generations living on the farm. Mother Wartenberg, Uncle Willie and Aunt Minna, their children Wernie and Ilse, their daughter Bärbel with her husband Manfred, and their son Michael. After Michael got married to Yvonne. that number increased to five generations living under the same roof when their son Julius was born in 2003. Mother Wartenberg died at the age of 99 in 2006.

Uncle Willie died before German reunification and never experienced his family flourishing in a free society on their again-privately owned estate.

Uncle Willie in Ebstorf

I only met Uncle Willie in 1958. He and his wife Ilse and their six children were living on a farm in Velgen in Lower Saxony, West Germany.

Uncle Willie and his family had been trapped in Poland after the war and my father was eager to see his cousin, whom I called Uncle Willie, again after more than 20 years. Uncle Willie's father-in-law was the manager, administrator and all-round, go-to man of the local dairy farm and creamery. He and Uncle Willie had managed the farm and the creamery throughout the war years. The Polish government did not allow them or their families to leave Pomerania to follow the rest of the Totzke clan to West Germany.

Only after his father-in-law died in 1957, and Ilse's brother, a farmer in West Germany, sponsored them to leave Poland, were they allowed to take their few belongings and board a train to West Berlin.

Uncle Willie was born in Pomerania in 1920 and married Ilse in 1940, shortly before their first daughter Dora was born later that same year. Eight more children were to follow.

In 1938, Uncle Willie joined the police force in Pomerania as a cadet. After he completed basic training, he was shipped to France in 1940 to police Paris as a member of the occupying force. Some autonomy was returned to the French, including local policing, after the Germans installed the Vichy government.

German police were slowly replaced by their French counterparts and by the middle of 1941 the last German police officers were decommissioned. Uncle Willie and others were given a choice, they could either join the regular army and be shipped to the Eastern Front or join the SS and be deployed behind the lines to fight local resistance groups or do other non-combat duties.

Very few accepted the offer to fight at the Eastern Front to face the Russians and the upcoming brutal winter.

After his basic training in the SS, he was assigned to fight the Yugoslavian Resistance Movement, one of the most feared and successful anti-Nazi movements during the Second World War.

He became friends with an Austrian named Anton, who had also been part of the police force in France and resented the war just as much as Uncle Willie did. One day they were lying in a fox-hole when Anton said, "I heard these Partisans are pretty good sharpshooters. So what do you think if we wave at them? They will shoot us in the arm, we'll go home and the war is over for us."

Uncle Willie argued that it would not be good to be shot in the hand as they'd be crippled for life. "No, no," Anton answered, "if you wave really fast, your lower arm is hardly moving and they always aim for the part that is not moving as fast." He raised his arm to demonstrate hoping to be only slightly injured.

What neither Anton nor Uncle Willie knew was that the partisan a few meters away was not a good shot, but had a great arm and could toss a hand grenade a long way. Knowing where the enemy was hiding, that is exactly what he did and for Uncle Willie and his friend Anton the war was now over.

Anton had severe injuries, but survived. Uncle Willie lost the heel of his left foot and had many shrapnel wounds. He walked with a limp for the rest of his life. After two months in hospital, he was discharged and returned home.

Upon his return to Pomerania, he had to start a new life. His dreams of being a policeman were over. He started working with his father-in-law at the dairy and quickly became an expert in most aspects of dairy farming and dairy products.

When Uncle Willie's family was denied permission to leave Poland, he lived in constant terror that the Polish authorities would find out about him being part of the SS. In the early days after the war, members of the SS were routinely charged with war crimes or simply executed by the Soviets without a trial. When joining the SS, recruits were required to be tattooed for identification purposes. After the war, that tattoo under their left arm made them easily recognizable. Most SS members had their tattoos removed or simply cut out but scars were an obvious giveaway. Uncle Willie always wore a shirt to conceal the fact that he was part of Hitler's elite troops responsible for most of the atrocities committed by Germans during the Third Reich.

I still remember meeting Uncle Willie and his family in 1958. My father had fond memories of taking him under his wing and introducing him to the mischievous things teenagers could get into, mainly alcohol, tobacco and girls. Dad, seven years older than his cousin, must have done a good job because the reunion was a weekend long affair with lots of booze, smoking and stories about the past. Uncle Willie's six children were proof that Dad had definitely taught him well about the art of love-making.

I had a great weekend as well. Uncle Willie spent a long time teaching me how to ride a horse bareback. There were no saddles on the farm and after a few lessons, I became pretty good. I had a great time trotting around, pretending to be the greatest cowboy to ever ride a horse. It wasn't until the next day that I discovered that every bone in my body was hurting and I could hardly walk.

After settling down in Germany, Uncle Willie and Tante Ilse had three more children. They bought a small house in nearby Ebstorf and life looked like there would only be happy days ahead of them.

Shortly after their last daughter Ute was born in 1966, the doctors gave them some terrible news. Tante Ilse had cancer and was told that she had less than a year to live.

She died in 1968 and Uncle Willie was left with eight children to look after. His oldest daughter Dora was married and had moved out of the house a few years earlier.

Uncle Willie picked himself up and reorganized his life to be a father and a mother. He had his children complete their education and helped them develop the skills to succeed in life. Nobody enjoyed life more than Uncle Willie. His bellicose laugh, his permanent smile and his positive outlook on life made him a joy to be around. Even though he never wanted to get married again, he loved the ladies and had some girlfriends after his wife died.

My mother told me that he even tried to seduce her when she came to visit him after my father died. When she reminded him that she was six years older than him and widowed, he said, "You are never too old to have a good time and you shouldn't live your life for the dead. They'll forgive you when you meet them in heaven again."

Uncle Willie never gave up trying to charm the ladies around him but struck out with my mother.

In 1990, we toured Germany with friends of ours, Joan and Willis, who were originally from Barbados. Uncle Willie had never had contact with black people before in his life and was fascinated with Joan, a stunning and beautiful black woman. When we left. she kissed him on the cheek. One of his sons told us later that he didn't wash his face for over a week after the kiss. He said he didn't want to wash the memories away of having been kissed by such a gorgeous woman.

On that visit, he also taught our then 16-year-old daughter Toni how to do shots of his homemade liqueur. Jackie and I were stunned when we saw that Toni had downed a few of them to my uncle's delight. He said his plum and herbal mixture wouldn't hurt her. I guess he was right because Toni had a good night's sleep and didn't wake up until early afternoon the next day after wobbling off to bed the night before.

Whenever we went to Germany, we always tried to visit him and his children, most of whom were married and living around Ebstorf. His daughter Gisela and her husband Georg as well as his son Ullie, his wife Anka and their son have visited us several times in Canada.

Uncle Willie died suddenly in 1999 of a heart attack at the age of 79. Even though I spent very little time with him over the years, he will always be one of my favourite relatives.

Nobody could resist his charm, his smile and his enthusiasm. He was a pleasure to be around.

Chapter 6

Growing Up Amongst The Ruins

Our apartment building on 32 Oderstrasse in Berlin was partially bombed-out with only the bottom three floors of the 5-storey building habitable. The top two floors and the whole building next door and most of the surrounding buildings were destroyed in the final days of the war.

On July 2nd 1946, the day of my arrival, the clean-up and rebuilding of the city was already in full swing. I saw my first sunrise through a window that had been installed the day before to let the sun shine into the apartment on a warm and pleasant summer day.

My parents were some of the lucky people to have an apartment in a city where 60% of the buildings were damaged by bombs and more than a third were uninhabitable. Sharing living quarters with others and living in basements and shelters was the rule.

My earliest memories of the rubble around us are fantastic. Talk about places to explore, play hide and seek, go treasure hunting, get scared, dare and be dared...

We had it all!

These ruins were our playground and made for a golden childhood. In our imagination, we transformed the bombed-out buildings into real fortresses to play Cowboys and Indians or into castles and pretended we were medieval knights. It depended on the movie we saw at the Sunday matinee at one of the many cinemas in our neighbourhood.

It didn't matter what we saw, everybody wanted to be the 'Hero'. We always had to draw sticks to determine who got to play one of the classic characters. These ranged from Robin Hood to Ivanhoe or Tom Mix to any of the German Wild-West Superstars created by Karl May. May was, at that time, the most widely-read German author of Wild West stories that always portrayed the Indian as a 'Noble Savage'.

The second most popular choice was playing the 'Villain'. After the two main characters were chosen we picked teams. Everybody had his homemade swords and shields to become a knight, or his water pistol to be able to play the role of a cowboy. A flexible tree branch, a piece of string and some dried straight twigs would give one of us the bow and arrows to become a proud Indian or one of 'Robin's Merry Men'.

Mom's broom became our horse and the clicking of our tongues made the sound of the hoofs as we rode into grim battles.

We played for hours and most of the time was spent in establishing who was shot and should be dead and who was granted a 'second life' because we ran out of players and the 'dead guys' didn't want to stay dead any longer. It was boring being dead.

Oh, and the girls seldom volunteered to be Maid Marion or a 'Squaw' unless the women in the movie participated in the fighting. There was full equality amongst us and some of the girls were the most aggressive warriors around, but I can't remember a girl ever being 'The Hero' or 'The Villain', that job was reserved for the boys.

The only serious injury I ever received in our games was from a girl. Martin's sister shoved me down a staircase in a sword fight. I split my head open and needed some stitches.

I still remember my mother hyperventilating when she saw the blood but Dr Brunner, who lived above his practice a couple of streets over from our building, reassured her that wounds at the top of the head tended to bleed a lot and promised her that I would survive and live a normal life.

I took great pride in showing my partially shaved head and the stitches to my friends to impress them with my injuries received in battle. It helped to make a point about my bravery.

We had several minor scrapes and bruises and in a sword fight you always ended up getting whacked across the knuckles and cries of 'that wasn't fair' were common when you got hurt.

It was breathtaking excitement to climb the scaffolding right up to the top floor, hoping to be out of mother's sight because she would surely spoil the fun. I can still hear 'Konraaaaad, get down from there!' or 'Haven't I told you not to climb up the scaffolding, you will break your neck!' or the constant threat of 'house arrest'.

Luckily for me, my mother was not very good at meting out punishment and by the time I was in second grade, she felt a little guilty about being so protective of her one and only son.

Most of the rubble had been cleaned up and the most dangerous walls had been demolished or secured by the time I was old enough to play with the other kids.

However, the warnings of our mothers screaming 'Don't play in the ruins' still ring in my ears.

It was exciting to climb up the semi-collapsed staircases, hide in dark basements with heavy bomb shelter doors still in place and occasionally interrupt some teenagers smooching in dark corners.

•••••

We helped the 'Big kids' hunt for copper, brass or metallic objects of any kind in the ruins for which the local scrap dealer gave us a few pennies. This was satisfying, because we felt we had 'earned' some money and could spend it on things we wanted.

I don't think we got our fair share from the big kids for the loot collected in those ruins. We didn't care as long as we had enough to buy broken cookies from the baker or penny-candies that we could pick out of the big jar at the local corner store.

The few pennies that we received as pocket money from our parents had to be accounted for and we were encouraged to save or spend it wisely, but this 'metal' money was ours to enjoy!

It was hard work for us little kids to use a hacksaw to cut off some brass fittings or swing a hammer to knock off more plaster to expose copper piping behind the walls.

We would often be chased away by Mr Lausman, the custodian of the building complex, who was always on the look-out to protect the neighbourhood from the plundering hordes of little kids. He didn't understand or like children of any age.

•••••

One thing that stands out in my memory is the 'Clubhouse' that the big kids built behind our building.

It took them days to gather up enough bricks, blocks and planks to construct this tiny hut, it even had a window and a roof. It was sufficiently concealed from plain view by big lush bushes. The smaller kids were not allowed in the clubhouse unless invited, because the big guys smoked, entertained their girlfriends and gambled with real money in there.

I still remember the day when I first puffed on a cigarette and the day when I gambled away my hard-earned scrap metal money. These adventures did make me feel grown-up and being part of the gang.

The 'Clubhouse' only lasted a few days. Mr Lausman discovered it and destroyed it, claiming it was unsafe and dangerous.

In retrospect, I have to agree with him but we didn't see it that way back then and our hatred for Mr Lausman grew even deeper.

•••••

Martin, my friend next door, once found a hand grenade left over from the last days of door-to-door combat. After playing catch with it for some time, Martin went to inform his dad about his terrific find.

We never found out if it was still in good working order because the Fire Department never came back to tell us. Martin was upset that his dad took this great-looking, iron egg away from him.

This was about the most dangerous situation we ever experienced. None of us ever sustained any serious injuries during our many pranks and only had a few scrapes and bruises and a stitch here or there. It must have been because of the warnings from our mothers that we didn't break our necks, poke our eyes out or kill ourselves.

By the mid to late fifties, everything around us had pretty much been rebuilt. The big mounds of construction sand that were our sandboxes, the scaffolding that were our monkey bars, and the bombed-out buildings that were our amusement parks, had disappeared and been replaced with a proper playground in the back of our apartment complex.

It wasn't as much fun!

Chapter 7

A Childhood Christmas In Berlin

Advent Time

The Christmas season started with the first Advent Sunday. This was the weekend when my parents bought our Advent wreath, decorated with red and gold ribbons, red bows and 4 white candles. It was placed on the living room table and the candles were lit every Sunday evening prior to Christmas Eve. We would sit in the living room singing carols, munching on cookies and preparing for the holidays.

On the first Advent Sunday, I would make my wish list for Santa, Mom and Dad made theirs, so Santa would fulfil their wishes as well as mine. My aunt Hanna never put anything on the lists, but I found it amazing that Santa always found the right thing to give to her.

The first Advent was also when we would get out the book of Christmas poems. It is a German custom that children learn a poem and recite it before receiving the gifts Santa had left for them under the tree. I was always very ambitious and tried to please everybody by picking a long and difficult one.

On the second Advent Sunday, we went to the Christmas markets. We had many of them in Berlin. There were the local ones, a few stalls along main street, selling several kinds of wooden and windup toys, tin soldiers, dolls, stuffed animals and crafts. Others offered decorations, flower arrangements, cookies and chocolates and even meats and poultry.

The food vendors prepared hot snacks like wieners, grilled sausages, meatballs, chips and waffles. And of course, no Christmas market would be complete without Glühwein (Glow Wine), a delicious mulled wine that would warm everyone up on those cold winter nights.

Back in those days, the neighbourhood Christmas markets were only lit up by street lamps. The vendors put up their own gas and kerosene lamps to illuminate the goods in their stalls.

There was no recorded music blaring from loudspeakers. A local choir, a brass band or an organ grinder filled the streets with the sounds of Christmas to get us into the holiday mood.

Santa travelled by streetcar between three of our local markets, stayed awhile at each one of them talking to the children and their parents and then caught the next tram to the next one on his route. I always wondered why he would take public transit and leave his reindeer and his sled at home.

I will never forget the sounds and the aromas drifting through the winter air as my parents bought some decorations for our home, a little toy for me and spoiled me with cookies, a wiener on a bun and even a glass of Glühwein, the alcohol-free kind of course.

The big Christmas market downtown around the Kaiser Wilhelm Memorial Church was much more commercial, but still had a lot of charm. It offered everything the local ones did but more of it. There were amusement rides for kids, beer-gardens and some mass-produced toys, sleds, skates and much more. A brass orchestra and a choir performed high up in the spire of the church and everybody could hear their beautiful carols and hymns across the square.

There were bright, colourful lights everywhere and a giant Christmas tree with thousands of white lights was placed in front of the church. There was a Santa with his elves in his castle. I got to sit on his lap and tell him what I would like him to put under our tree. It was something a little kid would not soon forget.

The third Advent weekend was reserved for visits to and from relatives and friends. Not one of my favourite things, because none of our relatives or my parents friends had children of my age to play with. I did a lot of reading, drawing and talking to boring adults, answering the same questions about school and what Santa would bring me for Christmas.

The fourth Advent weekend was certainly about getting ready for the holidays. We cleaned, cooked, shopped and baked and got the house ready for Christmas.

It started on Friday night. We had some serious shopping to do. Mom went to pick up the goose she had ordered weeks ago from our butcher. Dad had to first inspect the goose to make sure it wasn't overly fatty and wasn't one of those fish-fed geese which tasted terrible. Mom went home with the goose after Dad had given it his blessings and he and I went on to get the tree.

My father was particular about the tree, it had to be straight, the right height, without bare spots and freshly cut so it wouldn't needle or catch fire since we were using real candles. He also liked to bargain with the dealer to save a few D-Marks. I never liked that part, but Dad was always proud of his bargaining skills and with the money he'd save he would buy me a treat. He also would have a beer and a schnapps before we carried the tree home.

Saturday was a hectic day. Dad would go with Mom on her big shopping trip. From beer and wine to bread and cheese and everything in between had to be bought to get us through the holidays, because the stores closed early on Christmas Eve and stayed closed until after Boxing Day.

After shopping, Dad would beat the carpets, wash the floors and clean the lights. Mom would dust, clean and scrub. I helped a bit but I think my parents were happy when my friends came to go tobogganing with me. I think I was not a big help and got in their way most of the time. Everybody was ready to collapse when evening came.

Sunday was a bit quieter. The house was filled with the aromas of the Christmas season. Mom and I baked cookies. We would shape the dough into angels, trees and stars before we shoved them into the oven. I always got to lick the last little bit of dough out of the bowl. The cookies smelled delicious when they came out of the oven and none of us could resist sampling one or two of them.

Dad plucked and cleaned the goose. He singed the last few feathers off the goose and the smell of burning feathers would overpower the aroma of the freshly baked cookies.

Sunday evening we sat down for dinner and afterwards lit our Advent wreath for the last time. We had some of mother's great cookies or a slice of Advent Stollen, a German kind of Christmas cake, listened to stories Dad told us of Christmases gone by or sang along to our favourite Christmas songs on the radio.

I went to bed dreaming of Santa's arrival which was now just a few days away.

Christmas has arrived!

The 24th of December was finally here! Christmas Eve!

Lots of work had to be done before Santa arrived. Helping Dad put up the tree was always fun. We never decorated it before Christmas Eve. I'd hang glass ornaments, little figurines and knickknacks on the branches, use lots of tinsel and finish it off with a special ornament for the top of the tree. Dad would make sure that the candle holders were secure, so the candles wouldn't tip over and set our tree on fire.

It looked beautiful!

After the tree was done, I was no longer allowed to go into the living room. Dad had to make enough room under the tree for Santa to put his presents down. I had to either play outside or in my room. Mom and Aunt Hanna, who always joined us for Christmas, were busy working in the kitchen.

They were making potato salad, frying up meatballs or cutting up veggies. It was traditional to have a simple meal on Christmas Eve after Santa had left and kids had been able to play for an hour or two with their new toys. This also gave Mom a chance to enjoy the evening and not slave away in the kitchen.

By three o'clock we were getting ready for our bath. Dad had fired up the boiler in the bathroom and was the first one to climb into the tub, Mom followed and I was last. We had to time it right in between baths in order not to run out of hot water. Dad constantly stoked the fire and the bathroom was like a sauna. After the bath, Mom cut my nails, cleaned my ears and I got to put on new clothes.

At 5 o'clock the church bells would ring across Berlin to announce the arrival of the Christ Child and Santa Claus.

Even though I never saw Santa, I knew he had arrived. There was a loud knock on our door. Dad answered the door while Mom and I stayed in the kitchen. We heard Santa's jovial laugh as he stomped down our hallway. When he stopped laughing I could hear Dad talking to him and I heard them go into the living room.

A few minutes later, which seemed like an eternity to me, he shouted 'Merry Christmas' and left. Dad would open the kitchen door and ask me if I'm ready to come into the living room. Boy, was I ready!

Mom, Dad and Aunt Hanna sat down while I stared at my presents under the tree. An electric train was going around on an elaborate track. There was a little village of model houses with little cars and a train station with little people on the platform. There was also a new sled, books, lots of clothes and a colourful plate with many kinds of chocolates, cookies, gingerbread men, marzipan, nuts and fruit under the tree.

It was overwhelming!

The radio played *Silent Night*, the Christmas tree sparkled from the light of the flickering candles and then I realized that I had to recite my poem before I could enjoy any of my new toys.

Why did I have to pick such a long poem? It seemed like a good idea at the time but now I was stuttering, not being able to concentrate on the task at hand. It was torture! With a lot of help from Mom, who coaxed me along, I finally got through it.

I was enthralled with my train set and paid no attention to the presents that Santa had brought for Mom, Dad and Aunt Hanna. They were smiling and kissing each other, so they must have been happy with Santa too.

Munching on my sweets while playing I had no appetite when dinner was served. Mother insisted I had to eat something or I would get sick from the chocolates and cookies.

Dad was a great playmate and we played until late. It looked like he enjoyed the train set just as much as I did.

There was no curfew on Christmas Eve and I remember waking up in my bed on Christmas Day not knowing how I got there. Aunt Hanna slept over and now we had to start preparing the Christmas Dinner. Grandma arrived early in the afternoon and brought me, what she said, Santa had left for me under her tree.

I didn't believe it came from him because the sweater she gave me didn't fit. Santa knew my size because he had put a lot of clothes for me under our tree and I already owned the identical stuffed animal she gave me.

Grandma promised to exchange my presents for me. Surely, she wasn't going to go to the North Pole to get other stuff from Santa. His workshop must have been empty and his elves wouldn't start working again until after the holidays.

We could smell the goose broiling in the oven. Mom prepared the trimmings and we sat down to a great meal.

After the meal, Grandma insisted we sing songs to celebrate the birth of Christ and to remember what Christmas was all about. It would have been fun, if she didn't have such a shrill and piercing voice. She even drowned out Dad.

Dad didn't seem to care. I noticed that the bottle of brandy Santa had brought him was getting pretty low. When Grandma left, he was hardly able to say good-bye to her. It's not easy to say good-bye in German when you have imbibed too much of the Christmas Spirit. *'Auf Wiedersehen'* doesn't exactly roll off your tongue when you are inebriated.

On Boxing Day, we visited Uncle Karl and his family. I would have rather stayed at home to play with my new toys, but ended up having a great time. He had bought me an Erector set for Christmas and I played with it through the evening while the grown-ups sat around and talked.

My last thrill that Christmas was taking a taxi home, something we seldom did. Mom said that Dad didn't feel that good after all the celebrating and taking the subway home was not a good idea in his condition. He must have been sick because he fell asleep in the cab and Mom had a tough time waking him up and getting him up the stairs to our apartment.

He slept until noon the next day and didn't look very good when he got up. Thank goodness, he didn't have to go to work between Christmas and New Year.

Mom and Dad looked like they needed to recover from the hustle and bustle of the holidays.

Christmas was always a glorious time in Berlin!

Chapter 8

Home, Sweet Home

Growing up in an apartment building that is facing the runway of an international airport is not a memory too many people would share with me.

Our building faced Tempelhof Airport, possibly the only airport in the world in the middle of a city surrounded by apartment buildings. It was a busy airport, as it was the main airport for Berlin used mainly by British Airways, Pan Am and the US military.

Tempelhof Airport was made famous by the Berlin Airlift from 1948 to 1949 when the Soviet Union blocked access to Berlin by land and sea and attempted to starve the city into submission. For over a year, two million people had to be supplied by air with everything from fresh food to coal and gasoline. During that time a plane landed or took off every 90 seconds, 24 hours a day. Living on our street was a deafening experience.

After the Berlin Airlift, the airport only operated from 6.00 am to 11.00 pm. We could sleep at night without the noise of airplanes during the night. In the 1950's, we got soundproof windows in our apartments, which made it a bit more bearable.

Our balcony was close enough to the runway to look inside the cabin windows of the airplanes. We could even see if the pilot was wearing sunglasses. The planes taxied no more than 100 meters away and stopped right in front of our building to go through their final checks with the air traffic controllers before take-off. As a child, I used to stare across the airfield from our balcony watching the planes take off and disappear into the clouds.

Oderstrasse 32

I dreamt that one day I would be a pilot and fly to faraway places around the world. During my childhood, air travel was reserved for the rich and famous and unaffordable for our family.

Sitting on our balcony and having a conversation on a sunny summer day was almost impossible. The noise was unbearable and with a prevailing westerly wind you could smell the exhaust as the pilots revved their engines for takeoff.

I remember how differently people reacted when the powerful engines drowned out their voices.

My father hated to be interrupted and his voice became louder and louder to the point of screaming, with veins popping out of his head. My mother usually tried to wait until the plane had left and got extremely frustrated when she lost the gist of her story or people changed the subject after the two minutes it took for the roar of the engines to fade away.

The quiet between planes was when you heard the radios and the conversations of the neighbours. Many people did not bother to lower their voices or turn down their radios after the plane had left. What for? The next one was just a few minutes away. Most people on our street talked louder than people not living by an airport. I can't remember how often I've been told not to yell even though I thought I was talking in a normal voice.

Visitors who had never experienced being interrupted every few minutes got either very irritated or marvelled at the sounds and sights of the airplanes, but never failed to ask us how we could cope living in such an environment. We had gotten used to it and hardly noticed the noise anymore.

On foggy days, when there was no air traffic, the silence was eerie and bothered us probably more than the noise. When we woke up in the morning without hearing the engine of a plane, we knew we had bad weather and didn't need to listen to the weather report on the radio. The silence, as they say, was deafening.

When Tempelhof Airport closed in 2008, it was the oldest operating commercial airport in the world. The city converted it into a big inner city park.

The tenants of Oderstrasse are still complaining about noise and smoke coming from the former airfield because the city designated the area in front of them as the park's BBQ area. People now party until the early morning hours across the street from our old building and if westerly winds prevail, the smoke and smell of the BBQs drift into their apartments.

I guess you can't win, living at that address.

Our Neighbours

The apartments were all identical in size and layout, two tiny bedrooms, a large living room, a large kitchen, a nice big balcony and a bathroom. The people in our building were as different from each other as can be and every apartment had its own interesting stories to tell.

Maybe it was the deafening noise or the fumes from the jet engines that caused some of the people on our street to snap or display rather unusual behaviour.

Let me introduce you to our neighbours.

1st Floor

On the ground floor, we had the Strache and Breuer families.

The Breuers had two daughters, Marianne and Renate, and a son. I can hardly remember the son; he immigrated to Australia around 1950 and I never saw him again.

One of their daughters, Marianne, was a deaf mute, but both their daughters were the most beautiful and intelligent girls you'll ever meet.

My mother was friendly with Mrs Breuer and sometimes helped her with the sewing business she operated from her home. My parents, the Schmidts from the third floor and the Breuers used to get together to play cards on a regular basis and were good friends for a long time.

I remember the Breuers as a great family. They moved away to live closer to a school for the deaf on the other side of Berlin. We lost contact with them shortly after they moved.

Living in the other apartment on the first floor, Mr and Mrs Strache seemed to be a happily married couple. Mr Strache was a fun guy who liked to have the odd drink and socialized with most of the neighbours. Mrs Strache was rather quiet and shy.

One evening, Mr Strache went out to buy cigarettes. His wife reported him missing when he didn't come home. It was 6 months later that the police notified her that he had surfaced in Bavaria and did not want to be contacted. Mrs Strache got her life together and managed to build a new life without him.

Seven years later he came back, opened the door and yelled, "Darling, I'm home again!"

We heard the yelling and screaming throughout the night. A few things hit the wall and the sound of broken dishes could be heard a few times. Apparently, he had lived with another woman during that time but decided that he would return to his wife, beg for forgiveness and ask her to take him back. Incredibly, she did! They moved away shortly after his return to escape the gossip, head shaking, chuckling and finger pointing every time they walked down the street.

2nd Floor

Next to our apartment on the second floor lived the Hockun family. They had two girls, Bärbel and Gaby, and a son named Martin. Martin and I were the same age and were friends and playmates. If the story of our building would ever be made into a movie, the Hockun story would guarantee it an X rating.

Mr. Hockun was a truck driver for a brewery and an alcoholic. He was obnoxious and had the demeanour of a little weasel. He was also the manager and business partner of his wife.

Mrs Hockun was a professional hooker and call girl.

She was a stunning-looking woman. She had Rita Hayworth's long flowing red hair, Sofia Loren's body, an attractive smile and no shame or inhibitions. Her fashion sense was not on the conservative side. She wore miniskirts long before they were fashionable and together with her knee-high, red leather boots, it made her look like Irma la Douce. She certainly advertised and marketed her goods extremely well.

When she was 'off-duty' around the house, she wore next to nothing. She didn't mind opening the door to strangers, just dressed in a skimpy apron, barely covering her voluptuous bosom and leaving her derriere fully uncovered. She made no secret of her profession and you would find used condoms over her stove drying out after she had washed them out. She believed they would be OK for repeat performances and it cut down on overhead costs and consumables.

I would assume that the overuse of one of those condoms caused her to get pregnant rather late in life and provided her teenage children, Martin and Bärbel, with their baby sister Gaby.

They were the first family in our building to have a telephone. It was a regular occurrence to hear the phone ring in the middle of the night and 10 minutes later a cab would pull up. Mrs Hockun would jump in and return hours later, often early in the morning. On occasion, she supplied her services at her apartment.

There were times when we heard their front door banging and the yelling of either a dissatisfied customer or by Mr Hockun or both. Once shots were fired in the staircase and the bullet holes remained there for a long time. The story they told to the police about this incident was that somebody broke into their apartment and they fought the intruder off. The police interviewed all the tenants and asked if they had heard something. Nobody talked and nothing ever came of it.

When I had my first serious girlfriend at the age of 17, Mrs Hockun asked me one day if we had already made love. I must have blushed when I told her it was none of her business. She said that the reason for her asking was that she was willing to introduce me to the art of lovemaking, in order for my girlfriend and me to have a memorable first experience.

I was flabbergasted and declined the offer.

My mother told me that Mrs Hockun was active well into her late sixties.

Mr Hockun died in his eighties and the last I heard from Mrs Hockun was that, in her nineties, she was put into a home suffering from dementia. Nobody knows what happened to her daughters. Bärbel cut off all relations with her parents after she found her husband in bed with her own mother and Gaby moved out after she graduated from school.

Martin fathered two children and is now a widower living like a recluse, avoiding contact with his childhood friends and neighbours.

3rd Floor

Of all the families in our building, my parents socialized most with the Schmidt family. It was never a close friendship, but we were always friendly towards each other and had a good relationship over the years.

The Schmidts had two children, Lothar and Edeltraud or Traudchen as we used to call her. Lothar was the younger sibling and frequently ended up looking after me. Lothar was seven years older than me. When his parents and a few neighbours got together and inevitably ended up telling jokes, he and I were sent to the kitchen.

Lothar was supposed to entertain me and protect my sensitive ears from the dirty jokes flying around. I loved having Lothar look after me and looked forward to being exiled to the kitchen with him. However, he made no secret out of the fact that he detested having to babysit me.

What a thrill to have a big teenager as a playmate. Unfortunately, Lothar preferred to be with adults and didn't find it exciting to play kiddy games with a little boy. Without me, he might have been able to persuade his parents to let him listen to the jokes.

My father and Mr Schmidt were great storytellers and every couple of minutes we heard roaring laughter erupting in the living room.

Traudchen, Lothar's older sister, had fallen in love with Larry, an American GI. My parents adored Larry. My father said that he was not like the other Americans. He was humble, polite and agreeable and always smiled when you talked to him.

The smiling and his agreeable nods might have had something to do with the fact that Larry didn't speak any German. Traudchen and Larry got married and went to live in California.

Lothar finished his apprenticeship as a bricklayer and immigrated to the US. It was not much later that Lothar came back to Berlin, as a soldier in the US Army.

I still remember him pulling up in his Pontiac LeMans in front of our building and getting out in his spiffy uniform. It didn't take long until he left Berlin to be deployed to Vietnam. I stayed in touch with Lothar over the years and have visited him in California. I visited Traudchen in the hospital a few days before she died in 2004. Mr Schmidt died in the late 60s, but Mrs Schmidt always invited me and my family for afternoon coffee and cake when we visited my mother.

The other apartment on the third floor belonged to the Przyhodnik family.

Where do I begin?

My parents never liked any of the Przyhodniks.

It started with their eating habits. They loved horse meat. My mother almost fainted when I told her one day that Mrs Przyhodnik gave me a hamburger made from horse meat. My mother wouldn't touch or even look at horse meat. It repulsed her.

My mother would not even drink a cup of coffee at their apartment because of Mr Przyhodniks job.

Mr Przyhodnik considered himself almost a 'Doctor' due to his extensive knowledge of the human anatomy. He worked at the hospital in the pathology department and was in charge of stuffing human cadavers with sawdust and sewing them up after they had been dissected and the organs removed. My mother avoided shaking his hand and scrubbed up after any contact with him.

Mr Przyhodnik was very forthcoming with any diagnosis if he heard somebody was sick. He came up with the most bizarre illnesses that could have befallen that person and loved to describe in detail what it could do to the body and how the organs would deteriorate and rot away. His wife would smile like Igor in the Frankenstein movies and knowingly nod as he dispensed his bloodcurdling wisdom.

The fact that both of them looked like undertakers out of an Edgar Allen Poe novel made it all appear rather surreal when he talked about his gruesome job at the hospital.

Mr and Mrs Przyhodnik were either very laid back or just didn't care about parenting. According to them, their children never did anything wrong, did not need to be disciplined and had no restrictions on any of their activities.

Their two boys, Juergen and Wilfried, were absolute terrors in the neighbourhood. How they ended up without a criminal record was incomprehensible to everyone.

Wilfried was caught vandalizing our cemetery, breaking brass letters out of gravestones and selling them. He stole from many kids on our street and was a bully who threatened children when they tried telling on him. Juergen, the older of the two, protected him from the bigger kids. Juergen also had a destructive side and was full of mischief, bordering on criminal behaviour.

Mr Przyhodnik was able to keep both of them out of the juvenile court system, proclaiming they were going through a 'phase' and most times denying any wrongdoings by his boys.

Their oldest child was their daughter Inge. Inge's dream was to marry a rich American and live in the USA. She once applied to emigrate but was turned down since she didn't complete an apprenticeship or have any qualifications to acquire an immigration visa. Her only chance was to find an American to marry her.

She frequented every bar where you could find US soldiers and came home with a different one every week. It didn't matter what size, colour, shape or religion they were. She must have slept with half the US Army stationed in Berlin. The rumours about her frequent stays in hospital were all about miscarriages, abortions and bouts with VD.

To everybody's surprise, she found somebody to marry her and take her to Wisconsin where she is still living today, happily married with two children. Her dream of Prince Charming carrying her off to a new land certainly came true.

Juergen settled down, married and had two beautiful children. He died at the age of 42, after a heart attack.

Wilfried got divorced in his early 60s after a long marriage and after his two children had left home. He is now living in a remote mountain village in the Bavarian Alps.

4th Floor

Mr and Mrs Dutschke's daughter, Helga, was a gorgeous young woman. She had trained as a ballet dancer and was a showgirl at the Friedrichstadt Palace in Berlin. The Friedrichstadt Palace is still the largest stage in Europe and can only be compared to Radio City Music Hall in New York or the Lido in Paris.

Helga had the smile, the figure, the legs and the talent to be a member of this most prestigious ensemble.

Mr Dutschke sometimes got free tickets from his daughter and often gave them to neighbours to watch her perform.

I remember him as condescending, preachy and rather full of himself. I have no idea why he thought of himself as a touch above everybody else. He was a construction worker specializing in reinforced steel. My parents did occasionally socialize with them but Mr Dutschke was not somebody you wanted to be around when he had one too many drinks. He was most certainly not a happy drunk and his wife had to gently tell him to go home when he entered his obnoxious phase during a get-together. She had great difficulty controlling him.

In Germany, you only address close friends and relatives by their first name. Children and adolescents certainly didn't address adults by their first name. If an adult felt especially close to a child, they might offer to be addressed by their first name with the prefix uncle or aunt. For example my friend Kalle always called my mother 'Aunt Hedwig'.

I visited my mother in 1980 and met Mr Dutschke in the street on his way home from work. I could tell that he had been drinking. We engaged in some small talk and he asked me many questions about Canada. As I said 'Good bye, Mr Dutschke' he squeezed my hand, looked straight into my eyes and said: "You know Konrad, you shouldn't call me Mr Dutschke anymore, you can call me Uncle Rudy."

I was taken aback. Here I was, a man of 34 years of age and he still saw me as a snot-nosed little kid in *lederhosen.* I just looked at him and said, "Thank you very much, but I will stick with Mr Dutschke." That was Mr Dutschke, he would never regard you as his equal.

On the other side of the staircase on the 4th floor lived Mrs Sommerfeld. She was my mother's age and a spinster, but preferred to be called Mrs rather than Ms Sommerfeld.

She was a nice lady and everybody liked her. My father renovated her apartment once and said she was a pleasant woman. My mother invited her sometimes for a cup of coffee and a chat.

She had a good job as an office manager in a small company and seemed content with her life.

One Sunday afternoon she sat down in front of her stove, opened the oven door, turned on the gas and put her head in the oven.

Mr Grossman from the 5th floor smelled the gas as he was passing her apartment and banged on the door. He knew not to ring the doorbell or the sparks could have ignited the gas and blown up half the building. He broke down her door, pulled Mrs Sommerfeld's head out of the oven and tried to resuscitate her, but it was too late.

No suicide note was ever found.

5th Floor

I don't remember much about the Grossmanns. They were nice people, but very private. They always had a smile, a friendly greeting when they saw you and never complained about anything.

They hardly socialized and never picked a fight with anybody.

Their daughter Monika was the talk of the town when her boyfriend showed up in a shiny, red Porsche 356. In the 1950's, owning a car was something special and you didn't see too many brand new Porsches in our working class neighbourhood.

Everybody was impressed when she married into a rich family and entered Germany's 'High Society'. Nobody from our building was invited to the wedding. Everybody knew it was going to be a grand affair when a white, chauffeur-driven Mercedes 300s pulled up in front of our building to take the bride, dressed in a stunning designer gown, to church and marry into a life of privilege.

There was nothing traditional about the other couple on the 5th floor. They were Hilla Bester and Ulla Wolf, our neighbourhood's only same sex couple.

I was remotely related to Hilla through marriage. She was the niece of my uncle's wife.

Same sex couples were not common, nor readily accepted by society in the 1950s. Hilla and Ulla barely disguised the fact that they were lovers and it was not easy to understand what Hilla saw in Ulla.

Hilla was married before and had a son, Wolfgang Bester. She got divorced because she fell in love with Ulla and wanted to share her life with her.

Wolfgang lived partly with his mother, but mostly with his father and immigrated to Canada after he finished his apprenticeship. I visited him once in Toronto after I immigrated in 1968.

What attracted Hilla to Ulla is a mystery.

Hilla was a statuesque, good looking, friendly and educated lady. Ulla was built like a pitbull terrier, had the personality of a pitbull terrier and growled like a pitbull terrier. She was vulgar, loudmouthed and obnoxious.

Hilla dressed fashionably but conservatively. Ulla wore black construction boots and men's clothing that did not flatter her stout body and her rolled-up pant legs emphasized her already short stubby legs.

You could not find two people more different from each other than Hilla and Ulla, but people in our building were surprisingly tolerant of their sexuality and nobody ever caused any problems for them. They were accepted for who they were and lived happily together until Hilla died of cancer in the late 1970s.

Summary

I feel blessed to have grown up on Oderstrasse and not in a sterile suburban neighbourhood.

Life was different and simpler in those days. We were much more tolerant and understanding towards our neighbours, their needs, their opinions and their lives as a whole.

We knew each other, we helped each other. We laughed, cried and partied together and yes, we gossiped about each other. We lived a rich life during a tough time in a unique neighbourhood in a great city, Berlin.

Chapter 9

My 10th Birthday

My father was determined to have the biggest party the neighbourhood had ever seen to celebrate his son's 10th birthday.

It got bigger than he thought.

In those days most people still worked half days on Saturdays. My father had taken some time off to prepare for the party. He bought three 5-litre jugs of brandy from a friend who worked in a distillery and a few cases of beer, delivered by the brewery, together with lots of soft drinks for the children.

My mother was busy making tons of her famous potato salad, frying up *bouletten* (Berlin style hamburgers) and preparing sandwiches and *hors d'oeuvres* with the help of my aunt Hanna.

My cousin Margot was baking cakes. Dad was rearranging the furniture in the living room and setting up the chairs we had borrowed from the neighbours. He also prepared the punch, one for the adults and one for the kids. The kitchen looked like we were cooking for an army.

After all, we had invited our relatives from far and near and everybody in the neighbourhood.

We had scaffolding in front of our building. The facade was being re-plastered to get rid of the cracks that were left from the war. When the beer truck arrived, around 10:00 am, the construction workers enquired who the party was for; and my father proudly proclaimed that his son was turning ten and offered them a drink. Dad constantly refilled their glasses through the window and, not wanting to be a bad host, kept them company.

Since it was quitting time at noon, they hung around for a social drink to celebrate my birthday. They finally left when the clown, my parents had hired for the children's party, arrived. My mother dealt with him since my father's nose at this time was redder than the clown's and he stumbled around like he, and not the clown, was wearing those oversized funny shoes.

My mother, not too happy with my father's inebriated state, suggested he lie down for a while to sober up.

By two o'clock, the kids arrived and the clown entertained us for the next two hours with magic tricks, games and a sing-along in the backyard of the apartment complex. Mr. Lausman, the custodian of the complex, had given us permission to set up tables for the children's party and let us play on the lawn.

The 'Don't walk on the grass' signs, normally strictly enforced by him, could be ignored for the afternoon. He made sure to point out that this was a major concession on his part and worthy of a healthy gratuity. Most of his concessions and services warranted generous tips.

My father got up from his sobering nap just in time to help my mother serve the fruit punch and cake to the kids and give them their loot bags.

My Uncle Karl and Aunt Elfriede arrived with their daughter Inge and her fiancé.

Uncle Karl had brought his big accordion with him and was to be the entertainer for the evening. Inge's fiancee brought his guitar and we were looking forward to a great evening of entertainment. By 6:00 pm, most of the guests had arrived and since there were more people than our living room could accommodate, they mingled in the kitchen, on our large balcony and in the hallway.

My mother and Aunt Hanna put the food out in the kitchen and everybody helped themselves.

Uncle Karl and his future son-in-law started playing at around nine o'clock. Dad and Mr. Schmidt had good booming voices and loved to sing. They sang a few folk songs and got into the good German um-pah-pah and carnival music. The place was hopping in no time.

Dad got pots and wooden spoons out and we had a percussion section. Everybody was dancing, singing or just having the time of their life.

My 'invited' Birthday Guests, 1956

The policeman who patrolled the neighbourhood every night came up to talk to us. He said he was just warning us that we should tone it down a bit so he wouldn't get complaints. We pointed out to him that this was unlikely, with most of our neighbours attending the party. After he had a drink to celebrate with us he left, telling us to have a good time but to keep it down.

I don't remember if, how, where or when I fell asleep. However, I remember finding Dad sleeping in the bathtub early in the morning. Mr Stelling, from the building next door, had rolled himself up in our carpet and somebody, I forgot who, was sleeping in the stairwell half way down. Uncle Karl was sleeping in our armchair and Aunt Elfriede was snoring away on the chesterfield.

Mom was lying on her bed, fully dressed and wide awake, with Aunt Hanna curled up next to her.

I did try to wake up my father, but it was impossible.

I looked at him lying there in the bathtub, while I was doing my business on the toilet and started laughing. Somebody had brought him a pillow, but he still didn't look too comfortable. There was a knock on the bathroom door. Aunt Hanna had to have a pee, but refused to go with my father lying there in the bathtub.

Mom stood guard while Hanna did her business. She was safe as Dad didn't wake up for another hour.

When he finally awoke, he was almost paralysed by a giant hangover and stiff and sore from spending the night in a bathtub.

Mr. Stelling was gently unrolled out of the carpet when his wife came looking for him. He must have had a gallon of coffee before he went home, still holding his head and mumbling, "I'll never drink again." Uncle Karl went to get a taxi. He was in no shape to carry the accordion all the way to the subway.

Neighbours showed up to help us move the furniture back and to pick up their chairs.

Otto Schmidt, Mr. Strache and my father got straight back into celebrating with all the leftover libations, much to my mother's chagrin.

By early afternoon my mother had enough. She insisted on having a nap and threw everybody out. She needed some peace and quiet! I, dead tired myself, went to sleep beside her.

I don't know where my Dad and his two *amigos* went, but when I woke up late that afternoon my father was in bed snoring away. He didn't get up until Monday morning.

Mom was sitting on the balcony with Aunt Hanna enjoying coffee and cake. She asked me if I had a fun birthday.

I said yes, but I think I didn't have as much fun as Dad.

Chapter 10

Pranks

Just as in life, pranks don't always work out the way they are planned. The joyful anticipation when preparing a prank and the feeling of triumph and success when things go exactly as envisioned were priceless. It was as satisfying to achieve laughter, fun and amusement of everybody involved, or embarrassment and fury for our victims.

When things went wrong, and they often did, sadness, pain, regret and punishment could be the result.

But what would a childhood be without pranks?

•••••

The first prank I remember went terribly wrong.

Our streets were not busy in those days and playing soccer and other ballgames during the day was seldom interrupted.

A maintenance van was parked in front of the building next door, right in front of Mr Muecke's car. We had the great idea of taking our skipping ropes and tying them to the trailer hitch of the van and the bumper of Mr Muecke's car to see what would happen.

It was no contest; the van won.

The early cars built in post-war Germany were not too sturdy and a bumper was more a decoration than a safety device. When the driver of the van got going, we saw with horror that the little car only jerked a few inches before the bumper flew off and bounced merrily down the street behind the van. He immediately stopped, alarmed by the clanking of the bumper he was dragging.

My parents had to pay a quarter of the damages since we were caught by Mrs Stelling. She saw the whole thing and identified the culprits as Michael, Wilfried, Martin and myself to the owner of the van. There was no damage to the van but Mr Muecke was not happy. Neither were our parents who had to pay for the repairs.

I escaped a good hiding by pleading for mercy since I was an innocent bystander. It was Michael's rope, Wilfried's idea and Martin helped in tying the vehicles together.

In my mind, I didn't do a thing to deserve a beating, I was just a watcher. This was my first lesson that there was a thing called guilt by association.

•••••

Most apartment doors in our buildings opened to the inside from the staircase and we often tied the handles of doors that faced each other together and then rang the doorbells of both apartments. We had a ball when we watched the tug of war that followed. The tenants cursed and threatened us, but they never caught us mischievous little kids.

Not being able to open their doors more than a couple of inches, they went to a window and asked a passerby to untie or cut the rope. We often ran quickly down the street and turned around to slowly walk back up the street just as they started yelling for help. We offered a helping hand, telling our furious victims that we had seen some older kids come out of the building and run away laughing. We never got caught but the novelty wore off. Our mothers also noticed that their clotheslines were disappearing at an alarming rate and didn't allow us to play with them anymore.

•••••

The Przyhodnik brothers, Wilfried and Juergen, were known to be the local bad boys. The grown-ups on our street voted them most likely to end up in jail one day. Their pranks were a lot more vicious and designed to inflict pain or property damage.

The hallway in the basement of our building was pitch dark.

There were only a few dim light bulbs to barely illuminate these catacombs. They gave off just enough light to see the padlocks on the doors of the tenants' storage units.

Juergen once took out all the light bulbs. When my father made one of his frequent trips to the basement he had to feel his way to his unit, the second last one from the end of the hallway. When he reached for the padlock, he knew he was in trouble.

The big rat trap that Juergen had hung over the padlock snapped right across my father's fingers. The pain must have been excruciating. The swelling and the pain kept my father from using his hand for a few days. Luckily, no bones were broken. Juergen's father always believed his sons' pleas of innocence, and their deeds went unpunished. We later heard that Juergen bragged about having pulled off a good one on old Mr Brinck.

•••••

Another favourite prank of theirs, and I have to admit mine as well, was to stuff potatoes into car mufflers. On bigger cars, which were rare in those days, the potato would sometimes come flying out with a big bang and frighten everybody around. Most cars wouldn't start and we would watch puzzled drivers looking for hours under the hood to find the cause of their trouble. There weren't too many cars around in those days and word got around quickly. Soon drivers would first look for potatoes in their mufflers if their cars didn't start.

•••••

We still had organ-grinders in those days. They performed in the streets, sometimes with a monkey, wearing a little red bolero jacket and a cute little cap, chained to the organ. At other times, it could be with an old lady dressed like a Gypsy, singing and dancing to the gurgling sound and rhythm of the music.

It was the monkey's or the old lady's job to pick up coins that people would throw out of their windows and balconies while listening to the music and being entertained.

I never felt good about pranks that were designed to hurt people, but Wilfried thought it was funny to inflict pain.

It was his idea to heat up a 10 Pfennig piece over the gas stove until it was glowing hot and then throw it down to the monkey.

Neither Martin nor I were thrilled with the idea but you didn't disagree with Wilfried. He was a year older than us and was the local bully. Nobody wanted him as an enemy, so most of us went along with him.

I can still hear the poor little animal screaming in pain and see him going absolutely wild on his long chain, jumping up and down. It took the organ-grinder a long time to calm him down. Martin and I felt sorry for the little monkey and couldn't understand that Wilfried thought that this was amusing.

The organ-grinder never found out what happened to his monkey. By the time he had consoled the animal and went to pick up the money himself, the coin had cooled down leaving no trace of this cruel prank.

•••••

We tried to stay away from Wilfried after that and went back to our, presumably, harmless and funny pranks. These included throwing balloons filled with water out of our balconies in front of passersby to give them a fright and a bit of a splash, or shoving stink-bombs through the mail slot of Mr Lausman's apartment door, the custodian we loved to hate.

I can't remember too many pranks from public school, but in High School... well, that's a whole other story!

Chapter 11

Recycling, Berlin Style

Recycling has been practised in Berlin for as long as I can remember. It had become a necessity because Berlin was landlocked and the high cost of shipping food and materials from West Germany was to be avoided if possible to make local goods more affordable.

In our childhood, we collected paper, tinfoil, bottles and anything for which the scrap dealer would give us a few pennies.

The most memorable and unique recycling program was the weekly appearance of our local farmer to trade for food scraps.

I have told this story to many people from all corners of the world and nobody has ever heard of anything like it in any other city but Berlin.

Almost all the farms we had in the city raised livestock, mainly pigs. There were no fields to grow corn, oats or vegetables to feed the animals. The farmers had to come up with a cheap and profitable way to provide food for them.

Most houses and apartment buildings in those days were without central heating. Every room had a tiled stove and the bathroom had a coal fired boiler to supply hot water for your weekly bath.

In the kitchen, we had a gas stove and an old-fashioned coal stove. In the winter, we cooked on the coal stove, which meant that our gas consumption was higher in the summer than it was in the winter. To get these boilers, furnaces, ovens and stoves going we needed a lot of kindling wood to light the fires every day.

To solve the problem of coming up with cheap food for the animals and the Berliners' need for firewood, the farmers had a brilliant idea. Why not exchange food scraps for kindling wood?

Germans eat potatoes every day, boiled, fried, baked or even as potato pancakes. The potato peels were put in a basket and once a week a horse drawn wagon would rumble through our streets and the farmhand driving it would ring a big bell and yell at the top of his voice, *"Brennholz für Kartoffelschalen"* (Kindling wood for potato peels).

His wagon would be loaded with firewood and all the housewives would rush to him carrying their little baskets with their weekly collection of potato peels and other fresh vegetable cutoffs in exchange for some kindling wood.

There was also a large barrel on the wagon in which the farmer collected stale bread, cake and other dry food items. No food scraps were ever wasted back in those days.

We loved it when the potato peel wagon came rumbling through our street, stopping every few buildings. It was fun to pet the horse and sometimes we were even allowed to give it a treat or, on a hot summer's day, bring a bucket of water for the thirsty beast to drink.

I don't remember the last time I heard the rumbling of the potato peel wagon and the ringing of the bell with that never to be forgotten phrase *'Brennholz für Kartoffelschalen'*. As more and more women entered the workforce, not enough people were at home to answer the bell to trade for kindling wood. Berlin's urban renewal program also converted many buildings to central gas heating and this ended the unique recycling program. Our food scraps, from then on, ended up in the garbage.

I guess that's the price of progress.

Chapter 12

My School Years

Section I

Karl Weise Public School 1953-1959

I have many good memories of my years in public school.

I was blessed with great teachers. Ms Löhnchen was our teacher from grade 1 through grade 3. She had just completed teachers college and we were her first class.

We adored Ms Löhnchen and felt that she adored all of us. We loved going to school and she was more than capable of handling a class of 33 little rambunctious kids.

I still remember the exquisite performances she helped us put on for our parents in the school auditorium. We loved to dance, sing and perform for her. We never felt she favoured any of us and to 'tattletale' was a no-no! She worked with kids that needed a bit more help but never neglected to stimulate the more advanced children.

After grade three, our class was split up with a parallel grade (there were always two classes of the same age group in our school). We dreaded the idea of losing our beloved Ms Löhnchen but she was going to take on the new crop of grade 1's. We also hated the idea of losing our friends by changing classes. We knew we were either getting Ms Schneider or Mr Ceranka for our last three years. Everybody shuddered at the idea of getting Ms Schneider. Ms Schneider was different from Ms Löhnchen. She was mean looking, she was old and she was tough.

Picture of my Grade I class

When the public assembly started at the beginning of the school year, my worst fears were confirmed. I ended up with Ms Schneider.

To make things worse, I lost three of my best friends, Martin Hockun, Horst Kliche and Horst Grudde were assigned to Mr Ceranka's class. My friends Kalle Bartscht and Ralph Klähn and the rest of our class stayed together for the next three years.

We were Ms Schneider's last class; she was going to retire after we graduated from public school.

It turned out that Ms Schneider was not at all what she was made out to be. She was tough but fair, she cared for the slow learners and the gifted pupils. She was an old spinster and in her spare time offered private tutoring at her home, at no charge to the parents. She also invited the more advanced kids to visit her and work on extracurricular projects.

That she lived across the street from the school helped a lot. Parents and her pupils loved her. She was very bad in concealing what was maybe her only flaw, she always picked two 'teacher's pets' in her class. Some people complained but nobody did anything about it. Her record as a teacher was apparently exemplary. She had the highest grade average in our school district and had won many merit awards in her career.

What was great was that, for her last class, the two teacher's pets she picked were Christel Ruh and me. I still credit her for my better than average knowledge in English and stimulating my interest in history.

In grade five, I noticed girls for the first time and had my first girlfriend. Her name was Gisela Pawelzik. She was as cute as a button and we stayed best friends right through public school.

It was true 'Puppy Love'. She was the first girl I kissed on a foggy, damp and cold night in our neighbourhood park after we had come from our local outdoor skating ring. We were three couples, Lothar König and Karin Mueller, Peter Olbricht and Heidrun Wartenberg and Gisela and myself.

We had talked about kissing the whole week, but couldn't decide when, where and how to do it and the girls needed a bit more persuasion.

The girls finally agreed that the big event would take place Friday evening after skating. I remember chewing on pine needles all the way to the park because I was afraid I would have bad breath and spoil the whole thing.

The tension was building as we settled down on the park bench and started hugging in our heavy winter clothes.

I saw Gisela closing her eyes when our lips touched. As we pressed our lips together with our mouths firmly closed we suddenly heard footsteps on the gravel pathway and Lothar jumped up and yelled "Police" and we ran for dear life out of the park to avoid being arrested for kissing in public, or under age or for whatever we thought was illegal about kissing and punishable by... well, we hadn't thought that one through yet.

We never looked back to find out if it was a policeman or just an old lady walking her dog that scared the living daylights out of us. I was always a good student and in grade 6, Ms Schneider urged my parents to send me to a scientific school of higher learning. My father was not opposed to higher education but he always wanted me to learn a trade first and then, through evening classes, achieve my grades to enter university.

He believed in having a trade to fall back on. My father had a job as a vocational teacher at a government-run training facility to train young people that had gotten into trouble or failed university. He gave them basic training in a trade to get them qualified to enter the workforce as semi-skilled labourers. He had seen too many adolescents become too old to enter the strongly regulated apprenticeship programs in Germany.

My mother always wanted me to be a dentist, I have no idea why, and Ms Schneider made the point that you don't become a plumber first on your way to Dental College.

Ms Schneider and my mother won the argument and I was enrolled in a scientific school.

I had a great time in public school and we were a tight-knit group of students. In 2009 a group of 26 pupils from Ms Schneider's and Mr Ceranka's class of 1959 got together for our 50th anniversary of graduating from public school.

Former classmates from all over Germany and Canada came to celebrate the event in our old schoolhouse. Ms Löhnchen, now in her 80's, came from Bavaria to see her first-ever class reunited after 50 years. The school offered the cafeteria and catering services for us and we had a great time. We had a lot to talk about and went to a pub to continue our reminiscing well into the night.

The owner of the pub asked us what the occasion was for our get-together. He was astonished and told us he had never heard of a 50 year class reunion and bought all of us a round of free drinks. It was a memorable day!

We assembled the class of 1953 one more time to celebrate the 60th anniversary of our first day in school in May of 2013. I remember having a great ball that day.

Section II

Ernst Abbe High School 1959-1962

My fun-filled and carefree school days were over the moment I left public school.

Germany had a system of streaming children after grade six, according to their expectations and the abilities they had demonstrated so far in their education.

There were 3 options:

1. Practical School to grade 9, followed by a 3-year apprenticeship, including attending a vocational school one day a week.
2. Technical School to grade 10, followed by either Community college or training in government or other white collar professions.
3. Scientific School to grade 13, to prepare you for University. These schools were divided into 'Arts and Language' and 'Science and Mathematics' schools.

It was easy to tell that my new school was no longer meant to be fun. I was shocked when, at our first assembly, we were addressed as 'Ladies and Gentlemen'. That is a surprise at age 12. It got worse! Almost all the teachers addressed me as Mister Brinck. I thought you had to be at least old enough to shave before anybody would call you 'Mister'.

There were only four students from a total of over 60 at our school that had chosen the academic path. Veronica Vahldiek was my only classmate to transfer with me to this school. I had not been close to her. Christel Ruh and Detlef Neuendorf had chosen the arts and language school. I felt lonely.

It took a long time to make new friends. We came from all corners of our school district and nobody lived close to me.

The biggest adjustment was that I was no longer one of the outstanding pupils. I was now just another kid in a class full of bright, above average children. The curriculum was tough and I had to study for the first time in my life. My mother had already been unable to help me after grade five. Chemistry, geometry, algebra, physics needed my full attention to be understood. German and English came fairly easily to me but French was '*un grand désastre*'. I hated it. My first report card that fall classified me as an 'average' student. Words like 'Konrad shows promise but has to study harder' and 'He has to apply himself' were sentences my parents had never seen before on my reports.

With my Grade 6 classmates

My father started mentioning a trade again but my homeroom teacher, Mrs Feldberg, convinced him I would adapt and that I was smart enough to succeed.

The year-end report card mentioned that my results in French were not acceptable and I needed to study harder. Most subjects were about average with German, English, history, music and geography above average. My father had a serious talk with me and told me that if I did not improve, he would not hesitate to put me into an apprenticeship program after grade 9.

My mother hired a tutor for French after the first semester report card of grade 8. There was only one problem. She was a gorgeous grade 11 student with great knowledge in French and in more than just the spoken word.

I was more interested in '*cherchez la femme*' than linguistic skills. She had a tough time fighting my amorous advances off, but she needed the tutoring money and worked deals with me to let me kiss and touch her if we studied first. The last ten minutes belonged to me. The odd kiss and squeezing her sweater was all I got, but for a horny little fourteen-year-old that was a lot.

My tutoring was successful and I passed French. The other subjects did not show any improvement and chemistry and physics got worse. We had a new teacher for those subjects and he didn't like me and I could not stand him. My father now had made up his mind: "Son, you are going to learn a trade first. I'm not going to take a chance with your future!" was his verdict.

My mother still believed I could become an exceptional student and tried to persuade him to change his mind.

I had pretty much conceded that my future would be an apprenticeship and my academic schooling would end after the current school year. The pressure was off and I concentrated on becoming the class clown. I did just enough to scrape by and get a passing grade at year-end.

The pranks I pulled were, in my eyes, hilarious. To the credit of my classmates I was never found out when I cut off the legs of a teacher's chair so she would come crashing down when she sat down. I also mislabelled a bottle of chemicals, I think it was magnesium, so we would have a minor explosion in our chemistry laboratory.

I was also the instigator of placing Mr Kriesel's Isetta, a bubble car with a single door that opened in the front, between a lamp post and a tree so that he could not open the door to get into his car. Six of us picked it up and carried it onto the sidewalk and fitted it perfectly between the post and an oak tree. Passersby just chuckled about the whole thing. A crowd gathered as everybody waited for the owner to arrive. We waited in the distance to watch our victim solve this little dilemma.

Mr Kriesel, our phys-ed teacher, smiled as he came down the steps of the school and saw his car parked between the tree and the post. He asked for volunteers in the crowd to lift his car back onto the road. The crowd applauded as he drove off waving good bye. We were standing about 50 meters away. He knew it was us, but had a good sense of humour about it and gave us a 'Thumbs up' as he drove past.

Mr Reinhardt was a great teacher, he taught history and geography and was one of the few who made it fun to be in his class. He too had a great sense of humour and I was about to test it.

I bought a couple of stink bombs at a novelty shop and placed one under his desk and one by the blackboard. As he entered the classroom, he got a whiff of the nauseating smell and decided to teach us a lesson of his own.

It was a warm June day and the windows were wide open. He immediately ordered them closed by mentioning that he felt a chill. He then proceeded to teach everything from the back of the classroom. He made the three most likely culprits, Hans Weiser, Manuel Hartwig and me, stand in front of the blackboard for most of the hour never mentioning the smell.

He made us write on the blackboard, recite passages from books while sitting at his desk and other chores that required us to stand in front of the class where he would normally be. The smell was sickening and I had a tough time not throwing up. My classmates were not happy with me.

The last year at school was possibly my happiest. I became popular among the students and I discovered my sense of humour. My attempts at being funny or controversial were often interpreted as being a contrarian thinker or a devil's advocate.

Even though my teachers noted that my behaviour was often not acceptable and my grades did not improve, I was given a passing grade when my parents announced I would leave the school after grade nine to pursue an apprenticeship program.

My mother's dream of me becoming a dentist was over.

A couple of my teachers approached me and expressed their disappointment and told me that they hated to see me leave.

I didn't keep in touch with any of my classmates. In retrospect, I don't think that my father's decision was all bad but I do sometimes wonder if I had it in me and what my life would have been like if I had become a dentist.

My decision to become a 'Brewer and Maltster' made my father happy. I was going to learn a recession-proof trade in a country with over 2,000 breweries.

Little did he know how things would turn out.

But that too is another story.

Chapter 13

A Boy And His Dog

In the summer of 1961, my parents went on their first vacation without me. My cousin Margot, who lived next door, was supposed to check up on me every day and make sure I didn't starve to death during their absence.

The souvenir my parents brought home was a miniature dachshund. She was barely big enough to crawl out of the little box she travelled in from Bavaria to Berlin. I fell in love with her the moment I laid eyes on her.

If you ever looked into the eyes of a 3-month-old little dachshund you would know that nobody can resist their loving looks and affectionate whimpering as they lick your face and pee all over. We bonded immediately.

We named her Senta, a popular German name for dogs. I had a great time playing with her whenever there was a spare moment. She learned the usual tricks from giving a paw to rolling over. I knew, like every kid that has a dog, that my dog was the cutest, smartest and most playful dog in the world.

We soon found out that dachshunds are bred to be hunting dogs.

In the spring of the following year, my friend Martin and I took Senta to the park and let her run without a leash.

This is when she spotted a rabbit for the first time in her life.

Calling out the well taught commands, like 'sit', 'stay' and 'come here', didn't register with her. All she saw was something to be chased and caught. All I saw were her ears flapping in the wind chasing that little rabbit zigzagging across the field until the rabbit disappeared into a rabbit hole... and so did Senta!

When we came to the rabbit hole we heard a faint crying and whimpering from below. Senta was stuck and couldn't get out. She was so deep inside the rabbit hole that I could not even grab her tail.

I sent Martin to the public gardening plots to ask one of the gardeners to lend us a shovel. Martin returned within minutes and we started digging.

A small crowd started forming. Some people had seen the whole episode and others stopped to find out why we were digging up the park. Soon the park warden and a policeman arrived to lecture us about the 'leash law' and why it had to be enforced. They talked while we dug deeper and deeper.

It took us a while to unearth Senta. When we pulled her out she was the most frightened, dirty and sorry looking dog you can imagine. It took her only a few minutes to shake the soil out of her fur and lick herself clean to be her old playful self again. The policeman gave me a leash-law violation citation. The park ranger took down my address to send my parents the bill for returning the park back to its original condition.

My father paid the bills but was not happy. He didn't punish me but told me to be more careful the next time I would take her to the park. He too hated to keep Senta on a leash.

My mother, as expected, found a new object of her affection in Senta and spoiled her to no end.

It wasn't long before we noticed that Senta was not a toy or miniature dachshund!

It couldn't have been the treats and table scraps my mother and I gave her that made her grow to be not only one of the biggest dachshunds you have ever seen, but also one of the fattest. She was no longer a lapdog, because there wasn't a lap big enough to accommodate her.

We called her 'Dicke', an affectionate German term for Chubby or Fatso. She soon responded to both names. She had become a real 'Sausage-dog'!

Senta was a terrific watchdog. Visitors could move around freely as long as one of us was in the room with them, but as soon as she was alone with them they were not allowed to move. She would growl and snarl if they moved or even snap and bark at them if they got up. One of us would have to come back to calm her down.

She was stubborn and we knew when she had done something wrong. Her attempts to hide her guilt by cocking her head and looking at us with an angelic and innocent expression on her face was a dead give-away that she had been up to no good.

The children in the neighbourhood loved her. No ball, stick or doll was safe from her. She loved to be chased and never growled at or harmed a child.

The chasing and running around became less as she grew fatter and fatter but she would still try to steal toys from children. Knowing she couldn't outrun them anymore, she would try to sneak away hoping nobody would see her. Kids would give her a head start and then chase her down. Senta loved playing this little game.

The whole family shared the duties of taking Senta for walks. We had a set routine. The early morning walk was with my mother. I took her out when I came home from school. The late evening walk belonged to my father. He would walk her for almost an hour every night, or so we thought.

When my father died suddenly and unexpected, it was I who took Senta out for her late evening walk the next day.

Senta came out of the house and started leading the whole way as if she knew where she was going. After leading me around the corner and down the street she marched straight into the local pub. I could hear the innkeeper and the regulars shouting 'Hi Senta' as she waddled through the open door into the pub. The innkeeper had already put a large ashtray filled with beer in front of her as I walked in.

Everybody in the pub was unaware that my father had died

suddenly and they were shocked when I told them the news. I found out that my father's late evening 'long walks' with Senta were, in reality, short walks to the pub where he had his beer and schnapps and Senta had her beer and a nightly snack of a wiener or a meatball.

My dog and my dad had one thing in common, they loved their beer!

Senta took it very hard when I left for Canada. I had driven a Mercedes 200D in Germany and every diesel engine made a distinct knocking and pinging sound.

Senta knew that sound. Most taxis in Berlin are diesel-powered and every time a Mercedes diesel taxi pulled up to our building, Senta would bark assuming it was me returning home.

Once Senta jumped into a taxi and refused to get out even after much coaxing. She missed not only me but also our little car rides around town. She would curl up on the backseat where the road noise and the gentle rocking of the moving car would put her to sleep within seconds.

When I did come home for a visit four years later and my mother opened our front door, Senta just stared at me, started to cry uncontrollably, squatted down and peed over our hallway carpet. I hugged her and started to cry with her.

I thought she would have forgotten me and didn't expect her reaction to seeing me again. Senta would not let me out of her sight for the two weeks of my visit.

I'll never forget her face when she saw us packing our suitcases to go home again. There was a quiet acceptance and resignation in her eyes when we left.

She knew I was deserting her again. It broke my heart!

In her first letter to me, my mother told me that Senta had found one of my handkerchiefs and put it in her basket. She was guarding it and wouldn't let anybody touch it.

She even growled at my mother when she tried to grab it, and she had never growled at my mother before. This was her memento of me. She kept it for weeks before my mother had a chance to take it away and wash it. She didn't want it back after it was washed.

To paraphrase B.B. King:

The smell is gone
The smell is gone away
The smell is gone away from me
Although I'll still live on
But so lonely I'll be.

Even though Senta was grossly overweight and ate mainly people food, including cookies, chocolate and beer, she lived for 14 years and died peacefully in her sleep the following year.

Chapter 14

Television

Even though the first television broadcast in Germany was in 1936 for the Olympics, regular programming did not start officially until 1954.

Every night people stood on the sidewalks pressing their noses against the store windows of the radio shops to watch this novelty.

My first memory of television was sitting on my father's shoulders to watch one of Germany's games of the 1954 World Cup on a crowded sidewalk in front of the local radio store.

It was in 1956 that my father bought our first TV and our lives changed. I remember the dealer delivering the console TV and adjusting the picture after installing the antenna on the outside of our living room window, announcing to the neighbourhood that television had arrived at the Brincks.

We were the first family to have a television set in our neighbourhood and word got around quickly.

In those days we had two channels, East German and West German TV. There were only about five hours of programming a day, one hour for children in the afternoon and about four hours at night for adults. We hardly watched East German TV except for their *'Mr. Sandman's Good Night Story'* at night for the children and the Monday night movies of old German comedies from the 1930's and 40's.

Hordes of kids started showing up at our apartment just before four o'clock for the children's shows. The TV set had to be turned on 10 minutes before the show started, it took about seven minutes for it to warm up and for the picture to appear.

I had more friends than ever before and more than my mother could tolerate. *'Children's Hour'* with Ilse Olbricht was the most popular show for kids and my mother had a full house for every one of her shows.

My popularity was replaced by hostility when my mother insisted that I couldn't have more than four friends at any time watching with me. I guess her budget for cookies and lemonade had exceeded its limits. Picking only four friends was tough. The good part was, that after telling them that they were no longer invited to watch TV, they decided they were no longer my friends.

The children cleared out when the kiddy programs ended by around 5.00 pm, leaving Mother enough time to clean and tidy up and get ready for the evening shows.

Programming started at 7:00 pm with the local news followed by a sitcom, most often an American show. I loved *'Rin Tin Tin'* and *'Father Knows Best'*.

For the first few weeks, it was nice to have the neighbours come over to watch television with us. They started arriving during the nightly national news at 8.00 pm. Most popular were live broadcast of stage productions, thrillers, game and variety shows, just about everything except political debates. That meant a full house almost every night.

Some neighbours were very thoughtful, they brought some cookies or cake, some even brought one or two bottles of beer. Some expected just a cup of coffee, others expected refreshments and snacks to be served by my parents. There were suggestions of a little penny jar where everybody could donate a few pennies for my mother's trouble. We rearranged the furniture every night to make room for up to 20 people and asked some people to bring their own chairs.

The shows were watched in total silence and darkness. Hysterical laughter or shrieks of horror could be heard depending on the movie. Some, like my aunt, shrieked at the tiniest bit of tension and others like Mrs. Strache laughed like a hyena at the most banal jokes. It was always followed by the crowd telling the offender to keep quiet.

It got so bad that when my father came home late from his evening jobs and tried to greet everybody he was told to *'shush'* and keep quiet. He had to eat in the kitchen because he didn't want to eat in the dark and turning on the light would have disturbed everybody.

Smoking and drinking was much more prevalent in those days. I can't remember anybody not smoking, except for some of the women. Our apartment smelled like a beer hall every morning.

My mother was forever sweeping, vacuuming and washing dishes from the night before.

Our Persian carpet was covered with beer, pop and coffee stains. Mother vacuumed daily to get rid of ground-in cookies and cake. It wasn't easy to avoid being messy when snacking in the dark.

My parents had a tough time and decided to limit our audiences to about six guests per evening. My sleep was interrupted due to the noise when the programs were over and people left for home. We tried to make it clear that we would like to keep it quiet during the week. Some took the hint and others felt rejected.

My parents were closest to the Schmidt Family who lived in the apartment above us.

My father and Otto Schmidt got along famously. Both liked their drink and a good time. My mother and Mrs. Schmidt had a good relationship. Mrs. Schmidt had a a little dog called Purtzel. It was a Pomeranian and not the friendliest dog. He yapped at everything and was extremely nervous. The most objectionable thing about him was that he shed like a dried-up Christmas tree.

There was dog hair on the carpet, on the sofa, the armchair and blowing around on the hardwood floor.

When my mother asked Mrs. Schmidt if she wouldn't mind to leave Purtzel at home, the friendship came to an abrupt end. We never realized how much Purtzel meant to her. She made it clear that if Purtzel was a problem she would certainly not bother to come any longer. They bought their own TV a few days later.

I don't think Mrs. Schmidt ever realized what a relief it was for us that our neighbours now had a choice whose snacks to eat, whose carpet to mess up and where to get their nightly entertainment.

It took my mother a while to reassure Mrs. Schmidt that we still loved Purtzel and after that they stayed friends forever.

TV changed our lives. We didn't socialize as much anymore. Playing games or just sitting down to talk was reserved for evenings when there was nothing on TV.

As more and more antennas went up on our roof, we didn't even get the nightly visitors anymore to watch that little flickering black and white screen in our living room.

Television had opened a window to the world but made us feel a little bit more alone at night. Thank God, we had only four hours of programming and only two channels, that left us with time to talk and read and still listen to the radio.

Radio never disappeared from our evening entertainment. I preferred a good radio play to TV. My imagination was much more engaged as I listened to the German version of *'Dragnet'* and the weekly satirical radio show *'Die Stachelschweine'* (The Porcupines) on the radio.

TV didn't replace good radio shows until the 1960's. It is too bad that commercial radio and television have forced radio plays into extinction.

I miss them.

Chapter 15

My Sporting Life

Part I

The thrill of competition, the joy of winning and the gracious acceptance of losing.

I love sports and have always believed that I was better than most of my competitors. My competitive spirit and my perceived better-than-average natural abilities convinced me I'd be a superstar in something someday. I tried my luck in many sports and hardly ever lived up to my expectations. I rose to the level of mediocrity in many, gave up on most, succeeded in a few and never achieved stardom in any.

Even though I possessed great hand-eye coordination, was quick to react and had great stamina, there was one thing that kept me back: my speed was deceiving, I was slower than I looked.

My chubbiness held me back in many sports, including my favourite, soccer.

I always believed it was my coach who wouldn't let me move up to the 'Elite Teams' because he was blind to my great abilities and talent and placed me in the 4th ranked team out of five in my age group.

It was only due to my success as a goalkeeper on my school

team that I moved up to the 3rd team in my final season.

In high school, I made the junior team as a goalie in soccer and team handball. In handball, we even went right up to the regional finals due to my sensational performance in goal, I think.

Even though my best results were in table tennis, a second place in our club championships, I had to give it up to pursue my dream of becoming the next Pele to be worshipped by my fans around the world. In my mind this was a realistic goal. I guess I should have trained harder.

My best and worst memories of my soccer career did not come as a player but as the coach of my daughter's team in my later years. Coaching your own child is not something I would recommend to any parent.

Stories about my coaching days are much better told by my daughter. I don't think I would agree with her description of me as a coach. I was always seen as either favouring my daughter or being too hard on her. That view was shared by my daughter, the other players and their parents.

Rowing

Rowing sounded like a great sport and a friend in high school convinced me to give it a try.

Ahhh, being out on the water on a sunny morning gliding across the lake and watching the world go by... what could be more exhilarating?

Reality proved to be different! After a short lesson on dry land, I was off in the coxed four.

I thought my arms would fall off, my lungs would explode and I came close to fainting as the cox yelled out the stroke rhythm. Everybody had to pull at the same time. There was no way to relax or slack off.

I know that everybody looked at me, shaking their head and some even snickered as I couldn't get the oars out of the water due to sheer exhaustion. We had to stop for me to get my breath back and get some feeling back in my arms, I couldn't even raise my arms to wipe the sweat off my face.

The humiliation I felt holding my oars out of the water as the others rowed back to the club house was adding to my physical pain. My career in rowing had ended even before I got out of the boat. However, my worst experience was yet to come.

Boxing

At my last physical examination before moving to Wiesbaden, West Germany, my blood pressure and my weight were above average and my doctor recommended an exercise program. My years of drinking beer while working in the brewery had at last caught up with me.

When I arrived in Wiesbaden, a colleague recommended joining a boxing club as a great way to lose weight and get into shape. Living in a new city, where I didn't know anybody, this sounded like a great idea to meet new friends and improve my health.

I enjoyed my three workouts a week, did some sparring, lost weight and my more muscular-looking body started to impress me after my first six months in the club.

A competition had been scheduled with an Austrian club at the local arena for the fall of that year. Our heavyweight boxer broke his leg in an accident earlier that year and was unable to box. When the second heavyweight was admitted to hospital with appendicitis two weeks before the meet, the coach came to me and asked me if I would take his place.

Knowing that the boxer I was supposed to fight was the former runner up in the Austrian championships of 1956, it didn't make me feel confident that I had much of a chance to win. I had only been boxing for six months and never fought other than as a sparring partner. I figured I had a slight disadvantage.

My coach told me it would look bad if we have to cancel the heavyweight fight, which is always the most popular weight class. He suggested for me to take a dive if I should get hit hard by a punch. 'Just be on your toes, don't get hit and don't try to be a hero,' he said. Good advice!

•••••

My adrenalin is rising as I enter the ring. The announcer introduces me with his booming voice, "And in the red corner weighing in at 93.5 Kilograms, originally from Berlin, in his first fight, give a warm welcome to Konrad Brinck". I study my opponent in his corner. He looks out of shape, a bit flabby but much bigger than me.

The referee gives us his instructions, the bell rings and we are on!

For the first minute nothing happens, a few jabs, I dance around him, he is almost stationary.

The crowd starts booing.

I take a chance with a right jab followed by a left hook to the body. He winces as he gasps for air. My hook had connected with his liver.

This is where I make my big mistake! I think I can beat him!

It takes him a while to recover, but he does.

I don't remember hitting the canvas after a wicked uppercut and I am not clear where the yelling and screaming is coming from as I regain some consciousness. I just feel I have to get up.

I am still dazed as the referee grabs my gloves and asks me if I am OK.

I don't understand the question but say 'Yes'. Another mistake! He yells, "Box."

I am pretty defenceless hanging on to the ropes as my opponent pummels me. The bell saves me.

My coach is furious! "Why didn't you stay down? He's gonna kill you."

I have no explanation, just that I didn't know where I was when I was lying on the floor. I don't mention that I still think that I can maybe put him down with one more good punch.

The bell rings! Round two!

The second round is ten seconds old when he knocks one of my contact lenses out.

I don't know if the blood dripping into my eye, the loss of the contact lens or the swelling limiting my vision makes me unable to see that right hook coming towards my chin.

It doesn't matter that I am back on my wobbly legs by the time the ref counts to nine, my trainer throws in the towel to end the massacre.

I went home after the doctor fixed me up with a few stitches, put cold compresses on my swollen eyes and cheekbones and checked if I had suffered a concussion or broken any ribs.

I didn't recognize the guy who stared back at me from my mirror in the bathroom.

It didn't make me feel any better that the newspaper the next day described me as 'The new kid from Berlin with a lot of heart, but no style'.

I never boxed again!

Part II

Canada introduced me to sports that were not popular and almost unknown in Germany.

I had never seen a baseball game or knew much about curling or lacrosse but was fascinated by football and hockey.

It was my wife Jackie who awakened my interest in baseball. She loved the Pittsburgh Pirates and adored their star player Roberto Clemente.

We later became great fans of the Blue Jays and spent many hours in the stands of the old Exhibition Stadium in Toronto. I still remember their first game on a snowy, cold afternoon on April 7th, 1977.

We didn't know if we should get up and exercise with Toronto's mascot 'BJ Birdy' to get some circulation back into our frozen toes and fingers or just simply stay seated wrapped up in our blankets.

I was already a hockey fan in Germany with Berlin having two competitive teams and my good friend Horst Grudde playing for one of them. He later became the goalie of the German National Team. I was amazed by the skill level, speed and the hard body checking in the professional game. I joined the band of Maple Leaf supporters. After being a fan of the Maple Leafs for over 44 years I have come to the conclusion that I can't support a team that is specializing in only three things: Making money, losing and disappointing their fans! I've given up on the Leafs.

In the world of sales, 'Team Building' is part of the game.

Every sales organization I worked for had some kind of extracurricular activities for their employees to promote camaraderie and team spirit. I was always keen to join these groups as they were fun and a great way to get to know your colleagues in a social environment and have a few drinks together after the game.

At Olivetti, we had two hockey teams, sales and service. They were both in competitive Industrial leagues and very skilled players.

Management had the brilliant idea to stage an interoffice tournament between the three Toronto branches, Hamilton and the two Montreal branches. They tried to involve all employees but noticed a lack of interest amongst the non-Canadians who had not grown up with hockey. To create some interest and excitement they decided that each branch should have a 'non skating line'.

The rules were simple, you had to be an immigrant from anywhere but North America, could never have been a member of a hockey team and you had to have a good sense of humour.

We had four weeks to put our team together.

The first training session, if you can call it that, was painful or hilarious to watch, depending if you were the coach or a spectator. There were about 12 of us trying out for our team.

Most of the brave volunteers couldn't even stand on the ice. The coach cut half of us within five minutes. He had to use all his coaching skills to simply teach us how to skate.

I had skated as a child and remembered enough to get around the rink without falling down too often.

Johnny Carroll, the English player in our international line-up, tried using his soccer skills to play the game, he used the stick to balance himself and tried to kick the puck forward. Ernie Tommasetti, playing with great enthusiasm, was getting around by walking on the side of his skates with the blades hardly touching the ice and his arms flailing, swinging his stick wildly while literally running across the rink.

Dip Chakroborti, our Indian representative, was an amazing character. He played wearing figure skates and pushed himself off with one foot gliding along the ice, but the coach had a tough time teaching him that a hockey stick is not a cricket bat and the grip and shooting action are different from cricket.

Nizar was from Uganda, he learned to skate with his children when he came to Canada and got around fairly well. He was afraid of contact and never carried the puck but got rid of it the moment he touched it.

We got to wear full hockey gear for the first time at the tournament. None of us had ever worn knee-pads or gloves. It is pretty tough to get up after a fall when wearing full gear. I remember a few of the players having to crawl to the side of the rink to pull themselves up on the boards.

We only got about five minutes of ice-time in each game but the cheering in the stands was replaced by howling laughter when we were on the ice.

There have been fewer tears shed by Maple Leaf fans for their incompetence over the years than the tears of laughter shed on those two nights in Montreal for our comical version of hockey.

I don't remember who won the tournament and I don't think anybody else does, but nobody will ever forget those 'Non Skating Lines'.

Skiing

I won a complete ski package in a sales contest. I had never skied before and was willing to give it a try. I thought it would be a good idea for the whole family to take up skiing and enrolled us all in lessons. Toni, my daughter, loved skiing but Jackie, a native South African who had not seen snow until she came to Canada in her 20's, was not thrilled with the idea of spending any time outside when the temperature did not warrant wearing a bikini.

The idea of having fun in the snow seemed rather far-fetched to her. Adding a mild fear of heights to the equation and skiing was not something she would consider an enjoyable activity but voluntary torture.

She realized after a short lesson that skiing was not something for people born in Africa.

Jackie would still join us sometimes on trips to a ski resort and enjoyed the apres-ski activities. The thrill of shushing down a ski run was not something she would ever experience.

I loved skiing with Toni. Our ski trips to Quebec and Vermont as well as our day trips to the many ski hills here in Ontario were always fun. There came a time when Dad was just not wanted or needed anymore and her skiing activities were with her teenage friends. Old people like Dad just didn't fit into that mix. Watching her growing up from afar was not easy. I miss our times together.

•••••

I don't know if my most painful memory of my sporting days is from boxing or skiing.

It was the last run of the day down Jay Peak in Vermont. The sun was setting, the shadows were getting longer and there was hardly a skier left on the hill. I decided to let it all hang out and let my skis run. I did not see that mogul in the middle of the two intersecting trails and hit it in full flight.

I knew the landing was not going to be perfect as I was flying through the air with my ski-tips pointing skywards. The safety bindings released as I hit the packed snow landing hard on my back, and was somersaulting down the mountain being tossed around like a rag doll.

I don't know what was more debilitating, my inability to breathe due to two cracked ribs, my lack of mobility due to a dislocated knee-cap or the problem of being unable to move my arm properly due to a severely bruised shoulder.

The ski patrol recommended that I go to the hospital but I decided I could tolerate the pain and would be able to drive home. Luckily, it was my left knee that was immobile so I could still operate the brake and gas pedals.

My breathing was okay as long as I didn't laugh or cough and my shoulder didn't hurt that much as long as I did not try to raise my arm.

The drive back home the next day was torturous. I had only one restroom break because getting in and out of the car was coupled with excruciating pain. I was never more thankful for reclining power seats so I could glide in and out of the car without having to bend my knee.

The emergency doctor in Peel Memorial Hospital couldn't believe I had driven such a long way back from Vermont. I think he questioned my sanity a few times. I thanked him for the painkillers, the crutches and the handicap parking sticker. I needed them for the next few weeks.

Golf

My sport of choice these days is golf. My handicap puts me on an equal footing with everybody. It doesn't matter how bad I play because I know that on every hole there is one shot of mine that Tiger Woods couldn't have done any better than me.

The last one.

My wife Jackie has experienced the greatest thrill in golf: A Hole In One!

She will never ever let me forget that I have not. Well, not yet anyway. I'm still trying!

In my heart I know that one day the 'Golfing Gods' will smile upon me and grant me that moment of ecstasy when I make that perfect shot and see my ball take one bounce on the green and then disappear into that little hole about 180 yards away.

Chapter 16

What Was He Thinking?

My father was an emotional man and made decisions that he later regretted. He often admitted that he had not thought things through. Here are a couple of examples.

The Piano

When my father took on extra jobs, his customers were not the wealthiest people around and he often accepted goods and services in kind.

One lady offered him a piano for his services. Her husband had died and she had no use for it any longer. She didn't know if it was worth enough to pay for the renovations. It was over 20 years old and out of tune.

Since my father felt that I should learn an instrument, he agreed to take it and a few days later he rented a hand cart and a few strong friends helped him to move the piano into our apartment.

I was not interested in learning the piano. I wanted an instrument to play at picnics, campfires and at my friend's homes, like a guitar or an accordion, not one I couldn't carry around with me.

After a couple of weeks of trying to convince me that playing the piano would be fun, he gave up and put a 'For Sale' ad in the local paper. He would have charged the old lady 300.00DM for labour and materials and the cost of getting the piano moved to our home was another 50.00DM. A few extra Marks on top would be prudent in case he would be bargained down by an interested buyer. So the ad read:

PIANO FOR SALE
400.00DM
Kurt Brinck
Berlin, Oderstr 32
Sunday 10:00 am-5:00 pm

We had no phones in those days. People came to the apartment hoping the items had not been sold already.

The first person showed up at 10:00 am on Sunday morning and looked at the piano and said, “I'll buy it. Here is a 50.00DM deposit and I'll be here tomorrow to pick it up.”

My father was elated! He didn't even have to bargain!

It was noon when the doorbell rang and my father told the prospective buyer that the piano was sold. The man asked if he could at least have a look at it and my father let him in.

The man looked at the piano and said, “I would have given you 500.00DM for it!”

My father took a deep breath and said, “You can have it! I'll just tell the other guy I changed my mind and want to keep it.” He took a 100.00DM down payment and told the guy not to worry about the other buyer. He'd handle it. The man told him he would be back the following weekend to pick it up.

The excitement over the extra 100.00DM lasted only a short while.

When the local used furniture and junk dealer showed up my father told him he was too late. He proudly added that he had sold it for more than the advertised price. The dealer asked my dad what make the piano was and in what kind of condition it was. Dad told him the name on the piano was ‘Grotrian’ and other than a couple of scratches it looked perfect.

The dealer looked at my father and asked to see it. After playing a few notes on it he turned to my father and said, “ You don't know anything about pianos, do you?” My father shook his head.

He continued telling my Dad that he would gladly pay 1000.00DM for this classic model. My father swallowed hard and got mad.

Outraged about the previous buyers taking advantage of his ignorance, he proclaimed, "That last guy knew exactly what he was doing, he tried to screw me. There is no way I'll sell him my piano, he is a crook! If you are serious about buying the piano and think that it's worth a 1000.00DM you can have it!"

The dealer gladly gave my Dad a sizeable deposit and said he'd be back to pick it up.

Unfortunately, things didn't go well from then on.

Dad ended up in court for breach of contract.

My father complained bitterly about having been taken advantage of by the first two buyers. He argued that they should be punished for knowingly trying to conceal the true value of the piano.

The judge didn't share my father's point of view and awarded the piano to the first buyer for the agreed price of 400.00DM. My Dad had to compensate the second buyer for his loss and return the down payment. The dealer did get his deposit back but was not awarded any damages.

My father also had to pay everybody's court costs.

In the end, it cost him over a 1000.00DM to renovate that old lady's apartment. It wasn't, of course, his fault!

I still got an accordion for my birthday.

•••••

I had a paper route when I was in grade 8. I delivered magazines to houses and apartments in Tempelhof, a borough of Berlin. I had to deliver and also collect the money upon delivery. Some people paid me monthly in advance, which I preferred, but most paid weekly.

To cycle to Tempelhof was almost a 30-minute ride and my deliveries took me well over two hours. I could choose any day from Thursday to Saturday to finish my weekly route.

Weather always played a big role in choosing my day since it was no fun to ride in bad weather with 50 magazines on my bike's luggage rack. We had four days of rain in a row and Saturday morning was another rainy and blustery day. I asked my Dad if he would drive me to deliver my magazines. Even though he had a bit of a hangover from the night before he agreed to take me.

I started my deliveries and he drove from house to house. When we got to the apartment buildings at the end of my route, he said he would drive ahead and wait for me in the pub at the corner.

An hour or so later I was finished and joined him in the pub. He bought me a Coke and a snack and after he finished his beer, we got into to the car to drive home.

We came to the first major intersection and had to turn left. My father was in the left turn lane when a VW Beetle passed us too close on our right hand side and ripped off the right front bumper of my father's car.

It must be said that the Lloyd Alexander TS my father owned was not the sturdiest car and the right front aluminium bumper cost only 14.95DM to replace, as we later found out.

The car was my father's pride. Its 2-cylinder 600cc engine could reach a top speed of 100km per hour and it's 25 horse power made it almost a muscle-car amongst the anaemic mini-cars built in Europe in the 1950's.

When my father saw the mangled bumper, he yelled at the other driver, who had stopped and stepped out of his car to inspect the damage. There was not a scratch on his VW. He accused my father of having pulled out of his lane. A yelling match ensued.

The other driver challenged my father to call the police and, not thinking right, my father agreed.

The officer just shook his head as he inspected the minimal damage. When he took my father's information down, he said, 'Sir, have you been drinking?' My father quickly explained that he had a quick beer in a pub while waiting for his son to finish his paper route. The officer then asked if he would mind blowing into the newly introduced breathalyzer. My father didn't object.

Back in those days, the breathalyzer only had a green, yellow or red zone indicating your level of intoxication and was in itself not admissible in court. It was used as a guideline to indicate if a blood test should be administered to establish the real level of alcohol in the blood.

My father blew well into the red zone.

The residual alcohol from the night before and a couple of drinks in the pub must have done the trick.

The policeman called for a paddy wagon and Dad was taken for a blood test. My father's objections and his constant insistence that the accident was not his fault fell on deaf ears. His car was towed to the police pound and I was given a ride home by the police.

The 1958 Lloyd Alexander TS

My mother was beside herself. My father arrived home that evening and assured my mother that the accident was not caused by him being drunk and the test will show that he was under the legal limit of 0.8 promille. He only had a beer and a brandy!

A few days later, he was notified by mail that his alcohol level was 0.98 promille and he was charged with 'driving under the influence of alcohol and driving while intoxicated'.

My father was looking forward to his day in court.

Even though everybody urged him to hire a lawyer, my father was convinced he could talk himself out of it by explaining his innocence and the fact that there had to be a mistake since he only had a beer and a brandy.

To my father's surprise, the judge was not interested in who had caused the accident; the other driver wasn't even subpoenaed to appear at the trial. My father insisted and had a note from the pub owner, that he consumed only one beer and one brandy that day at the pub. When the judge asked him about his consumption on Friday night, my Dad was honest. We had company that night and he did have a few drinks.

The judge was patient as he explained to him about the residual alcohol in his bloodstream and at his height of 168 cm (5' 6"inches) he would reach 0.8 promille even without having sinned the night before. He then showed some mercy. He dropped the charge of 'driving while intoxicated' because the police had not performed a sobriety test and intoxication could not be proven.

The verdict still came as a shock to my Dad.

- 90 days' licence suspension
- 500.00DM fine
- 480.00DM in court costs
- He had already paid the impounding and towing fees of 130.00DM
- Total cost: 1110.00 DM plus subway tokens for 3 months.
- I forgot, he still had to buy a brand new, shiny aluminium bumper for 14.95DM!

Chapter 17

Who Were They?

People always talked about 'The War Years' while I was growing up. They talked about the horror that civilians experienced during the bombing of our cities, the hardships suffered by our soldiers on the front, the restrictions of freedoms under the 'Third Reich', but nobody ever talked about the atrocities and crimes committed by Germans.

I became more and more aware of Germany's immediate past by reading books, watching documentaries on TV and the odd mention in the papers of 'Nazi-hunters'. I also learned about the history of our own family, having had an aunt interned in a concentration camp and an uncle jailed for being a member of the KPD (Communist Party of Germany) in the 1930's.

I became obsessed with the Holocaust, when Adolf Eichman was captured in Argentina and subsequently tried for genocide in Israel. The newspapers, radio and TV ran constant reports, discussions and documentaries about the trial and Germany's past.

I could not understand that almost everybody claimed they did not know what was going on during that time.

How could six million people have been slaughtered and nobody knew?

Who and where were these Germans today?

Where were the people that ordered, executed, assisted , knew, collaborated, promoted and justified these murderous crimes?

I could never find anybody who at least admitted to have known about it or knew somebody who was a participant in the killings. Yes there were rumours, some said, but who could have believed them? We were civilized people and would not kill people for their race, religion, political beliefs, mental or physical condition or sexual orientation.

I had learned in school that Germany was a land of progressive thinkers and rulers in the past. Rulers like Frederick the Great who offered refuge to oppressed and persecuted minorities from across Europe. Otto von Bismarck's social insurance programs were the first in the world and became the model for other countries and the basis of the modern welfare state. Bismarck introduced old age pensions, accident insurance, medical care and unemployment insurance for all Germans.

Kaiser Wilhelm I guaranteed freedom of religion in 1871 and the Weimar Constitution of 1919 enshrined these rights after WWI.

Great minds like Martin Luther, Immanuel Kant, Johann Wolfgang von Goethe, Albert Schweitzer and many more were idolized and worshipped by Germans.

Was everybody living in denial during and after the Third Reich?

Did they forget their heritage, morals and ethics?

My father told me that even though he listened to the German Service of the BBC while stationed in Norway, he never heard any reports about genocide of Jews or minorities.

My history teacher did not help me either. German history studies in those days ended with Bismarck and current history, called contemporary studies, started with the founding of the German Federal Republic in 1949.

I asked questions of my pastor during my confirmation classes. He offered no explanations, but hid behind the Bible and claimed the church helped during that time with spiritual guidance.

My Uncle Fritz, who was imprisoned by the Nazis for 'Subversive Activities', said that he could not believe that these death camps existed when he heard rumours about them.

Nobody knew, nobody wanted to know and nobody would ask any questions.

What disturbed me even more was the fact that all these crimes had been confirmed. There were survivors, witnesses, movies, documents and people like Adolf Eichman admitting to having been an architect of this genocide but very few people were held responsible for their actions.

The Memorial at the Dachau Concentration Camp

I often looked down from our balcony and watched people walking by thinking, 'Were any of them involved?' When I walked the streets, I looked at people and wondered how many had participated in the slaughter?

How many people does it take to kill millions? It can't just be a handful, there must be thousands of them walking around with blood on their hands.

It frightened me that anybody I met could have been a mass murderer and would look just as nice and friendly as everybody else. I did not understand the moral implications and detested the, in my eyes, cowardly excuses of just having followed orders.

It bothered me that very few of my friends felt as strongly

about this as I did. The general attitude was that it was about time that they caught and convicted the man who was to blame for the genocide, Adolph Eichman. Everybody wanted to forget and carry on with their lives.

There were those who talked about collective German guilt. I didn't feel guilt! I felt ashamed about a people that did let this happen, but I was not to blame. That period in my life shaped my political convictions and made me become involved in politics later on in my youth.

I will never understand why genocides still occur and why we let them happen. The inscription on the Memorial at the Dachau Concentration Camp is already obsolete, it reads:

'NEVER AGAIN'

Chapter 18

The Berlin Wall

Part 1 - Caged Inside The City

August 13th 1961. It felt like any other Sunday.

I woke up and thought how nice it was to wake up in my own bed this Sunday. The previous week I spent Saturday night in East Berlin in the holding cell of a police station.

I never thought that I would be arrested and thrown into jail at the tender age of sixteen.

I turned on the radio to listen to some music and heard the news that the East German Government was preventing all access to and from West Berlin. All streets were blocked by barbed wire and they were in the process of building a wall.

West Berliners were caged inside their city. East Germans were no longer able to leave the German Democratic Republic (DDR).

I knew that everybody's life on both sides of the border had just changed.

•••••

We loved going to the East where our money bought five times more than in the West.

The quality of goods available in the DDR was horrible. Luxury items and even food like beef, coffee and tropical fruits were unavailable most of the time. Products like Coca Cola, jeans and most things manufactured in the West were never sold in the government-controlled stores.

My friend Kalle and I went often to the East. We attended the theatre, the opera and visited the zoo and amusement parks. We were not able to afford these things on our meagre incomes as apprentices in the West. East Berlin had great cultural institutions and lots of things to offer that were just as good as anything we had in the West at a fraction of the cost.

It was illegal to take East German money into the DDR. The country needed hard western currency and tried to force tourists and visitors to exchange West German Marks at par at East German banks. In the West we received five East Marks for every West Mark. There were no controls when you crossed into the East. The city was wide open, only signs indicated that you were leaving the West and were entering the Soviet controlled sector of the city.

My friends and I had gone camping on the outskirts of East Berlin the weekend before August 13th. We went into the local village to purchase a few supplies, namely horrible tasting but cheap East German cigarettes and drinkable but watery beer. These were things that you were allowed to consume in the East at the age of 16 but only at 18 in the West.

As I mentioned before, there were often shortages in the East, one of them was toilet paper.

When we walked through the village, we noticed a sign in the window of the State controlled supermarket:

"Today, fresh toilet paper!"

We thought that was hilarious. As we were walking down the street, we started yelling things like 'Don't hold it in any longer, you can wipe now!' and other juvenile remarks revolving around bowel movements and excrement. It was just the kind of thing you would expect from a bunch of teenagers with bravado and a herd mentality.

A group of the Free German Youth (FDJ), the Communist Party's version of a Boy Scout organization, came towards us.

They did not share our sense of humour and accused us of ridiculing the German Democratic Republic. I have no idea who threw the first punch. The police arrived within minutes. When we heard the sirens we tried to run away. The young socialists stopped brawling and tried to hold us down until the police had a chance to get us into the paddy wagon. Most of us were arrested, but nobody from the Socialist Youth group.

To say that we were scared is an understatement. We sure felt that we would need some of that toilet paper.

One of the officers told us that we would be charged with several crimes and misdemeanours, from disturbing the peace to assault.

They kept us in a holding cell for the night where we hardly slept a wink. No sense in asking for a telephone call, there were no direct lines to the West. We got very little to eat but were allowed to drink as much water as we wanted.

The officer in charge was not the nicest human being we had ever met. When we asked when we could go home, he said, "It's up to the judge, anywhere from tomorrow to five years from now," followed by a cynical giggle.

On Sunday morning, we were brought into a meeting room. What must have been a high ranking police or party official gave us a three-hour lecture on the advantages of the socialist system, the purity and humanistic values of Marxism and the glory of the first German Workers' and Farmers' Paradise called the German Democratic Republic.

We had to acknowledge that we were truly sorry and appreciated the achievements of the Communist Regime. Due to our age, we only received a warning and were sent home.

That was my last visit to East Berlin for many years.

•••••

The morning The Wall started going up, I found my father in the kitchen reading his Sunday newspaper. He hadn't been listening to the radio. We switched on the TV. The usual Sunday morning religious programming had been cancelled and live reports were broadcast from several locations in Berlin.

We stared at the pictures in disbelief. This could not be happening. My father turned towards me and said, "I'm sure glad you didn't go camping over there this weekend."

I swallowed hard to try to get rid of that lump in my throat.
My thoughts turned to our relatives in East Germany.
What would happen to them?
What would happen to us?
Would there be another blockade like in 1948?
Would there be war?
The Wall would divide a people for the next 28 years!

Part II - Symbol Of Freedom & Resistance

West Berliners never accepted The Wall as a permanent dividing line of their country, their city or their families. They just learned to live with it.

I can never forget the headlines in the newspapers when people were shot by the East German border guards as they were trying to escape. It happened with frightening regularity in the early years.

Berliners often witnessed the brutal murders at the wall or watched people drown as they tried to swim across the canals and rivers that in some places formed the border between East and West.

One of the most gruesome deaths was that of Peter Fechter, a young East German who had already climbed to the top of the wall and was mowed down by the bullets of three border guards as he attempted to jump to the West. He fell back onto the east side of the wall and was left lying there to die.

He screamed for help for over an hour but the soldiers ignored his cries until he bled to death.

This happened within sight of the famous Checkpoint Charlie, one of the few crossing points of the wall, and in full view of American soldiers. Hundreds of West Berliner citizens and policemen watched him die and were unable to help. I watched the whole sad episode unfold on the evening news.

Thousands, including myself, attended memorials and protests but nothing changed.

The successful escape attempts became less frequent as the wall was reinforced with minefields, electrified fences, death-strips and watchtowers, equipped with powerful searchlights. Tripwires were installed between towers, setting off alarms when touched by escapees. With time the wall became almost impregnable.

The escape attempts became more daring, imaginative and desperate. Tunnels, armoured trucks, buses, homemade balloons and modified cars to hide people were used to escape. Secret networks and organizations specialized in bringing people across by any means.

The morale of West Berliners was strong and determined and withstood the pressure of the Soviets and their East German puppet regime.

All of Germany's allies pledged their support to keep Berlin a free city. There were moments of tension when Soviet and American tanks faced each other, battle-ready at the border. At times, war seemed inevitable but the Soviets blinked first and withdrew their tanks, giving in to American determination.

The biggest morale booster was President Kennedy's visit to our city in June of 1963.

I remember getting up early in the morning to secure a place close to the steps of the Schöneberg Rathaus, West Berlin's city hall, to hear him speak.

In my mind, I was going to see and hear four giants of world and German history, President Kennedy, Willy Brandt, the Mayor of West Berlin, Konrad Adenauer, Germany's first post-war chancellor and General Clay, hailed by the citizens of West Berlin as the saviour of the city during the Berlin Airlift.

My friend Gerd Mueller and I got there before 9 o'clock in the morning. The square in front of city hall was already starting to fill up. The ceremonies weren't supposed to start until 2:00 pm. By midday, the square was full and the side streets started filling up. People climbed trees, walls, roofs and lamp posts to get a better view of President Kennedy and the other dignitaries.

When Kennedy arrived just before 3 o'clock, I felt a shiver run down my spine.

Looking back, I think I was acutely aware that I was about to witness a speech that would remain part of global history and become one of the most famous speeches of Kennedy's life. He reassured us that everybody knew what Berliners were enduring and that Berlin and its people had become a symbol for freedom and resistance around the world.

When he uttered the unforgettable words, *"Ich bin ein Berliner"*, we knew he was one of us!

It was in 1975 that I was able to cross the wall and visit East Berlin on a day visa. Foreigners, I was a Canadian citizen now, could enter East Berlin for 24 hours after buying a visa and being forced to exchange a fixed amount of western currency at exorbitant rates as 'spending money'. Any money not spent during a visit had to be donated to the Vietnam Freedom Fund upon leaving. No refunds were given and taking East German currency out of the country was illegal.

It was always exciting and nerve-wracking to go through the checkpoints. The border-guards never smiled and treated everybody like a criminal. They looked for any reasons to extort money by levying fines, imposing import duties for certain items or confiscating personal belongings as illegal imports.

On the way back into the West they ripped your car apart looking for escapees in the trunk, checking with mirrors under the car to see that nobody was hanging on to the undercarriage and everybody had to take out their backseats. Even the fuel tank was measured to make sure the car was not modified to hide East Germans trying to flee their republic, which they advertised as a workers and farmers paradise.

One year, we were lined up at Checkpoint Charlie on a blistering hot summer day to cross over into the East. My rental car had no air conditioning and I opened the door to step out and get some fresh air.

All I heard was the clicking of machine guns and when I looked up I saw that they were pointed at me. An officer, with his gun drawn, started yelling at me, "Who told you that you can get out of your car? Get back in or we will shoot!" I raised my arms and quickly retreated back into my car.

The wall did not only exist above ground but also beneath the surface. Let me paraphrase from an article that described what went on below ground:

"Berlin, like many major cities, has an underground or subway system. After construction of the Berlin Wall, trains could only operate on the side in which they were based. Some trains either ran purely on the west side or the east side.

"Trains which previously crossed the border would now go no further than its respective border and then turn back. There were three lines that went through East Berlin for a small part of their journeys. The trains travelled through several stations which became known as Ghost Stations, dimly lit and heavily guarded stations that they were unable to stop at.

"Friedrichstasse Station, which was situated in East Berlin, was used as a transfer station for passengers to get onto other trains travelling to locations in West Berlin. Passengers could also enter East Berlin at this station if they had the relevant permits. Friedrichstasse was regarded as a border crossing and was heavily guarded. When the Ghost Stations were reopened after the fall of the Berlin Wall, the first people using them found them preserved as they were when they closed in 1961 with the same signage and advertisements on the walls.

"The sewage system predated Berlin's division and had to be closed and barricaded by the East. Canals, rivers and lakes dividing the city had to be fortified to prevent boats, swimmers and scuba divers escaping the East."

On a more humorous note, West Berliners used the Berlin Wall as an ideal way to get rid of rubbish. If they had anything that needed throwing away, they threw it over the wall. After all, it wasn't as if they would be made to go over it to fetch it back.

I visited Berlin just three weeks before the wall came down and was harassed for the last time by the humourless guardians of the wall when I crossed to meet family for lunch in the East.

On November 19th 1989, after weeks of tension in the German Democratic Republic with citizens demanding more freedoms, the wall opened up without warning or bloodshed.

I heard the news in my car and rushed home and watched the events unfolding on television.

Tears of joy were running down my face as I watched in disbelief as masses of East Germans crossed into the West being greeted by their brothers and sisters on the other side with flowers, cheers and the biggest smiles I have ever seen!

The Wall, and its ugliness, is gone today. Only a 200-metre strip of it remains as a memorial. It's called the East Side Gallery and showcases graffiti of artists from around the world to remind us with humourous, satirical and depressing images of the tyranny, brutality and oppression this city had to endure.

Chapter 19

The Apprenticeship

Mr Hockun worked as a truck driver for one of our local breweries. His son Martin had a tough childhood and dreamed of becoming a brew master. His father assured him that he would get him an apprenticeship at the brewery he was working for.

Martin told me for the longest time what an exciting career it would be. It involved a large knowledge of biology, physics, biochemistry, mathematics and he would be producing a product that was recession proof, Beer!

Martin had one problem, he didn't get accepted because he did not pass the brewery's entry exams.

When my father insisted on me quitting school and choosing a profession, Martin convinced me that being a brewer was the best thing in the world. My father loved the idea and I still hear his words, "Son, they'll always drink beer, you'll never be out of work."

I wrote my entry exam for the local brewery with the majestic name of: *Löwenbrauerei Böhmisches Brauhaus AG Berlin* or, translated into English: Lions Brewery Bohemian Brewhouse Inc. Berlin.

I was accepted and started my apprenticeship in the spring of 1962. I soon noticed that being a brewer was not what I had expected. My favorite part was the brewhouse. It was interesting work to get the process started and it involved lots of manual calculations, biochemical tests and everything from milling the barleymalt, adding the hops, activating enzymes and producing the mash ready to be fermented.

As interesting as it was, this was a process that took 24 hours and involved shift work for five days which pretty much ruined my social life, especially my soccer career.

The worst part of the job was working in the fermentation cellar. I went underground for the whole day in temperatures of 8C (46F) working mostly with water, dressed in rubber boots and wrapped in a heavy apron.

A good deal of my time was spent crawling into huge metal vats and cleaning them, scrubbing floors, walls and pulling heavy hoses. Not a fun environment. Working in the cellars in the winter meant you didn't see more than an hour of daylight.

Apprentices were sent to the local malting plant for four months to learn the process of converting barley into the many kinds of barley malt.

Once a week we had to attend the Food Industry Vocational School in Berlin.

Towards the end of our apprenticeship, the school arranged a trip to different breweries in West Germany to teach us about the many regional specialty beers not produced in Berlin, like wheat beer from southern Germany, Kölsch from Cologne and Rauchbier (smoked-beer) from the Ruhr area.

Overall, I enjoyed my apprenticeship but it became clear to me that I was not going to run around in rubber boots, knee-deep in water in dark, dingy and freezing cold cellars for the rest of my life.

During my apprenticeship, I became involved in Labour Unions and Politics and that opened up a whole new world to me.

Having joined the 'Food Industry Trade Union', I participated in their youth groups program. In my second year, I became the group leader for Berlin South.

I finished my apprenticeship at the top of my class and was offered a permanent position at my brewery. My Brewmaster offered me the opportunity to stay with the company and to pursue a master degree. Wanting to explore the world, I decided to leave Berlin. Breweries from all over the world advertised in our trade paper to attract young brewers. I explored offers from as far as Bolivia, Australia and South Africa.

The job offers from overseas included multi-year commitments to cover the costs of relocating, which the companies offered to pay for. Leaving Berlin was adventurous enough for me at the time and I didn't want to commit to a lengthy contract and, consequently, accepted a position in Wiesbaden, West Germany. It was only a train ride away, in case I got homesick.

I had more than one reason to leave my hometown. I wanted to get out of Berlin, learn to stand on my own two feet and experience independent living.

Another reason was a girl named Rosie.

Chapter 20

Rosie

My cousin Margot lived next door to us. Her daughter Elvira was a year younger than me and was terribly good looking. She was tall, had long shapely legs, a winning smile, short black hair and a giggly personality that she used to cover up her shyness.

When she had her first serious boyfriend at 15, we would practice kissing. I remember her being rather unemotional about the whole thing but I would get extremely excited during our sessions. I always tried to talk her into more advanced sexual experiments, but was denied any further exploratory and intimate encounters.

Elvira suggested I should meet her girlfriends, Annegret and Rosie. It was Annegret's birthday and her mother was throwing her a birthday party at the pub she owned. Elvira got me an invitation.

She introduced me first to Annegret's mother, then to her daughter and then to her girlfriend Rosie.

I thought my heart stood still when I looked at Rosie. She had a shy smile that lit up her face and her long, wavy, blond hair made her look like Jane Fonda.

I tried hard to get her to dance and I think we danced once, but she was rather stand-offish towards me or any boy who approached her.

I ended up asking Annegret for a date and she accepted. I didn't' know if I should be happy for having landed a girlfriend whose mother owned a pub or be upset that I didn't get the girl I wanted.

Annegret and I went out a couple of times but there was no spark. Her mother didn't trust any boy who lusted after her daughter nor any man, after having divorced an abusive husband who left her alone bringing up two children and running the family pub.

I was still thinking of Rosie and mentioned it to Elvira. She suggested that she would ask Rosie if she would go out with me. I told her she could try but I was rather pessimistic of getting a favourable reply.

To my surprise, she agreed to go to a movie with me.

I fell head over heels in love!

We stayed together for over a year and I thought we were made for each other.

Rosie was never as committed to me as I was to her. Even though she did well in school, we did not share many interests, Rosie never cared for politics, sports or literature, but she was fun-loving and did overcome her shyness.

Rosie had a one-year-old stepbrother, Alexander. Her mother had gotten pregnant after marrying her second husband. Rosie's parents were both professional waiters and worked shifts. Her mother worked at a local restaurant and her stepfather was the headwaiter at the famous Hotel Kempinski. Every second week they worked afternoons on weekends and I would spend the evening until midnight with Rosie alone, while we were baby-sitting little Alexander.

I don't know why Rosie's mother trusted me. We were always sitting nicely dressed on the sofa when they came home around midnight, trying to look innocent and sleepy.

I wished everybody a good night and left happy taking the last streetcar home.

When her parents worked the day shift we took little Alexander to the park or went to my home and often had lunch or dinner there. My mother loved playing with little Alexander and would babysit him so Rosie and I could have some moments alone.

Having little Alexander with us most weekends and pushing a tram around made for good gossiping in our neighbourhood about me having a girlfriend with a child out of wedlock. There was even talk about me having been the father.

Everything looked rosy in my life and I often talked about our future. Rosie was non-committal even though I told her I was ready to marry her as soon as I had finished my apprenticeship and she would finish her's two years later. I was 18 years old and thought I had found the love of my life. I went and bought an engagement ring in November of 1964. I knew I wanted to leave Berlin to work in West Germany for at least a year and wanted to make it clear to her that I would always be there for her and would come back to Berlin as often as possible.

I never had a chance to give her the ring. She told me at the end of November that she wanted to explore other relationships and didn't want me to feel tied to her while I was away.

I offered to stay in Berlin, but it was over.

Nothing I said would change her mind, so we broke up.

I was devastated and heartbroken, and so were both our mothers. They thought we were made for each other.

It took me a long time to get over Rosie. Elvira told me that it was not my leaving Berlin that caused our breakup. Rosie wanted a life of luxury and wanted to marry a doctor or a lawyer. She did end up marrying an architect, but got divorced after having two children. Her ex-husband ended up in a home for alcoholics and Rosie only got her life of luxury for about eight years before losing everything.

I met Rosie again when I was in Berlin for my mother's funeral in 1986 and we kept in touch afterwards. I introduced Rosie to my wife Jackie on a subsequent visit to Berlin in 1989. Her son Holger came to visit us in Canada and in the 1990's she and her fiancé also came to visit. We travelled to Las Vegas together, where they got married in a wedding chapel on Las Vegas Boulevard. Jackie and I were their witnesses.

It was the tackiest wedding I've ever attended.

The chapel was decorated in pink with Cupids suspended from

the ceiling. A Wurlitzer Jukebox in the back of the chapel had a large choice of prerecorded wedding songs ranging from Classical to Elvis Presley. A large collection of fake flowers was tastefully placed around the altar.

For an Elvis impersonator to sing *'Crying in the Chapel'* would have been an extra $100.00 and might have been worth it just to give the ceremony that final 'Over the Top' Las Vegas touch.

Rosie and I still didn't have much in common. Other than reminiscing about the past and general small talk on trivial subjects, there was not much that attracted us to each other.

We visited her and her husband once more in Berlin. They were still happily married. After that, we drifted apart and have lost contact over the last few years.

Rosie was my first love and she gave me a year of happiness.

Jackie is my last love and she has given me a lifetime of happiness.

But that is another long, long story!

Chapter 21

Leaving The Nest

I had learned all that I could from my teachers, my mentors and my parents.

It was time to leave the nest and experience life and learn from it, without parental supervision!

With my brewing diploma in my pocket, I applied for a job at the 'Germania Brewery' in Wiesbaden, West Germany.

I was offered a room at the brewery at no charge. My room was huge in what must have been part of the malting plant of the brewery that was no longer used. It was now a storage facility. The offices had been converted into an apartment with a kitchen, bedroom, living room and a dining area. Except for the bathroom, it had no walls. It was totally open. Today, it would be called a loft with 12-foot ceilings.

The job was everything I had hoped for. My colleagues accepted me right away. Living in the brewery was convenient, fun and cheap.

The only other people living in the brewery were the head brewmaster and his wife. They lived in a separate building and kept an eye on me to make sure I did not entertain female guests, which they considered immoral and sinful.

The brewery was located in an industrial area on Mainzer

Strasse and was also the business area for the ladies of the night who paraded up and down the street to strut their stuff to attract customers.

The head brewmaster was a religious man and warned me on my first day that he did not allow any working girls on the premises. I assured him that my moral standards were of the highest order and that I could control my hormones and be a good tenant. He went to bed by eight o'clock every night and never found a working girl in my room. The action on the street never got going until much later.

At 18 years of age, away from home and free at last, this was almost paradise.

Friday nights, my apartment became party central when many of my colleagues stopped by for a beer and we discussed everything from politics to the weekend soccer games. Some nights, we ended up playing cards and other nights we just partied and made sure that the beer we had brewed was still cold and drinkable... and it always was!

It didn't take long for me to find out that there were many domestic skills my mother had failed to teach me.

Cooking was not a problem since the brewery had a very good cafeteria. Breakfast, lunch and sandwiches were available at very reasonable prices from Monday to Friday. Every night the cook would ask me if I wanted some leftovers for dinner or she would have to throw them out.

Co-workers and friends invited me frequently for dinner on the weekends and I kept a small supply of cans, bread and cold cuts on hand. Washing dishes was not a regular activity in my life.

I needed only a knife to make the odd sandwich, a spoon to eat the macaroni right out of the can (why dirty a plate?), a cup to make an instant coffee in the morning and beer tasted much better when you drank it out of the bottle.

The first time I missed my mother was when I noticed that there wasn't anybody anymore to pick up after me. My place seldom looked clean and tidy, clothes everywhere and the bed was never made. The next time I missed my mother was when I ran out of clothes. Laundry started piling up, I ran out of towels and underwear and it was time to change the sheets again. I hadn't noticed that the apartment didn't have a washing machine. Nobody had mentioned laundry facilities to me. I asked the caretaker if he could give me a tub or a big pot to do my laundry in.

He came up with a huge zinc pot that barely fit on my stove. The pot covered the burners so I used two burners to heat the water and did my entire laundry in a single batch.

My mother used to boil laundry in the communal washing kitchens in our building, so I threw my shirts, socks, pants, woollen sweaters, sheets, towels and everything else I had into that pot of boiling water. I added a good portion of detergent to get it clean and then I let it boil, and boil, and boil. It made perfect sense to me that the longer it boils the cleaner it will get.

The water turned into a nice greenish, purplish sauce.

After a few hours, I thought it was a good time to give it a rinse.

I could not lift the pot off of the stove, it was much too heavy. Standing on a footstool, armed with a pair of tongs, I fished every item out of this giant pot and dropped it in the sink.

Noticing that most of the laundry had taken on this purplish green colour of the water I hoped that a good rinse would turn my shirts, underwear, towels and sheets back to a brilliant white.

I was mistaken.

I also assumed that my woollen sweater, socks and various other pieces of clothing would return to their original size if I would stretch and pull them a bit.

That too was an assumption that was wrong.

Some things would hardly fit a midget and my sweater was too small to fit a poodle.

My formerly white shirts, underwear, towels and sheets were now purplish green.

I think my red track suit and my green woollen sweater might have been responsible for the tinting effect.

Monday morning, I asked the cook to come to my apartment and give me some advice on how to reverse some of my obviously failed attempts to wash my clothes.

After she stopped laughing and wiped the tears off of her face, she told me about sorting laundry and what to boil and what not to boil. Why didn't anybody tell me that before?

I replaced my discoloured clothes as quickly as I could, starting with shirts and a new sweater. I still lived with my greenish purple sheets and underwear for a while.

The cook also mentioned that I could give her my sheets and towels in future. The laundry service the brewery used for the cafeteria would do them for me and she would not even charge me for it. A laundry service in town could do the rest for me and I wouldn't even have to iron anything.

For what it cost me to replace my clothes I could have used the laundry service for many years.

I had a great time in Wiesbaden and learned a lot about myself. It taught me how to be responsible and independent.

I would have stayed longer in Wiesbaden but the Military wanted me to spend 18 months with them.

This was one invitation I did not want to accept.

Berlin was subject to the Potsdam agreement and officially not part of the Federal Republic of Germany. Berliners were exempt from the draft as long as they were registered as residents of the city. To avoid being drafted, I had to return to Berlin on rather short notice. The draft board gave me two weeks to get back or wear a uniform for the next 18 months. My friend Kalle came to drive me home where a new and tumultuous part of my life was about to begin.

The Germania Brewery was later bought out by a rival brewery and demolished.

There is nothing left to remind me of my nine months of coming of age, with one exception: The working girls are still around and practising the oldest profession in the world. They have moved indoors now and the site of the old brewery is now surrounded by sex clubs and bordellos.

Germany has lost over 1800 breweries since I entered the profession in 1965 and many brewers have been replaced by computers and unskilled labourers. Most of them retrained and entered different professions and I was one of them.

Brewing is one of the oldest professions in the world and was first mentioned by the Sumerians six thousand years ago.

The sex trade is even older and growing everywhere. No well trained professional in that trade will ever be replaced by a computer or an unskilled labourer. Makes you think that when it comes to sex and alcohol, most people will choose sex.

Call me old-fashioned, but when I say I'd like to enjoy a cool blonde, I am talking about a beer!

Chapter 22

Fun And Turmoil In Berlin

My mother was delirious with joy when I returned home again. I did not object to her spoiling me after nine months of living by myself. I found a job right away at a brewery, but stayed only for three months.

I did not get along with the brewmaster. He hated the Unions and told me once he thought of me as an agitator because I tried to interest some apprentices in joining the youth group of the Food Workers Labour Union. With him being my boss, I would have to work in the cellar forever, and that is the worst job in a brewery.

There were only two independent companies in Berlin that owned all the breweries. I knew that my choice of employers was limited if I decided to live in Berlin and stay in my profession.

A friend told me about an opening at the Schindler Elevator Company and I accepted a position as a trainee metalworker and cabin builder. I received three months of on-the-job training.

It came as a surprise to me when I was promoted to team leader after one year when my predecessor became the full time Shop Steward of the company. We were paid on an hourly basis and given a quota to complete a certain number of elevator cabins per week. If we were slow we had to put in extra time but if we exceeded our quota we were paid for the extra cabins. We always made our quota and got paid handsomely for our over-achievements. I had a terrific team and loved my job and the company.

After returning from Wiesbaden, I had resumed my Labour Union activities and became politically active again.

I had met Werner, the leader of a local Rock & Roll band, who just got started and didn't have much experience other than school dances and a gig at a local pub in our neighbourhood. They called themselves 'The Mustangs' and were not bad. I talked them into playing at one of our dances for free with the idea of talking our Union executive into sponsoring a big dance for our young members and non-members at the main hall downtown.

The Union officials thought that was a good idea and agreed to have a dance to recruit more members and as a fundraiser for youth activities.

It was a great success.

Other Unions approached me to have The Mustangs perform for them. Soon after that I became their manager and was busy arranging dances for various unions across Berlin. I was also approached by other promoters to have my band perform as opening acts for their shows and became involved in the entertainment industry.

It was a great part-time job and soon I had a great second income.

My weekends were very busy and sleep was a luxury.

I started meeting famous performers, bought a Mercedes, used of course, and earned more money than I had thought was possible from a little job on the side. Life was great.

Things had become more politically polarized in our Union group and the ideas and goals of the very strong student movement in Berlin under the leadership of Rudy Dutschke made us begin to question our political system and the values of society.

Rudi Dutschke was an East German refugee and a charismatic and intellectual leader. He believed in the basic teachings of Karl Marx but was also a believer of the teachings of Jesus Christ and called him the greatest revolutionary of mankind. He detested authoritarian and brutal dictatorships, including the DDR and the Soviet Union. He was always looking for peaceful resolutions of conflicts. Our youth groups in the labour movement started joining the students in their protests and many of us joined left-leaning political clubs and groups that combined the student movement with labour unions, human rights groups and the women's rights movement.

I became increasingly involved with these groups. The conservative Labour Union leadership did not like the idea of the more activist approach of their youth wing.

We started questioning the support of the German Federal Republic for things like the Vietnam War, the Shah of Iran and South Africa.

The refusal by the West Germans to recognize the existence of an East German State or negotiate anything with them that could lead to normalization between the two Germanies was unacceptable to me.

I participated in more and more demonstrations. They became more confrontational and police now started using billy-clubs, horses and water cannons against the demonstrators.

It was the middle of 1967 when things started falling apart for me. I started rethinking my future and if the movement and my part in it made a difference.

It was the demonstration against the Shah of Iran and the aftermath of it that changed everything.

During that protest, a young Berliner by the name of Benno Ohnesorg was shot by a police officer. This was the catalyst for the radicalization of many of us.

Demonstrations were largely peaceful until then. Films and photos, suppressed by the authorities for many years, prove that during the protest against the Shah and his brutal regime, agents of his government provoked students and the police overreacted by using unprecedented brutal force.

After 1989, it was revealed that the officer who shot the student was an agent of the East German Secret Police (STASI) and that it was a case of premeditated murder to escalate the violence in Berlin. The officer was charged with manslaughter at the time, but was acquitted due to a massive cover up by the West Berlin Senate and the Berlin Police who, at that time, were unaware of him being a double agent. Double jeopardy protected him from being retried after 1989.

Berlin politics and the student movement were in a mess.

There were calls for the resignation of the Mayor after it became clear a cover up was going on. Berlin's Chief of Police retired voluntarily shortly after the incident and the student movement split. The tone at our meetings had changed and calls for more aggressive demonstrations were heard, but resisted by the leadership of most organizations. More radical groups were formed, laying the foundation for terrorist groups like the Red Army Faction, the Baader-Meinhof Gang, Kommune 1 and individuals like Fritz Teufel (the first left wing urban terrorist to be convicted in Germany).

I was at a crossroad!

My mother was worried about my safety and urged me to stop participating in any more protests. She did not understand nor cared much about politics and saw me as misguided and naive. I know my father, who had died the previous year, always appreciated my involvement and idealistic beliefs and would have told me to follow my conscience, but also to consider my future and my enjoyment of life.

Many saw us as East German sympathizers and Communist agitators. How could I be a Communist defending East Germany and the Soviet Union? I was living in West Berlin, where I was reminded daily of the inhumane policies that denied the East Germans many rights and freedoms and imprisoned them behind a wall. Not to mention, the killing of their citizens by East German soldiers for trying to escape to the West.

Many saw us as anti-American. How could I be? The USA saved Berlin twice by their resolve to protect our existence in West Berlin during the Blockade and after the building of the Wall. We disagreed with many of their policies and the Vietnam War, but we never doubted that the American presence in Germany was protecting us from the bigger evil of Soviet occupation.

After being questioned by the Political Police about my activities, I knew I had to decide what I had to do about my future within the movement. The Labour Union was not comfortable with my involvement and was looking to somehow discredit me and lessen my influence in the youth groups.

They found an ingenious way to do that.

In early September of 1967, I was summoned to a meeting of the executive and was asked if I knew that all my positions were voluntary. They stressed the point that I was not allowed to profit from my activities as a delegate, youth leader or any of my voluntary positions.

I immediately knew what was about to happen.

I admitted that I charged for the performances of the Band, but that I acted as the manager of the band and not as a volunteer or a member of the Union. Therefore I was entitled to be paid. I never contacted any of the Unions to arrange dances for them but was approached by them as the manager of The Mustangs and asked if they were available to play at their functions. I did not see a conflict.

The Union did see a conflict and told me I would be relieved of my duties as a youth delegate to the Labour Council and that my own Food Workers Union could impose further penalties on me.

I resigned from all positions but kept my membership in the Food Workers Union.

The Mustangs had now lost their steady gigs through the Unions and were signed by a local promoter. They did not need me any longer and my short but profitable involvement in the entertainment business came to an end.

In early November of 1967, my friends Horst and Detlef gave me an idea that would solve my moral dilemma and change my life.

Chapter 23

A New Challenge!

It was just another Saturday night in our local pub. I was sitting at the table reserved for the regulars when Horst and Detlef marched in and told us they had a big announcement to make.

They ordered their beer and Horst announced with great fanfare that they had decided to immigrate to Canada.

Everybody raised their glass and wished them good luck and asked the usual array of questions:

Why? Are you planning on coming back? Do you know anybody over there? Etc, etc, etc...

I thought about it for a minute before asking them if I could join them. They didn't seem to mind and I was excited about the idea.

What did I have to lose? I had no girlfriend, Berlin's political future as well as my own was in shambles and I was looking for something to get me out of the doldrums.

I had known lots of people who had emigrated and none of them had returned. Everybody who ever left must have loved their new countries.

In our building alone, five people had immigrated to different countries. Lothar, Trautchen and Ingried went to the USA, Wolfgang to Canada and the Breuer's son to Australia.

The Arndt family, that lived around the corner from our building went to Canada and now had a big turkey farm just outside of Toronto.

Immigration seemed to be the road to happiness and prosperity.

I had forgotten to consider one person in my sudden enthusiasm, my mother. How would she take the news that I was leaving home again?

I knew it would be hard on her. My father had died the previous year and losing her only son would break her heart. I told her that we were just thinking of going for two years and if our lives wouldn't improve, we'd be coming home again.

Mother never tried to talk me out of going to Canada. She told me that if I thought my future was in Canada, she would not stand in my way.

The time from my decision to join Horst and Detlef to the day of our departure flew by. I somehow had to get some money together. Saving had never been my strong suit, so instead I sold everything I couldn't take with me:

- My beloved Mercedes;
- My stamp collection;
- My model train set, including the accessories my father had built over the years;
- My model cars;
- My extensive record collection, including every Elvis and Little Richard single released in Germany;
- My 72 bass Hohner accordion went for a bargain basement price to my friend Horst Grudde;
- My collection of Steiff stuffed animals, about 25 of them, went for 250.00DM (CDN $62.50 in 1968), they would be worth well over $10,000.00 today.

I turned the memories and treasures of my childhood and youth into cash.

We were told that medical care was not free in Canada, so Horst and I checked into a hospital to have some minor surgery done before leaving. I had problems with ingrown toenails for years and had them removed twice before. Now I wanted them permanently removed. Horst had a condition called Gynecomastia, an abnormally large breast, and had male breast reduction surgery. His left breast was larger than the breasts of some of my girlfriends and it was a challenge not to stare at it when we were wearing nothing but swim trunks.

We also took some English lessons from the daughter of one of my mother's friends to build on our school English that we had already partially forgotten.

We had several interviews at the Canadian Consulate in Berlin and the immigration officer assured us that we would all be good additions to Canadian society and promised a prosperous future in our new country.

We needed a police report to prove we had no criminal record and had to show that we had at least $400.00 each to survive the first few weeks until we found a job.

He told us that German craftsmen like ourselves were in high demand in Canada and that finding work would be no problem.

The immigration officer told me that the skills of German brewmasters were in great demand in Canada. He said that German style beer was getting more popular every year due to the return of Canadian soldiers who had been stationed in Germany and from tourists having developed a taste for German beer while vacationing in Europe. Little did he know that getting a job in a Canadian brewery as a brewer would prove next to impossible, as I would find out later on.

We passed our medical tests and the basic English language skills requirement and received our visas to start a new life in Canada.

A plane ticket was all we needed and we were ready to go.

I loved my job at Schindler Elevator Co. and had kept my immigration plans secret from everybody. Three weeks before leaving I gave my two weeks' notice and was surprised about their reaction. They wished me luck, told me I could come back anytime and gave me a glowing reference letter, in English, to help me get off to a good start in Canada.

When the taxi pulled up in front of our door on July 13th 1968, I was so excited that I hardly noticed my mother quietly fighting back her tears, apparently, she had none left after crying all night. We hugged and kissed for a last time and I promised her I would send her a plane ticket to come and visit me as soon as I got settled into that great job that was surely waiting for me in Toronto.

My cousin Margot and her husband Ferry and their daughter Elvira were there to say good bye.

Ferry gave me the name and address of his old boss Alfred Harmsen who had left Germany after the war, and suggested that he might be able to help me if I ever needed somebody to give me a hand to get started. He told me that Alfred was a nice chap but to avoid talking politics with him because he was a former SS officer and a staunch Nazi.

Many of our neighbours stood on their balconies and waved good-bye to me as we drove off.

The short drive to the terminal of Tempelhof Airport took less than ten minutes. It wasn't more than an hour after leaving home that I looked out of the tiny airplane window as it taxied past our apartment building. I was hoping to get a final glimpse of my mother looking out from our balcony to wave to me.

She wasn't there.

The engines roared and the plane quickly accelerated and lifted off into the blue summer sky.

For a moment, I felt sadness and wondered if I had done the right thing and whether I would ever come back again.

As the city began to disappear in the distance, I suddenly got all excited about the thought that I would be in a new country before the day was over and tomorrow would truly be the first day of the rest of my life.

Gunther Arndt, who had immigrated to Canada with his family a few years earlier and had been a schoolmate of Detlef's, was going to welcome us at the airport and help us get settled.

I didn't think that was necessary because surely the Canadian Immigration authorities would have a welcome kiosk set up to greet arriving immigrants to assist them with starting a new life in Canada.

Canadians, however, didn't think that was necessary.

We were on our own!

Chapter 24

Welcome To Canada

Air Canada flight 847 arrived on time, on Saturday July 13th 1968, at Toronto International Airport with Horst, Detlef and me on board eager to start a new life in a new country.

After clearing Canadian customs and immigration, we collected our luggage and walked into the crowded arrival area of the terminal. We spotted Gunther, Detlef's old schoolmate, who greeted us with enthusiasm and welcomed us to Canada. After the great welcoming scene, he asked us where we wanted to go.

Good question!

We asked him to take us to the welcoming and orientation centre for newcomers to Canada. They would help us find lodging and assist us with finding jobs.

He smiled and told us there was no such thing at the airport and the manpower office would only open on Monday. He said he'd love to offer us lodging for the night but he lived with his parents, an hour's drive away from Toronto. He suggested that we look for a hotel or a hostel for the night.

My cousin Ferri had given me the name of his former boss. I thought of looking him up in the telephone directory and hoped he was still living in Toronto. Ferri had lost contact with him years earlier and didn't know his whereabouts in Canada anymore.

Eureka! There was an A. Harmsen listed on Dovercourt Road in Toronto.

The first dime I ever spent on Canadian soil was to make a call to Alfred Harmsen.

Somebody answered the line on the other end and I said in my best broken English, "Excuse me, but you don't know me. I am the cousin of Ferri Hunger who used to work for you in Berlin. Do you still speak German? My English is not so good."

He replied in German and wanted to know the reason for the call. I told him that I was at the airport and wondering if he could help me since I had just arrived and had nowhere to go.

His reaction overwhelmed me. He invited me to come to his home and spend the night and said he would help me in the morning to get settled. I told him that this was very kind of him but I was not alone and had arrived with two friends. He told me not to worry and to take a taxi and come to his house.

Gunther's little VW couldn't accommodate us and our luggage but he followed our taxi to Toronto to make sure we were taken care of.

Our first cab ride was unbelievably exciting. We had seen American cars in movies but sitting in a car the size of a small house was breathtaking. There was nothing like this Lincoln Town Car in Germany.

Ali Harmsen and his wife Gertrud welcomed us with open arms. After the introductions, Gunther left and we were invited to stay at the Harmsens for the night. They lived in a small double-storey house with three bedrooms. I don't think his two teenage daughters were too happy that they had to vacate their bedrooms and sleep on the sofa in the living room to accommodate these intruders.

We had supper with them and chatted about Berlin, my cousin's family and made plans for Sunday when Ali offered to take us on a tour of Toronto and help us find a place of our own.

We were exhausted and were given our room assignments. Detlef and Horst slept in the room of their older daughter that had a small single bed and a chesterfield and I got to sleep in the room of their younger daughter that had only a single bed.

I was sure I would fall asleep right away, but the events of the day, the new surroundings and the excitement and anticipation of what the next day would bring kept me awake for a long time.

We got up early the next morning, our bodies hadn't adjusted to the 5-hour time difference yet.

We had our first Canadian breakfast and tasted Canadian bacon for the first time. The smell and the taste was delicious.

Well fed, we were off to explore Toronto and start our search for a place to live.

After checking out a few flats around High Park, an area with a large German population, we settled on a furnished two-bedroom flat on Dorval Road and made arrangements to move in the following day.

Ali was a letter-carrier and got home fairly early from his route. To our surprise, he told us on Monday morning that he had called his employer and taken the rest of the week off. He said he was in the process of building a new house in the country and wanted to take some time off anyway. He would also use that time to help us get settled.

He had a few connections in the building trades and was able to help find jobs for Horst and Detlef.

I had a problem!

When I arrived in 1968, the breweries were on strike and I was not even able to fill out an application at any of the three breweries in Toronto.

Until the strike was over, I decided to find a job in the elevator industry. With my good references from Schindler Elevators in Berlin, I was offered a position at Pape Elevator Co.

Within a week, we had jobs, a flat and felt like we were settling in nicely.

Horst, Detlef and myself could have been described as a mixture of the Three Stooges and the Odd Couple with an extra Felix Unger thrown in for good measure. There was no question who the Oscar Madison was, I filled that role perfectly.

My housekeeping skills and lack of seeing the need for being tidy were diametrically opposed to Horst's sense of neatness and strict division of refrigerator space. Detlef was a bit more easy-going but also felt that dishes should be washed right after the meal. My philosophy of 'why wash dishes when there is still a cup left in the cupboard' did not meet with their approval.

I was glad to have gotten the second bedroom to myself. They took turns to make up their bed every morning with great care and precision. I believed this to be a great waste of time because it would get messed up again the next night anyway. Horst even went as far as to measure if the bedspread was hanging evenly off of each side of the bed.

Detlef complained that Horst infringed on his space during the night and at one point put a clothesline down the centre of the bed to prevent Horst's nightly invasion of his side of the bed. I guess Horst wanted more blanket and Detlef didn't want to cuddle.

It didn't take them long to realize that it was in their best interest to find an apartment for themselves.

It was left up to Horst to give me the news that they had already signed a lease on an apartment in a highrise and I had a week to find myself new quarters to live in.

I was disappointed at first to be left behind, but realized that I would probably be happier by myself. There was more Oscar Madison in me than I wanted to admit.

We had some good times together and I was not going to break up our friendship over this split.

I still remember some great laughs we had at Dorval Road, none more than Detlef trying to cook a great meal for himself on a hot and humid Sunday afternoon, dressed in nothing but a pair of gym shorts and flip-flops. It ended up being a total disaster.

He first prepared the home-fried potatoes, put them on a plate, turned on the gas in the oven and put the plate into the oven to keep them warm.

His mistake was that he did not light the gas in the oven, assuming it would light automatically like the burners on top of the stove.

He then proceeded to fry up a great steak with onions. I still remember the smell of the fried onions and the steak wafting into my room and thinking that his meal would probably be a better choice than my can of Chef Boyardee Ravioli I was going to eat right out of the can to avoid dish-washing duty. That's when I heard and felt the explosion.

Horst and I had been watching television and arrived in the kitchen at the same time.

I will never forget the scene we faced.

I don't think anybody had ever moved the stove to clean behind it. Soot, which had accumulated for the past 30 years, was blown into the air by the explosion and engulfed the kitchen in a black fog. As it settled, we saw Detlef standing next to the stove, covered in soot. Every hair had been singed off his body, and he was one hairy guy. He stood there, frozen like a statue, with a spatula in his hand staring into empty space. There was no response when we called him. The explosion had deafened him temporarily and he was in total shock.

He was lucky that he was standing next to the stove when it exploded because the oven door was blown right across the kitchen by the force of the blast and cracked the drywall on the other side. It surely would have broken his kneecap if he had been standing in front of it. We noticed that the kitchen window had disappeared and was lying in the backyard next to our landlord, who was sitting in a lawn chair sunning himself.

I rushed downstairs to retrieve it. Our landlord, an elderly man from an eastern European country who spoke less English than we did, was hard of hearing. He looked at me as I picked up the window and said in broken English, "Me sleepink, hear bang and veendow fall down, but it no break. Is all OK?" I just nodded, smiled and ran back upstairs. The landlord smiled back at me and went back to sleep.

I still can't understand how the glass in the window didn't break after being blown out of its frame and falling onto the lawn from the second floor.

Horst was still trying to get Detlef out of his daze. Slowly, he regained his grip on reality and got his hearing back. He still had a ringing in his ears, but was now able to put a smile on his face. We started laughing. Detlef looked like a semi-nude Al Jolson in the *'Jazz Singer'*.

The next day, we had to paint the kitchen ceiling, wash the

walls, fix the drywall and reinstall the window. Detlef regained all his faculties within a few hours and ended up eating a can of Chef Boyardee Ravioli for dinner that he borrowed from me. However, he ate his out of a bowl that he had to wash first because our dishes were covered in soot.

Another anecdote of our short stay with our patient and understanding landlord also revolved around Detlef.

We were anxious to see our first hockey game in Canada. We had heard that Canadian hockey was the best in the world and far superior to anything we had ever seen at the World Championships, where Canada was only represented by amateurs.

The Toronto Maple Leafs were the reigning and defending Stanley Cup champions. We were ready to sit down and watch our first NHL game on TV.

Detlef wanted to have a bath before the game and started filling the tub. However, he ran late and started watching the game. Getting caught up in the excitement, he forgot about the running water.

The bathtub was ancient and we had never noticed that it did not have an overflow that would lead into a floor drain.

Ten minutes into the game there was a knock on our living room door and our landlord politely asked us about the water running down the staircase into the foyer.

We never saw the end of the first period. We were busy drying the carpet, mopping up the standing water in the hall and hoping the ceiling downstairs would not be ruined. We did get back to watch the end of the game, the Leafs beat Detroit 2:1.

The landlord never got excited or complained or expressed his objection to anything we ever did. We hardly knew he was there. He lived downstairs by himself and his son would show up occasionally to do some work around the house, collect the rent and leave.

On a full moon day, our landlord's son would spend the night at the house. In the middle of the night the old man would get up and start running into the walls head first with flailing arms, howling and screaming like an animal.

It baffled us at first and we didn't know what to do. His son explained later that he suffered from some kind of mental disorder that made him behave like that on a full moon day.

The next morning we would see him with bandages pasted over his face and bruises on his forehead and arms.

I don't believe in werewolves, but I sure came close to thinking they were real and that one of them was living with us on Dorval Road.

Chapter 25

Jobs, Jobs, Jobs!

My first job in Canada was not what I expected.

We arrived in this country when all the breweries in Ontario were on strike. There was no indication how long it would last. There was not even an opportunity for a job interview since none of them would accept employment applications until after the strike was settled.

The only brewery not affected by the labour dispute was the Formosa Brewery in Formosa, Ontario, about 180 km north west of Toronto.

The agent at the unemployment office pointed to my last job in the elevator industry and sent me to apply for a position at the Pape Elevator Company in Toronto.

Every new immigrant to Canada faced the same question at their job interviews: Do you have any Canadian experience?

This question has driven many newcomers crazy. It is given as the reason for not hiring new arrivals and, therefore, denying them the opportunity to get some of this precious commodity called Canadian experience.

In my case, that question was never asked and I was hired on the strength of my reference letter from Schindler Elevator in Berlin.

Big mistake on their part.

My starting wage was $2.10 per hour with an increase of $0.50 cents an hour after three months.

I wouldn't last that long, my lack of Canadian experience would do me in!

On my second day on the job I had to cut a heavy double T-beam 14 feet and 4 inches long (I'll never forget this measurement until the day I die).

I moved the heavy bar onto the saw table to be cut.

On the blueprint the measurement was expressed as 14'4." That to me and my metric mind meant 144 inches. I proceeded to cut and then started drilling holes at the indicated distances as marked on the drawing. Soon I ran out of beam. I called the foreman over and showed him the drawing. He looked and then measured and started yelling, "You idiot, you have cut the damn thing 2 feet 4 inches too short!" I protested by pointing to the drawing that clearly stated 14'4"... that's when it dawned on me that every foot had 12 inches.

The next day, I was on sweeping, cleaning and gofer duty. There is only so much to sweep, clean and go for in such a small company. Nobody trusted me with anything that involved imperial measurements. After just two weeks, I had cleaned, sorted and swept everything clean and my boss handed me my notice.

In a way, I was lucky to get fired because it just so happened that the strike at the breweries had ended and I could finally apply for a job in my profession.

I now learned about the second peculiarity in Canada.

Being overqualified for a job means that you won't be hired for any other job either.

I was definitely overqualified for what they had to offer. There are no real brewers in Canada, only brewmasters hired from the UK or trained in Chicago as an extension to a university program to run the whole brewing operation and for that I was definitely underqualified. Most jobs were, and still are, performed by semi-skilled labourers for which I was overqualified.

I was caught in a Catch 22 dilemma.

Carling O'Keefe Breweries offered me a job in Michigan and

said they would help me obtain a work permit for the US. I declined. Leaving Canada after just three weeks was not what I had in mind.

There was still Formosa Brewery in Formosa, Ontario. Ali loaned me his car and I was off to Formosa. To my surprise the brewmaster offered me a job, $2.00 an hour, including a room at the brewery.

It didn't take me long to decline the offer. Formosa was a town of less than 500 people and country living did not appeal to me. I already had a job offer of $2.20 cents at Tri-Metal, a company owned by Ali Harmsen's son in law, Hans Berger.

I worked for Hans Berger until late fall, when I heard from a friend that Alcan was hiring truck body assemblers and punch press operators. Tri-Metal was located in Milliken, more than 50 km away from where I lived and the Alcan job offered better wages and was only five minutes away from my boarding house. Hans understood my reasons for quitting.

I enjoyed my stay at Alcan. I worked the morning shift one week and afternoons the following week. Working on piece-work, I averaged well over $3.00 per hour and considering that my first job only paid me $2.10 per hour, I had now increased my income by almost 50%. Things were beginning to look up for me.

In the spring of 1969, Horst approached me and said, "Konnie, your father was a painter, didn't he ever let you work with him? If you could work as a painter you could make almost $6.00 an hour. I could introduce you to the owner of Amsterdam Painting and maybe you could get a job with him."

My interest was piqued.

After a chat with Martijn Amsterdam, the owner who everybody called Marty, things were definitely more of a challenge.

Marty explained to me that in order for him to hire me, I had to first join the Union and prove to them that I was a qualified painter.

This didn't look good. How was I going to prove that I was a qualified painter?

There had to be a way. What did I have to lose by trying to fake it?

I wrote to my mother to send some of my father's old letterhead and his rubber stamp that said 'Master Painter Kurt Brinck'.

I typed up my own letter of qualification and a letter of reference, forged my father's signature and marched down to the Manpower Translation Services on Spadina Road in Toronto. They translated my letters into English on official Government letterhead and stated that these letters were true translations from the German originals.

The Union as well as Marty had no doubt that this was legitimate and I instantly became a qualified painter and member of the International Brotherhood of Painters.

I got hired and on Monday morning I met Marty at the shop. He drove me to a house on Cummer Ave. We unloaded the paint and materials. He gave me a bunch of paint chits and on every one he noted the room that had to be painted in that colour.

He told me he'd pick me up again in the evening.

My total experience was helping my father a few times painting but I had never mixed paints and was staring at these gallon cans and those little tubes of tints and colourants, without a clue about what to do.

I decided to start on the smallest room that was to be painted in a light purple.

After opening the first can of paint I wondered if that little tube would be enough to achieve the light purple tint they wanted. It had to be enough because I had only one tube with me.

The result, after squeezing the tint into the paint and giving it a good stir, was unbelievable. The paint turned a dark purple. How could a little tube have such a dramatic effect?

I was stunned and started perspiring.

I now took an empty bucket and poured another gallon of white paint into it and added just a touch from my dark purple gallon. After adding just a cupful I had achieved the tone I needed, but there was now an almost full gallon of royal purple paint I had no use for.

I decided to do the ceilings for the rest of the day, they were all in white.

When Marty arrived at around 4:00 pm in the afternoon and

looked at my work, he turned to me and said: "Kid, you are no painter, are you?" It was obvious, I guess. I came clean with him and told him that I had helped my father often, but was not a qualified tradesman and had faked my papers. To my surprise, he didn't fire me.

He just said in his strong Dutch accent: "You are unbelievable, but I like you. I will keep you on as a 3rd year apprentice, but I'll pay you only $4.10 per hour."

I couldn't agree quickly enough, that was still more than my previous job at Alcan building truck bodies. I learned quickly but when November rolled around, the jobs got scarce and since I was the last one hired, I was the first one to be let go. Marty assured me he'd get me back in the spring. He was fond of me and had almost become a father figure to me.

We went for a great night out on my last day and he wanted to prove to me that an old Dutchman could drink a young German brewmaster under the table on any day of the week. The last thing Marty taught me was that gin will give you a hell of a hangover.

Good thing I didn't have to go to work the next day.

•••••

Finding a job in November as a painter in Canada is almost impossible. So it was back to the Manpower office looking for work.

The Manpower agent was looking at my file with my experience in brewing, metal work and now painting on my record. When one of his colleagues walked by and handed him an index card saying that an engineering company is looking for a second or third class engineer rather urgently.

I had no idea what a third class engineer did but anything third class sounded rather easy to me. So I said to the agent that I had studied some engineering in Germany and might just be qualified enough to do this job. He just looked at me and said, "You want to tell me that you are a brewmaster, a metalworker, a painter and now an engineer and you are barely 23 years old?"

He chuckled and gave me the card and said, "See if you can bullshit your way into this company."

To my surprise, I got the job! No papers needed, no questions asked, just the referral from Manpower and my German accent did the trick. God bless Canadian prejudices, because it is assumed that all Germans are great engineers. They explained that my duties were to install and test heat exchangers and that my crew was experienced and would give me a heads-up should I have any problems or questions on the job site.

Monday morning I met my welder Gerhard, a German tradesman, and my helper Aldo, an older Italian chap, in the cafeteria. We were introduced and given our assignment.

Our destination was the oil refinery in Oakville where we were greeted by a gentleman in a white coat. I assumed he knew my colleagues from previous jobs. After introducing himself to me, he told me that everything had been cordoned off in a 300 feet diameter and precautions had been taken to avoid an explosion.

Explosion?

I stopped him right there and asked to have a word with Gerhard.

Gerhard had a great sense of humour and found it amusing how I had conned myself into the job. He assured me he had done this many times and to just let him do the job and wait in the truck after letting the gentleman in the white coat know that we would be finished in about four hours.

While Gerhard and our helper did what they had to do, and I still don't know what that was, I waited in the truck praying that there wouldn't be an explosion blowing the refinery and the town of Oakville to smithereens. On our drive back to the plant, Gerhard promised he would help me find a job in the plant by explaining to management that I had developed nerves working in the refinery.

The chief engineer apologized to me for not mentioning that there was an element of danger involved and offered me the supervisory position for the permanent afternoon shift in the shop, which I gladly accepted.

This was one of the easiest jobs I've ever had!

My duties were checking the setup of presses, drills and other heavy machinery to templates or drawings. My workers were all experienced and it was just a formality. Other duties included signing worksheets, enforcing safety rules, filling out general reports and paperwork for which I was trained.

For the first time in my life, hiring was part of my job description. When my forklift operator quit, I hired my friend Haiko.

Life was great until a new plant manager was hired for the afternoon shift.

He and I did not get along from the beginning. Borys was a polish immigrant with a very heavy accent. I assume he hated anything German. One of my co-workers told me once that his parents had been shot during WWII by the SS. I never talked to him about it since he avoided my company and any personal contact by barricading himself in his office.

Nothing I did was good enough. He criticized me for hiring and keeping Haiko on my team, even though he was seen as being lazy an uncooperative. There were many complaints received about his attitude and working habits. He fired Haiko without consulting me.

After many abusive confrontations and angry shouting matches I walked out one night. I regretted losing the job.

One evening, my good friend Reggie told me to stop hunting for jobs and use, what he called, my extraordinary gift of the gab to pursue a career in sales.

This was one of the best pieces of advice I'd ever been given in my life!

Chapter 26

Love At First Sight

If it wasn't for love at first sight I would most likely not be married to Jacqueline today.

The power of love brought us together and made us learn to love each other. Let me explain.

Horst and Detlef came to me and asked if I would be willing to arrange a blind date for two South African girls they had met at a friend's place. I knew two young single Germans, Haiko and Reinhard, who were also recent immigrants and unattached as far as I knew. I spoke to them and they agreed to a blind date.

It turned out to be only a partial success. Haiko showed no interest in his date Jackie and neither did she in him.

However, Reinhard and his date Madge fell head over heels in love! There was one major problem for Reinhard and Madge. Neither one owned a car and Reinhard lived in Toronto and Madge in Hamilton.

How could these two lovers get together in a country where public transport was in its infancy? Was this love affair condemned to die due to lack of transportation?

Reinhard approached me and mentioned that Jackie showed absolutely no interest in Haiko and that Haiko was not willing to work on the relationship because his girlfriend was immigrating to Canada shortly and he felt he had to be faithful to her.

Reinhard asked me to go on a date with Jackie. He described her as a beautiful young woman and reminded me that I had no girlfriend at the present time.

This was only partially true.

I was having a convenient and weird affair with my landlady.

She was a mother of a 4-year-old boy and a wife to a husband who, as it is called today, had erectile difficulties due to prolonged health problems.

He knew what was going on during his wife's frequent visits to my room. He never mentioned to me that he felt uncomfortable with the situation. His wife told me she had needs and he understood they needed to be addressed. He loved her very much and did not want to risk losing her due to his, hopefully only temporary, condition due to severe bleeding ulcers.

Being 22 years old, I felt that I was doing both of them a favour. There was no need to spend a lot of money on dates when room service was included in my rent. I was, therefore, not too interested in becoming a substitute blind date.

Reinhard begged me to just give him a chance to cement his relationship with Madge and convince her to move to Toronto to live with him. I agreed to tag along for a few weeks.

It was Monday, August 4th 1969, when Reinhard and I travelled to the Scarborough apartment of the Lesch family to meet my date.

The apartment was a madhouse. Reginald and Merle Lesch, also recent immigrants from South Africa, were living in the apartment with their five teenage children. They must have been very popular people. They had at least a dozen visitors in their apartment that day, which was normal for them, as I found out later.

I was introduced to a Jenny and, not paying attention with all the commotion going on around me, I understood Jackie.

Wow, what a sight! Jenny was a tall olive skinned woman with a short white leather miniskirt and matching white knee-high boots. Her long auburn wavy hair cascaded over her shoulders and the white cotton blouse barely concealed her lacy bra. I didn't notice her boyfriend Joseph and his friend Wolfgang, two young

Austrians, arriving with her. Reinhard pulled me over and said he wanted to introduce me to Jackie. I was confused, this wasn't Jackie?

He said that this was Jenny and, while I was still drooling over one gorgeous woman, he introduced me to another.

Jacqueline Simons.

She was definitely less provocatively dressed than Jenny, and was wearing coral caprice pants with a yellow top. She also had an olive skin complexion and shoulder length jet-black hair and a terrific figure. Jackie did not smile but seemed rather agitated, trying to get us out of the apartment.

She didn't look like she was excited to have been introduced to me. I almost felt like she wanted us out of there and get rid of us. Later, I learned that Merle was a bit stressed that afternoon with so many visitors in her apartment. Remarking on the large German speaking contingent, she said that she felt as if Hitler's Army had invaded her living room.

After being introduced to the whole Lesch family and their guests, we left right away.

The moment we got into the car it was obvious that Reinhard and Madge were very much in love. It looked like there was a kissing contest going on in the backseat of my car. At times I thought they were trying to suck each other's faces off.

Jackie and I decided to drive to High Park in Toronto's west-end where we could leave them alone for a couple of hours. We didn't ask if that was OK with them in order not to disturb their necking in the back of my car. It was almost embarrassing to listen to the moaning and groaning noises emanating from the backseat while sitting next to a young lady I had just met.

To drown out the two smooching lovers, we turned up the volume of the radio and listened to CHUM, an oldies type station in Toronto. We discovered that we both had the same taste in music.

After we arrived at the park, we agreed to meet Reinhard and Madge again in about two hours and they disappeared into the more private areas of the park. Jackie and I sat by the edge of Grenadier pond and talked.

When I was first introduced to Jackie, there were no sparks flying between us. As a matter of fact, Jackie did not look like she was very interested in me and, maybe due to her rather cool demeanour towards me, I cannot say that I was falling head over heels in love with her either.

As we were sitting by the pond we started talking and I found her very interesting. Her stories of her life in South Africa fascinated me. Even though I knew a fair bit about South Africa, I was pretty much unaware of the full impact of Apartheid on the people in that country.

I was astonished to find out that Jackie and I would not have been able to date in her home country, because she was not white but classified as coloured or of mixed race and, therefore, not allowed to marry or even date a white man. We would not even be allowed to sit on the same park bench, ride in the same taxi or go to the movies together.

I was captivated by her and her stories.

She agreed to have another date and I gladly agreed to drive Reinhard to Hamilton the following week to spend some more time with Jackie. We were pretty much by ourselves the whole day, chatting about her and my families, South Africa, Germany's history, current events and sports. It was a pleasure to be with somebody who was well versed on so many topics and willing to listen to new ideas and opinions. We enjoyed our time together and had fun and a few laughs.

By the third date, I had fallen in love with her and I could sense that she had also grown very fond of me.

It was only on the fourth date that we kissed for the first time and as one says: The rest is history.

So it is true that Jackie and I are together due to love at first sight. It just wasn't ours, we needed a bit more time to find out that we were made for each other.

Chapter 27

A Tale Of Two Friendships

When Jackie and I became close, it was natural that we introduce our best friends and their families to each other.

In my case, it was the Harmsen family. When I arrived in Canada not knowing a soul, they had opened their door to me and given me a home away from home and enjoy being part of a family. I spent my first Canadian Christmas with them. They celebrated my birthday with me and I helped them almost every weekend building their new house in the country.

They had practically adopted me as a family member even though the subject of politics was hardly ever discussed due to his still strong beliefs in the philosophies of Nazi Germany.

Maybe that should have been a sign of things to come.

Jackie was very close with the Lesch family. Their ties went a long way back to South Africa where Jackie had worked together with Merle Lesch and established a great relationship with the whole family.

It was amazing how differently these two families reacted when we were introduced to them.

I can truly say that I was shocked at the way the Harmsens reacted when I introduced Jackie as my girlfriend.

Ali Harmsen was courteous, but cool, and his wife Gertrud ignored Jackie completely and did not engage her in conversation or make her feel comfortable in her home.

When we left after a short visit, Jackie said right away that these people were racists and rejected her because she was not white.

Even though I had noticed the icy atmosphere surrounding our visit, I thought they might have had a fight before we arrived and were in a bad mood. Jackie told me that she had lived with racism her whole life and certainly knew when she was being discriminated against.

I only saw the Harmsens once more after our visit and it became clear to me that their belief in Aryan supremacy and racial hatred would end our friendship. They made it pretty clear to me that they could never accept anybody from outside their racial background.

The family had cut ties with one of their older daughters when she married a Portuguese immigrant. They had never talked about her with me since she was a *persona non grata* and shunned by her parents. It now became clear that their Nazi philosophy was so deeply rooted that they were willing to not only destroy our friendship but their own family over it.

Ali Harmsen went as far as to write to my mother to tell her that she should try to convince me to look for a nice 'white' girlfriend. In his mind even a non-German girl would be fine as long as she was white.

My mother did not dignify that letter with a reply.

This was not the first or last time that I was confronted with racism in my life but I had never experienced it directed towards me or my friends before. I grew up in the 60s, a decade where tolerance and open mindedness was the flavour amongst young people.

•••••

Jackie and her friends and family had grown up in South Africa, where the official policy of Apartheid promoted racial inequality and racism.

The Lesch family welcomed me with open arms with the motto that any friend of Jackie's was a friend of theirs. There was a warm and friendly atmosphere in their home and everybody seemed to enjoy life. They judged everyone as their equal and even though I took a lot of kidding for being German, they never prejudged me for being white or German.

There was no boredom or apathy, only a true interest in all aspects of life. We had many open, and sometimes, heated discussions on topics like politics, sports, music or any other subject that was worth talking about.

Their house was open to everybody and there was always a good time to be had. Reggie was the intellectual patriarch of the family and Merle was the fun-loving hostess with a wicked sense of humour and the sharpest tongue, keeping everybody on their toes. Reggie was also an accomplished piano player and we enjoyed listening to him and had many sing-a-longs.

One could truly say there was a party atmosphere in their house almost every weekend. Their home became not only the meeting place for South Africans, but also for anybody who loved a good time.

Jackie's and my life pretty much revolved around the Lesch family for many years. There will be many more stories about the Lesches and the good times we shared with them.

This is the last time the Harmsens will be mentioned in my memoirs. It certainly is a shame when a closed mind refuses to learn from the wrongs of the past and misses out on the joys that other cultures can add to your life.

Chapter 28

Life With A Girlfriend

It was on our third date after another day at the park and dinner, that I invited Jackie and the lovebirds Reinhard and Madge to my room to have a drink before the girls went home to Hamilton.

The next day, my landlord approached me and casually asked me if that girl I had up in my room was my date. I told him that she was and his reply was that due to the circumstances it would be better for me to find another room.

I had until the end of the following week to move out.

Since I had started to fall in love with Jackie, I was thankful that my landlord took it upon himself to end the rather awkward situation with his wife.

I found a nice apartment on High Park Boulevard just a few blocks away and moved the following weekend. The landlady was a middle-aged German woman and seemed rather nice.

The first Saturday evening I invited Jackie, Reinhard and Madge to my new place after we had been to a movie. We had a few laughs and the girls left about midnight.

The following week we again decided to have a drink at my place before the long drive to Hamilton. We had the shock of our lives as we came through the front door.

The landlady, who was hiding under the staircase, saw that I had company and she jumped out and started yelling in a very agitated voice, "I am not running a whorehouse here. Do you think you can bring all kinds of women into my house? We are decent people living here and we don't condone this kind of thing. I want you out of here by next week."

Her rotund figure, the excessive gesturing and the hysterical screaming reminded me of Brunhilde and I guess Richard Wagner would have been proud of her performance.

The four of us just looked at each other. Judging by her frenzied behaviour, there was no point trying to talk any sense into her. I told her that these were my guests and, as long as my rent was paid and we didn't disturb anybody, I had the right to have visitors. We walked past her and up the stairs to my apartment to enjoy the rest of the evening. We also had a good laugh talking about the hysterical antics of my moralistic landlady.

It was on that day that Madge had agreed to move in with Reinhard on the following weekend, the same weekend my mother was arriving on her first ever visit to Canada.

What a hectic week this was going to be!

I found a lovely room with a kitchenette just down the road and planned to move for the second time in three weeks.

Reinhard asked me to move Madge to Toronto on the Friday evening and said he would help me all day Saturday to get ready for my mother's arrival the next day. Since it gave me a chance to spend an hour with Jackie, I agreed and picked him up after work and we drove to Hamilton.

We finished the move late that night and Reinhard and Madge couldn't get me out the door quick enough to do the thing young lovers do. After all, this was their first night together.

I left for my last night at Brunhilde's castle. I hardly slept a wink that night. All kinds of things were going through my head. Jackie, my mother, moving... my life was in turmoil!

The next morning, I got up early and had everything packed when Reinhard, Madge and Haiko arrived. Reinhard announced right away that it looked like I had everything under control and that Haiko and I could manage without them and they left.

He didn't even ask if their help was needed, they just walked away. I was pretty pissed off. It was obvious that he didn't need me any longer.

Haiko and I got the moving chores done quickly. My belongings comprised of a few boxes, a suitcase, a TV and a small stereo system. He helped me with the unpacking and organizing. We were done by dinnertime and went to our favourite restaurant for a great meal. That night, I slept like a baby. I was exhausted.

My mother's plane arrived on time. She was overjoyed to see me and I had a tough time getting her to stop crying. On the way to my apartment, I told her about my hectic week. She asked me many questions, especially about the girlfriend I had mentioned in my letters. I told her she would meet her the following Saturday.

We talked until late evening when jet-lag caught up with her and she went to sleep.

I had taken the Monday off to show my Mom around the neighbourhood and point out the stores where the staff spoke German, since she didn't speak a word of English.

Mom got right back into spoiling me. Dinner was ready when I came home from work and she bought little knick-knacks to give my apartment a homey look. We went for walks in High Park and she felt right at home in Canada.

We planned our itinerary for her stay, including the usual sights like Niagara Falls, a 30,000 Island tour in Georgian Bay and other attractions. We also decided to go to Montreal for a weekend during her four-week vacation.

Saturday came and I invited Horst and his girlfriend Maria over to my place for the afternoon to meet Jackie as well as having somebody to speak German to my mother.

Jackie was supposed to arrive by two o'clock. That time came and went and Jackie was nowhere to be found.

I got worried and was ready to call the police to find out if there was an accident between Hamilton and Toronto when she arrived just after 4 o'clock. Jackie was reluctant to talk about the reason for her delay but indicated that she was not feeling well. She didn't mention that she suffered from menstrual cramps and was unable to drive. This is not the kind of thing you want to discuss when meeting your future mother-in-law.

We felt tense and my mother's introduction to Jackie did not go over well. The language barrier and Jackie's not so happy disposition made for a less than pleasant afternoon. Towards the end of the evening, I mentioned that I was going to take my mother to Montreal for a weekend and asked her if she wanted to come along.

To my surprise, she agreed to join us. The excitement and anticipation of the trip almost killed me.

The whole trip was very stressful for me. Both my mother and Jackie tried their best to get along and bond with each other but the language barrier was hard to overcome.

I now had to work out the sleeping arrangements. Let me point out that I had not spent a night together with Jackie at that point.

My mother was agreeable to take a single room and let me share a room with my girlfriend. She was a very liberal and open-minded person when it came to sexual things.

I booked a single and a double room at the Hotel Nelson at Place Jacques-Cartier in old Montreal. Our rooms were adjacent to each other and had a connecting door.

I was not happy about this arrangement. To say that my first night with Jackie was less than what I had expected is an understatement. Every sound could be heard in the next room. For my mother to be able to listen in on everything that went on in our room did not lend itself to the sensuous, wild and raucous activities I had envisioned for my first night with the love of my life.

There is not much else I remember about this trip except that I knew then that Jackie was the one I would marry.

My mother left in the middle of October and I promised to go and visit her as soon as I was settled. She told me to look after Jackie. She knew that Jackie was most likely the reason for me to not move back to Germany. It took me two more years to take my new bride to my home country. But that too is another story.

Chapter 29

Love, Lust And Happiness

The Commute

Friday nights were never like this before.

Working permanent afternoon shifts until 10:00 pm every Friday meant that I could get to Hamilton just in time for the 11 o'clock news. However, watching the news was not what I had in mind when I walked into Jackie's apartment and greeted her with a passionate kiss and a loving embrace.

The weekends belonged to us and on most weekends, I didn't leave until Monday morning.

We spent our time visiting friends, mostly her friends Sally and Derek in Dundas Ontario or we drove back to Toronto to be with the Lesch family and spent the nights at my flat in High Park.

We always made sure that we had enough time together to do the things that young lovers do, and lots of it!

My landlord was a real nice guy and didn't mind that my girlfriend stayed overnight. He was very fond of Jackie and me.

We were having a great time together, but I wanted her to come to Toronto and move in with me. Jackie agreed but first she had to find a job in Toronto.

It was the middle of April and I felt that mailing resumes and having to wait for replies was too long a process. I was impatient and so I became proactive and started looking for a job for her.

Jackie is a social worker and had been working for the Hamilton Housing Authority at that time.

I took advantage of being free that day and started canvassing the employment offices in Toronto, trying to at least get an interview for her. Jackie had given me a resume and some references and I started making calls at various municipal and provincial agencies on her behalf.

My second call was to the human resources office for social services at the city of Toronto.

The employment councillor was amused about the fact that the boyfriend of an applicant was trying to find a job for his out-of-town girlfriend. He assured me that they were hiring and agreed to see Jackie the following week. If Jackie had the right qualifications and had as much desire to be with me as I had to be with her, he could almost guarantee her a job. That, I told him, would make me the happiest fellow on earth.

We drove to Toronto the following Monday and to my delight Jackie was hired as a welfare visitor.

I took the rest of the day off to celebrate with her and we started making plans for her big move to Toronto.

Three weeks later, we loaded all her belongings into our cars and made the trek from Hamilton down the Queen Elizabeth Highway to Toronto.

Learning to live together

Jackie has always been a very modern woman in many ways. Knowing my background, being an only child, spoiled by my mother and with limited housekeeping skills, she made it very clear that she was neither going to be my domestic slave nor my substitute mother.

It was understood that this was not going to be a traditional German relationship where the man wears the pants and the wife's only duty was to keep hubby happy. Our cooking skills had not reached a level that was sufficient to put a gourmet meal together. We were more comfortable trying to fry an egg or boil potatoes.

Jackie also made it clear that her parents were never to find out that we lived together, or lived in sin, as it was referred to in those days. Apparently, her mother was very religious and not very progressive when it came to sexual matters. Knowing that her daughter lived with a man would have killed her. That rule also extended to her work, since living common law was frowned upon by the Department of Social Services, not only for the welfare recipients but also for staff.

The first time, our lack of cooking skills and the rule of not admitting to our sinful relationship to relatives caused a problem was when a distant cousin of Jackie's vacationed in Canada and wanted to visit her in Toronto.

The day before his visit, we removed all visible evidence of our living together. Tooth brushes, razors and male toiletries, shoes and coats in the hall closet were hidden. All evidence of my presence in our combination living/bedroom and the mail and bills addressed to me had to be hidden.

We even told our landlord not to let on that I lived here in case he ran into Jackie's cousin on his way in or as he was leaving.

Jackie thought it would be nice to make him a South African dish, a soupy kind of oxtail stew. It turned out to be a disaster.

Jackie put the oxtail bones on to boil the evening before and forgot about them as we went to a movie. When we came home, four hours later, the water had almost boiled away and a brownish, blackish residue had formed on the bottom of the pot.

We added more water and Jackie said that if we add the onions, peppers and carrots and boiled it a bit longer the slightly burned taste would disappear.

After cooking this for another hour, it tasted a bit better but the burned aroma was still noticeable, presumably because the longer we boiled it more of the blackish, brownish goo at the bottom of the pot dissolved and reintroduced that burned flavour. We decided to let it stand overnight and add a few more things in the morning to improve the taste. I would have gone to buy different meat but since it was a Saturday night in 1968, the stores had long closed and Sunday shopping was still years away. No shops, other than restaurants, were open on Sundays. We had to do with what we had.

In the morning, Jackie went through the refrigerator and the cupboard to add whatever she thought would enhance the flavour of this by now cooked-to-death concoction. No Worcester sauce, vinegar or array of herbs and spices was going to make this dish any more palatable.

This witch's brew had now cooked for almost seven hours. The bones were so soft you could cut them with a fork. Jackie felt it was edible and served it to her cousin.

I can honestly say that I was unable to eat more than a spoonful of this failed stew and made it clear that I thought this was not fit for human consumption. Jackie's cousin felt he had to protect Jackie and proclaimed it wasn't that bad and ate everything on his plate.

When Jackie asked him if he wanted some more, he frantically waved his hands and arms, shook his head and made it very clear that he had had enough. His spontaneous reaction to Jackie's question made it hard for me to suppress a chuckle.

Luckily, we had lots of desserts and salads so none of us went hungry that evening.

I drove him back to his hotel that night, pretending I lived out that way and had to pass his place anyway. He had no clue about our co-habitation and reported to Jackie's mother what a nice person I was.

I never saw him again after that and he never asked to be invited back for another meal. I wonder why!

Jackie did most of the cooking in the early days and her abilities around the kitchen improved rapidly. Soon she began preparing delicious meals. She concentrated on curries and dishes she had grown up with in South Africa. If I wanted something German, like a schnitzel or a hearty goulash, I got the recipe, often by mail from my mother and prepared it for the two of us.

A few weeks after we had moved in together, our landlord asked us if we wanted a large, well furnished basement apartment in his other house just a block further down the street. After he showed it to us we gladly took it. The rooms were large. It had a separate entrance that gave us the privacy we lacked in his boarding house.

We now could throw parties and entertain in a big way. However, the first party that we threw, a stag party for my friend Haiko, got terribly out of hand.

Chapter 30

The Party

Even though Jackie and I gave many great parties in our life, the first one we ever gave was one of the more memorable ones.

My good friend Haiko and his Finnish girlfriend Pirkko had decided to get married. Pirkko had only been in Canada for a couple of months and Haiko had a rather rocky employment history. Money was not something they had a lot of.

We decided to throw them a big bridal shower and a stag party they would never forget.

The bridal shower was organized by Merle Lesch and the stag was my responsibility.

To raise some cash we arranged a cash bar, had two poker tables and rented a movie projector to show some movies that would not be featured in your local movie house. The admission price was $2.00 to cover the cost of snacks and incidentals.

The turnout was terrific. The Lesch boys brought a lot of their friends and word got out amongst the German community that this was going to be a hell of an event.

It was the end of the 60's, and no party was complete without having a joint or two during the night.

Let me also mention at this point that the legal drinking age in Ontario was still 21 in 1969.

Many of our guests still had some time to go to reach that milestone in their lives, including our 19-year-old friend, Joe Jilek.

He decided to go home at about 10:00 pm but couldn't find his car. He assumed it was stolen, so he called the police and we told him to wait outside to report the crime.

It was just before 11:00 pm that he walked into the apartment, followed by an officer of the Toronto police department.

Everybody turned to look at the officer. A sudden hush fell over the room as he surveyed the scene in front of him.

The smell of marijuana filled the room, people sitting at poker tables, not playing with chips but with real money, and the sign advertising our beer and liquor prices was easily spotted as it was pinned on the wall behind our makeshift bar. Luckily, the film projector had just finished playing one of the explicit sex education movies.

I scuttled Joe and the officer quickly into the bedroom. The officer looked at me and said, "Do you have a licence to sell alcoholic beverages? Those are liquor tickets out there, aren't they?"

I assured him they were food tickets and the smell of marijuana was explained away as awful smelling European cigarettes.

He looked at me and said, "And you're gonna tell me that you are playing poker just for fun and everybody gets his money back at the end of the day, right?"

Not knowing what to say, I just nodded.

He now sat down to fill out the police report. Looking at Joe's licence he said, "You are only 19 years old. Have you been drinking? I think I smelled liquor on your breath."

Joe shook his head, stuttering that somebody must have spilled a drink on him. The officer gave him a 'yeah right' kind of a look and started filling out his forms when the women that had attended the bridal shower arrived to crash our party.

Merle Lesch was leading the army of women down the stairs into the basement, yelling at the top her voice, "We want to see some dirty movies!"

This got the officer's his full attention. Merle was followed by her 14-year-old daughter, Lesley, who was carrying an open case of beer, followed by other young ladies carrying more liquor, wine and food. While some men desperately tried to shut her up, the policeman just looked at me and said, "You know that I could throw the book at you and have half your guests arrested on all kinds of illegal activities and misdemeanours."

I just nodded and hoped for leniency and mercy.

As he left, he said to me that he didn't expect any more calls or trouble coming from this address or he would have us all thrown into jail. I breathed a sigh of relief when he walked out the door.

It turned out that Joe's car was not stolen. He had parked in front of our neighbour's driveway, blocking it, and they had called the parking authorities to have it towed away.

After everybody crucified Joe for leading a cop into the apartment, I had to have a couple of stiff drinks to calm my nerves. I got pretty plastered and went to lie down not feeling too well.

Reggie Lesch was lying next me as I got sick in my sleep and threw up over him. Neither one of us woke up and I can't remember who discovered us but it certainly was one awful mess.

Both of us stank to high heaven. We threw the bedding away and tried to fit Reggie into some of my clothes. This was not easy since Reg was about six inches shorter than me and almost 100 pounds lighter.

After getting cleaned up, Reggie decided to drive home with his youngest daughter. They left around 2 o'clock in the morning.

The party was just about coming to an end shortly before 4 o'clock when the phone rang. It was Reggie.

He called to ask if somebody could come to the local police station to bail him out.

He had been going the wrong way on a one-way street and when the cop noticed that he had been drinking he arrested him for drunk driving.

Most of our guests had already left, some had passed out and others didn't want to go into a police station in an intoxicated state to bail out a friend who was being held for being drunk.

Since I had not had a drink for some time and the women had sobered me up by pumping me full of black coffee after my unfortunate vomiting episode, I volunteered to go and pick up Reggie and Leslie. This was the 1960s, and we believed that black coffee would sober you up and a couple hours of sleep would be enough to get back behind the wheel.

As I walked into the police station, I saw Lesley sitting dejectedly on a bench and she rushed over to tell me how glad she was to see me.

I told the desk sergeant that I was there to pick up Reginald Lesch. He turned around and yelled that Mr. Lesch's son was here to pick him up.

This was very comical, since we didn't look anything like father and son. I was a whiter shade of pale and the only thing German about Reggie was the spelling of his last name.

However, I had no time to correct him since the officer that had paid us a visit earlier the previous evening came around the corner and stopped in his tracks as he saw me.

"What are you doing here?" he said with a puzzled look on his face.

"I am here to pick up a friend of mine who got arrested for drunk driving," I mumbled.

"After leaving your party, I assume?" he added with a big grin on his face.

I just nodded. He walked away shaking his head once again.

Reggie pleaded guilty and got convicted of drunk driving, lost his licence and paid a hefty fine. We threw another party to raise money to cover the legal costs and pay for cab rides so he could get around town for the next three months.

We had the party at Joe's place at the other end of town, away from the vicinity of our police station and to avoid meeting the same cop.

After all, he was the reason most of the excitement happened in the first place.

Chapter 31

Road To The Altar

The Proposal

It wasn't a proposal in the literal meaning of the word. It was more a matter of fact, unromantic remark uttered while I was studying the Canadian tax system as part of my new career as a life insurance salesman.

We had been living together for four months by this point and I felt committed to Jackie. I always introduced her as my wife or wife-to-be. A marriage licence was nothing more than a piece of paper legitimizing our loving relationship for society.

We both felt that we would stay together and marriage didn't mean much to either one of us.

The old-fashioned attitudes were still strong in those days and many people would, for instance, guide us to separate bedrooms when we stayed over for the night. Some of our friends even told us that they felt uncomfortable letting us sleep together in their house without us being married. Jackie's parents and her employer were not supposed to find out that Jackie was living with me under one roof. It was still frowned upon by her parents, church and most of society.

The sexual revolution had not caught up with everybody by the end of the 1960s... When I learned that I could deduct Jackie as a dependant from my income tax if we got married late in December, I thought it would be great to take advantage of this financial windfall.

I think I said something like, " Do you know that we could save a lot of money on our taxes if we got married in December? It would also end that charade with your parents and your job pretending we don't live together. So what do you think? Should we get married?"

Jackie reacted very calmly and I think she was considering the advantages and said, "Yeah, why don't we?" It was much later that I found out that Jackie was taken aback because she had expected something a little more romantic.

There was no diamond engagement ring and no kneeling in front of my darling during a romantic candlelight dinner with violins, playing in the background, serenading our eternal love.

I was financially overextended in those days, living the good life without having an income to justify it. I had taken advantage of the freely available credit and bought everything from great cars to a colour TV and a stereo system. The monthly payments were drowning me. Getting a nice tax rebate was certainly something to look forward to. Jackie still kids me today that I married her for her money and a tax rebate.

The income tax rules have changed since then and nobody else will ever have the added advantage of being able to say to his sweetheart, "Hey Darling, would you like to be a major deduction on my income tax? Then, let's get married."

In retrospect, I would do it differently if I could do it over again but... *c'est la vie!*

We picked the wedding day that night, December 19th 1970.

Planning the Wedding

My clumsy but successful proposal had been made. Now what?

Neither one of us had ever been married before, we were not religious, had made few plans for a future together and that included a wedding. Our first decision was to have a nice modern apartment to begin our married life above ground. We both had good jobs and were by now able to afford to move out of the basement apartment.

Our landlord was very understanding when we told him we would be moving out at the end of October and he wished us luck. We signed a lease for a two-bedroom penthouse apartment, with a great view of downtown Toronto, on Lawrence Avenue in the north west of the city.

We felt like we had arrived and were moving on up.

The reception was the least of our worries. We had met Bill and Elsa Davidson through Merle Lesch. When Merle told them we were looking for a hall to have our reception, they offered their house. I guess they were partial to German/South African couples since they were one themselves.

They owned a huge house with a big store for their successful rug and carpet business on the ground floor, they lived on the second floor and the recreation room was in the basement. It was the size of a banquet hall with a bar and enough room to accommodate the 55 guests we had invited. We didn't know Bill and Elsa very well and were surprised when they offered their home to us. They even supplied the main course of the meal, lobster and salmon and, to top it, gave us a nine by twelve carpet as a wedding present. We were extremely thankful.

We both agreed not to get married in City Hall. Friends of ours told us it was a dreadful experience. We wanted to have a Justice of the Peace marry us at the reception, but were unable to convince a single one to show up on a Saturday afternoon a week before Christmas.

We then decided to get married in church and hoped to find a minister who would do it without too many religious trappings and keep it fairly secular.

We went to see the minister of the United Church just around the corner from us on Wright Avenue.

I started my request for a very simple ceremony, by saying, "We came to you because the Church has been in the business of marrying people for almost 2000 years. We aren't that religious and would like you to concentrate on the societal and personal aspects of marriage rather than the religious ones in your sermon."

The minister listened to what I had to say and when I was finished he looked at us in a very friendly way and said, "Well, I guess there are many ways to please the Lord. The fact that you came to me to be married in the house of the Lord is a start."

"So you are going to marry us?" I asked, surprised that he would not first try to ask us to join his congregation or make us disciples of Jesus Christ.

He looked at us with a stern expression as he said, "Jesus never turned nonbelievers away and neither will I. You have come to me to get married in the house of God and will receive the blessings of the Lord and hopefully one day you will find your way to Jesus Christ the Lord."

I told him that I looked at it more like a business deal and would pay him for his services. He just smiled and said that Jesus never accepted payments for his blessings and neither would he.

"However," he continued, "If you would like to make a donation to our church, you are more than welcome."

"How much does one donate when one gets married?" I enquired.

"The most we have ever received is $1,000.00 and the least is nothing," he replied.

I was getting a little impatient. This was like pulling teeth to get an acceptable amount out of him.

"A thousand is too much," I said. "Can you tell us how much people give on average?"

He said that around $25.00 was the usual donation for weddings and baptisms.

"That's a deal, $25.00 it is," I said as I stretched out my hand to shake his to finalize the negotiation.

"Well," he hesitated, as he lifted his index finger like a schoolteacher ready to enlighten his pupils, "there is also five dollars for the registrar, five dollars for the organist and five dollars for the janitor."

I just looked at him and was surprised about the sudden hidden charges that were not included in the original price, I mean donation. I told him that my friend Reggie was an accomplished pianist and used to be the church organist in his home country, therefore the five dollars for the organist was out. I also told him that we would instruct our guests not to throw rice or confetti and the five dollars for the janitor was out as well.

"Do we have a deal at $30.00?" I asked. He just nodded and we shook hands.

We were set for the big day.

The Wedding

We both woke up early on our wedding day.

I took Jackie to Merle's house to get ready for the march down the aisle. Merle's daughter Margot was the bridesmaid. She and her friend Jenny turned Jackie, in my eyes already the most beautiful woman alive, into a most stunning bride.

Jackie had told me that the wedding dress was not a traditional gown. She had bought a flowing off-white pantsuit that was tailored with wide flowing legs. It looked like an evening gown and the fact that it was not a dress was not easy to see. After dropping Jackie off, I went back to our apartment.

Many of my friends had told me I would get last minute jitters and doubts about getting married. No such thoughts ever entered my mind. On the contrary, I could hardly wait to say 'I do'.

I got dressed and waited for my best man, Derek Scott, to come and pick me up and get me to the church on time. He and his wife Sally showed up in plenty of time and we got to the church early. The minister went over some details with us and now the waiting game started.

To everybody's surprise, the bride arrived right on time but one very important person was missing. Our organist Reggie Lesch was nowhere to be seen.

The crowd of close to seventy guests was getting restless. The minister asked if his church organist, who was already playing while we were waiting, could play for our ceremony. I told him we would wait, something must have happened and we assured him Reggie would show up. He arrived almost half an hour late mumbling something about a flat tire, rushed to the organ and started playing. My heart almost stopped as I spotted Jackie coming down the aisle. She looked breathtakingly gorgeous.

I couldn't help but think of my parents. How proud they would have been to see a beaming Jackie floating down the aisle.

The Wedding Party

The minister's mouth dropped open as he saw Jackie and noticed the pantsuit.

Jackie was halfway down the aisle of this huge church when Reggie got warmed up on the organ and started to jazz-up the traditional wedding march, getting the crowd to sway and bop along to the music. The minister looked bewildered. He had never heard the wedding march played like this before.

He gave a short sermon, touching only fleetingly on Christian traditions that were, and still are, relevant in a secular world. He talked mainly about love, trust and faithfulness.

After the 'I do's' I was so emotional that I didn't hear him say, "You may now kiss the bride" and just stood there, almost in a trance, looking at my new wife. Jackie nudged me and said, "Don't you want to kiss me?" I grabbed her and gave her a long passionate kiss that I didn't want to end. The crowd applauded and, after what seemed like an eternity to everybody else, the minister tapped me on the shoulder, coughed awkwardly, and said, "I think that's enough!" Reluctantly, I let go.

Reggie again started playing the organ and I can only remember that it was a rousing, catchy piece of music that matched the happy feeling and spirit of the occasion.

When we went to sign the marriage papers, the minister said it was the most memorable ceremony he had ever performed and Jackie was the first woman to get married in a pants suit in his church. He loved the uniqueness of it, including the music and the enthusiastic congregation.

The reception at Bill and Elsa's home ended up being a great party. Jackie didn't want to go home, she was having so much fun. I, however, having finally become a romantic, was urging her to leave for home to complete the wedding day with the last of the still missing pieces, carrying her across the threshold and having a fantastic and unforgettable wedding night.

We didn't leave the party early. I only got to carry Jackie across the threshold because she had indulged a bit too much in the refreshments and, because of that, I'll never know if our wedding night would have been the most exhilarating, satisfying and romantic night of our lives.

I doubt it.

Chapter 32

Hospital Horror

After a year of marriage and a job that didn't demand much physical activity, my weight had ballooned to close to 250 pounds.

I had suffered from abdominal pain for almost a year but now my bouts became unbearable and more frequent. I visited a doctor who told me that if I lost some weight these pains would go away.

One day in the office the pain became excruciating. I asked my boss Don to drive me to the emergency at nearby North York General Hospital.

It got so bad that I was screaming in the reception area and a doctor administered a sedative to be able to take some x-rays.

His original diagnosis of a kidney stone was confirmed.

The stone was over two centimetres in length and embedded in one of the kidneys.

This was 1971 and shock wave lithotripsy, the crushing of kidney stones with ultrasonic shock waves had not been invented yet. My only option was open surgery.

The surgeon, Dr. Smythe, urged me to lose some weight before proceeding with the operation.

He prescribed diet pills. Every time I felt hungry, I was supposed to pop a pill. They were amphetamines, also known as 'Speed' in the illegal world of drugs. This was popular in the 1970s but is no longer allowed due to the horrendous side effects. It was magic.

I was 'On' all the time and talked a mile a minute. My sales activity and closing ratio increased. I worked long hours and always felt energized. My sex life was terrific. I was never tired and I got by on a few hours of sleep.

Except for some hyperactivity, irritability and clammy hands, I felt great. The formula worked, when hungry, have a slice of toast, pop a pill and drink some water.

I lost over forty pounds in six weeks.

It looked like everybody was happy.

This changed the minute I checked into the hospital the day before my surgery.

I was told I'd have to fast until the next day.

Then they took my diet pills away.

The only things my lips were allowed to touch for the next 24 hours were cigarettes and water. Smoking in a hospital room was still acceptable as long as none of the patients objected.

By eight o'clock that evening, I went almost ballistic. I demanded my pills back. I was shaking and soaked in perspiration. The nurse finally called a doctor who gave me a sedative.

I slept well but still felt tired and exhausted the next morning as they prepared me for surgery.

I was wide awake when the anaesthesiologist asked me to count backwards from ten to zero. When he saw that I was still conscious, he increased the dose and asked me to count again. I noticed his frustration when he saw that I was still awake. He sighed, increased the dosage again and told me to start counting backwards from 99. I was out before I got to 95.

This high dose caused me to take ages to recover and I was happy to see Jackie at my side when I opened my eyes.

I was pretty groggy for the rest of the day and beyond.

The first time I saw the size of the incision I was surprised. It was thirty centimetres long. The doctor told me that they removed a rib for easier access to my kidney, which they were able to save.

The real torture and misery, for me and the nursing staff as well as for Jackie, started the following day.

I was quickly becoming the most irritable, annoying, uncooperative patient in the history of North York General Hospital.

My plan was simple. I wanted everybody to leave me alone until I was healthy enough to go home.

The nurses had a different idea.

The first day they wanted me to start walking. I was in no mood but with the doctor's insistence I walked as little as necessary, grumbling and complaining incessantly.

I was not in a good mood. Everybody was amazed that I had gained four pounds on the intravenous after the operation. My body was that starved for nutrients.

Adding to my grumpiness, I was put on a liquid diet for the next few days.

I had rented a TV and was content to just watch it and stay out of everybody's way.

The second night at about 11:00 pm, the night nurse came in and said, "It's lights out and time to sleep". I objected and said I wasn't tired and always watched the Johnny Carson Show.

"Oh," she said, "if you aren't tired, I'll get you something to help you sleep."

As she trotted off, my roommate explained to me that the nurses liked to have a quiet night and didn't want to worry about patients being awake.

I told him I don't care and would watch TV until I felt like sleeping. He just smiled.

A minute later the nurse returned with two sleeping pills and told me to take them.

I refused and told her I was fine and wanted to be left alone.

She threatened to take my remote and switch off the TV, insisting it was lights out time.

Now, I was getting pissed off.

"Listen," I said, "I paid $10.00 a day for the TV. To me, that's 24 hours a day. If you want to deprive me of it for six hours, then you owe me $2.50. So you either reimburse me part of my rental fee or you don't switch off my television set."

She looked at me rather confused, mumbled something unintelligible and walked out. My roommate almost killed himself laughing.

No nurse ever tried to switch off my TV again.

Three days later, during his rounds, the doctor mentioned that I was ready to be put on solid foods.

Hallelujah, no more Jello, pudding and chicken broth.

It was too late to change my lunch order but I was looking forward to dinner, my first real food in more than five days.

When my dinner arrived it was, you guessed it, pudding, Jello and broth.

I called the nurse immediately and protested. I told her that the doctor had put me on a solid food diet that morning. She checked the chart and mumbled, "Nothing written down here, take it up with the doctor in the morning."

She refused to call a doctor to verify my story. I wasn't the most popular guy on the ward and she certainly wasn't motivated to do me a favour.

No problem, I thought, I have a phone and will call Pizza Pizza, a fledgling franchise with a catchy phone number, 967-11-11.

I gave them my room number and they promised to deliver within half an hour.

I grabbed my intravenous pole and moseyed down the aisle towards the elevator. Passing the nursing-station, the head nurse remarked how happy she was to see me up and about as I was not known for my willingness to exercise.

There was a bench by the elevator and I sat down and waited.

When the door opened, I stopped the delivery man from going any further, gave him the money, told him to keep the change and started shuffling back towards my room.

As I passed the nursing-station again, the lovely aroma of the pizza must have preceded me. The same nurse looked at me and said, "Mr. Brinck, is that a pizza?"

"Of course," I replied, "What else do you think comes in a box shaped like this?"

She stormed out from behind her desk and started yelling at me, "You know you aren't allowed to eat that, I will have to take it away from you."

I pulled it out of her reach and snarled, "Look here now, if you take my pizza away I will call the police and charge you with theft. This is my pizza, I paid for it and you have no right to take it away."

She stopped and stared at me.

"You wouldn't do that, would you?" she gasped.

"Damn right, I would!" I growled. "Just because you are the head nurse doesn't give you the right to steal patients' property."

She turned around trying to figure out how to handle this situation and said she'd call the doctor right away. She wasn't going to take a chance on having to explain to a policeman that she wasn't a criminal.

The doctor on call arrived half an hour, or to put it differently, a whole pizza later. At my bedside he looked at my chart and told me I should have asked for a doctor. Playing the innocent injured party, I assured him that I had asked for a doctor to rescind my liquid diet but was ignored by the nurses.

These are just a few highlights of my memorable stay at the hospital. I blame my bad disposition on the withdrawal symptoms from the amphetamines.

I barked, yelled and hissed at everybody, including my wife Jackie, who showed a lot more patience and understanding than the nursing staff.

My behaviour probably led to my earlier-than-recommended discharge and is possibly the reason why I ended up with a surgical hernia, which often bothers me today.

It took me a few weeks to return to the sweet, loving, easy going and humorous disposition that I have been known for ever since.

Chapter 33

Two Different Worlds

From the moment that Jackie and I met, we realized our cultural differences. We both looked forward to one day being able to explore those differences and experience each other's heritage, background and customs. We both knew it would take a while for us to be able to visit the countries of our birth. By 1973 we had saved enough money to take our first big trip.

Germany

My mother was eager to welcome me home for the first time since I left Berlin five years earlier. We arrived in Germany in late May and planned to stay for three weeks.

I wanted Jackie to get to know my last few family members, my friends and my neighbourhood. I was looking forward to walking her through the history of Germany, good and bad, as well as having her enjoy the beauty of the ever changing picturesque countryside from the North Sea to the Alps.

My aunt Hanna was the first family member Jackie met. She took to Jackie right away and the feeling was mutual. Tante Hanna, as we called my aunt, was enamoured with Jackie and wanted to show her the new apartment she had just moved into. She insisted that we come over for coffee and cake, which is comparable to the English custom of 4 o'clock tea. Even though there was a huge language barrier, and they never had a proper conversation other than smiles, hand signals and single words like yes, no and OK, I could sense an unspoken bond developing between them. Tante Hanna congratulated me more than once on my choice for a wife. My normally shy and withdrawn aunt was bubbling over in Jackie's presence.

My cousin Margot and her husband Ferri welcomed us into their home and their daughter Elvira, who spoke English rather well, lessened the language barrier.

Jackie was fascinated by the Berlin Wall. We crossed over into East Berlin at Checkpoint Charley to meet my cousin Ilse and her family. She was mesmerized by the elaborate security, the fortifications and the nerve-wracking, almost rude treatment we received from the East German border guards.

We did not have a visa and the tourist day pass we received granted us only access to East Berlin. We were not allowed to go to Potsdam where my cousin Ilse and her family lived on their farm. Instead, my mother had arranged to meet them at the famous Alexander Platz. This was the first time I had seen Ilse and her family since the wall went up in 1961.

We spent the day getting reacquainted, sightseeing and being introduced to life on the other side of the Iron Curtain. Ilse was so excited about meeting Jackie that she ignored the fact that Jackie didn't understand German and talked to her constantly not giving me a chance to translate. We were in tears when it was time to say good-bye after a memorable day.

Leaving East Berlin was even more dramatic than entering had been. Border guards practically disassembled our car to confirm that nobody was hidden inside the trunk or gas tank, stuffed and sewn into the upholstery or hanging on to the undercarriage of the car trying to flee. Once convinced, we were allowed to leave.

Jackie told me she felt like she was in a Cold War spy movie and the whole ordeal of crossing the border sent chills down her spine. She confessed it was exciting and, in a weird way, she had enjoyed the experience.

Back in the West, I introduced Jackie to my friends and my old hangout, the local pub. Jackie was welcomed and treated like one of the regulars from day one. The ability to communicate with my friends varied. Everyone around my age had taken at least five years of English in school but how much they remembered differed. Surprisingly, my best friend from childhood, Kalle, managed very well and succeeded in having some conversations with Jackie. Communication improved as the nights went on, mainly due to good German beer and schnapps loosening our tongues and ridding us of our inhibitions.

We had the best of times travelling through Germany. We explored the Rhine on a day cruise and sang along to drinking songs in quaint restaurants in medieval villages. We enjoyed Bavarian culture with their *um-pa-pa* music and *lederhosen*, which is so often falsely portrayed as being predominant across the country.

Wherever we went we experienced German *Gemütlichkeit*, that feeling of cordiality, comfortable friendliness and congeniality.

Topless and nude beaches were already socially acceptable in Germany back in the 70s. That, combined with our visit to the Red Light District, which is mandatory when you visit Hamburg, was an eye opener for Jackie.

We also visited landmarks celebrating Germany's glory days as well as its darker times. From visiting impressive castles like Neuschwanstein and memorials celebrating the military might of the Prussian Empire to visiting the Dachau concentration camp, we took in everything possible.

Jackie found the people a lot more relaxed and friendly than the few Germans she had met in Canada. She slowly realized that the younger people did not resemble those Germans in Canada from an earlier generation. The open-mindedness, from political to sexual attitudes, was certainly much further developed than in either Canada or South Africa.

The stereotype of the cool, rigid, unemotional German squarehead who doesn't know how to relax, was hard to find.

Jackie gained a lot of insight into the German psyche, its history and its people. We agreed that this would most certainly not be our last visit to the country of my forefathers.

South Africa

Jackie and I were planning to visit South Africa in March of 1978 when, on December 5th 1977 at four o'clock in the morning, the phone rang and woke us up. It was Jackie's sister.

I knew this was not going to be good news. Jackie had talked to her sister a few days earlier and knew her mother had been having abdominal pains and was scheduled to have some tests done.

She was diagnosed with cancer and passed away before doctors could treat her. She didn't even have enough time to get her affairs in order.

Thirty-six hours later, Jackie, Toni and I boarded a plane for the long journey to Pietermaritzburg, South Africa.

Jackie had told me a lot about South Africa and I assumed I was prepared for anything. After all, I had experienced racism, prejudice and exploitation before, in Canada as well as in Germany. There was one big difference. In South Africa, racism was the law, prejudice was a way of life and exploitation was what the country was built on.

I had no idea of the challenges that lay ahead.

In Johannesburg, I noticed an immediate change as we went from the international to the domestic airport terminal to continue our journey to Durban. There was a multitude of toilets and, for the first time, I not only had to watch for gender classification but also for my racial background to identify the place where I could relieve myself.

I had arranged for a rental car to be picked up at the airport in Durban. We could not have travelled together by cab since they were segregated. Travelling by bus or train would also have been impossible since seating was according to race. Waiting for Hertz to get my car ready was already problematic. I had to sit and wait away from my own wife and child, benches were marked for whites and non-whites. I never knew how hard it would be to explain to a three year old why Daddy couldn't sit with her. This was the first time I realized what a tough time we were going to have. My blood started to boil and I wondered if I would lose my temper in the days to come.

We arrived in Pietermaritzburg to a tearful welcome by Jackie's family. The mood was subdued and everybody was still in shock about the sudden and unexpected death of Ivy, their mother, sister and grandmother.

Walter, my father-in-law, looked weak and distraught. He was happy to see me again but was barely able to smile as he hugged me and thanked me for coming.

Even though we were exhausted, we stayed around to welcome the guests as they arrived in the afternoon for the wake and to pay their respects to the family. Toni found herself a little corner to catch up on her sleep.

I forgot who asked me if I had gotten permission from the authorities to stay at my in-laws' house since this was a 'coloured' area and, according to the 'Group Area Act' which divides residential areas by race, I was not supposed to be there. I was also asked if we weren't afraid of being arrested for violating the 'Immorality Act' that forbids interracial sexual relationships and marriage. Apparently, my Canadian passport did not exempt me from their racist laws. Jackie was still a South African citizen and the law would come down much harder on her, being a coloured woman than on me, a white male foreigner.

I was introduced to family, friends and neighbours. Late in the afternoon, the minister of the local church arrived to make arrangements for the funeral.

Having felt the heavy-handedness of Apartheid, I asked him if I could sit with my family during the service or if there was a section for whites in his church.

He smiled and said, "You can sit with your family. We don't segregate in our church. It's not necessary since you will be the first white person ever to attend a service in my church."

I was intrigued and asked, "So, there is no segregation in churches, they are integrated?"

"Oh no," he replied, "when there is a need for separate seating it will be implemented."

I was shocked again. I asked him how he could justify obeying these non-Christian laws and not rebel in the name of the Lord.

He just smiled and said, "As Jesus said, we give to Caesar what belongs to Caesar and to God what belongs to God. The law of the land was not written by our Lord and Saviour, he has put me here to save souls and not to fight the government."

I tried to convince him that in my view, Jesus was a revolutionary in spiritual and worldly matters. I tried to convince him by mentioning Jesus' outrage about the Pharisees and money changers. He just said that I didn't understand and walked away.

I was furious. Jackie's family and the people we met in Pietermaritzburg were very religious and they used their beliefs to endure injustice and oppression. They didn't agree with Apartheid, but somehow found a way to tolerate it. Even worse, they felt somewhat superior because they were of mixed race and not as lowly on the racial scale as black Africans. In this absurd society, Indians felt they were better than the coloureds since they were still a pure race. It was surreal.

There was no animosity towards me because I was white. Some may have felt a bit awkward having a white man amongst them but overall, I felt they were as comfortable around me as I was amongst them. I had to answer a lot of questions about life in Canada but hardly anybody was willing to condemn or even discuss Apartheid with me.

After the funeral, I tried to spend some time with my relatives, especially the children. It proved to be rather trying.

I wanted to take my nephews to a soccer game. They loved the idea but told me that they would have to sit in the seats behind the goal, which were reserved for non-whites, while my seat would be in the white section, the grandstand, the best seats in the stadium.

It broke my heart when I talked to my nephews about their future. They were twins, but had totally different personalities. Clinton was a lively and adventurous young boy and Quinton was quiet and loved mathematics. They were too young to realize their dreams of becoming a pilot or an accountant one day would not be realized. South Africa's 'Job Reservation Act' excluded non-whites from most careers and high paying jobs.

Yes, the good life was reserved for whites.

I tried to get to know my brother-in-law better by going to a bar and chatting over a couple of drinks, nope, there were bars for whites and there were bars for non-whites, and never the twain shall meet.

Treating the family for a nice meal in a fine restaurant, you guessed it, not in Pietermaritzburg.

It was a tearful good-bye. I loved Jackie's family but felt so hopeless and discouraged about their lives, their aspirations and their future. I also felt sorry and helpless for myself. Nothing I had said or done had made a difference in my view. I had not changed anybody's mind or broadened their horizons.

My father-in-law made me promise to come back to bury him. I did, knowing I would not be able to keep my promise. Three months later he died heartbroken, having lost his will to live.

We left to drive to Cape Town and Jackie promised me I would meet a different kind of coloured people among her friends. They were more educated, open minded and politically engaged.

We had planned to take it easy driving to Cape Town and enjoy the breathtaking scenery along the way.

Stopping to eat along the way proved to be a challenge. We had to buy take-out food and eat in our car or along the roadside, there were no multiracial restaurants along the way. Even the benches in the many picturesque parks wouldn't let us sit together and enjoy a meal as a family.

Before leaving Canada we had acquired a list of 'International Hotels' from the South African embassy in Ottawa. An international hotel was allowed to offer rooms to couples of mixed race as long as one person had a foreign passport. All other hotels were strictly segregated.

Our first stop was Port Elizabeth. We arrived at the Elizabeth Hotel as darkness fell.

The next morning we marvelled at the view from our 10th storey window. It was breathtaking. The day was sunny, without a cloud in the porcelain blue sky. Our room overlooked the deep blue ocean and a gorgeous beach.

Since it was such a lovely day, I suggested we go for a swim before checking out. Jackie cautioned me that she and Toni probably couldn't join me on what was likely a 'Whites Only' beach.

I was incredulous. How could an international, multiracial hotel not have a beach that all their guests could use?

What happened next absolutely astounded me.

The clerk at the front desk smiled at me when I asked him if 'anybody' could use the beach at the hotel and said, "Of course you can sir, why do you ask?"

"Because we are a racially mixed family," I replied.

His facial expression changed as he pointed to a remote corner of the lobby and asked me to take a seat there. He would get somebody else to come out and talk to me.

He clearly tried to get me out of earshot from the front desk to avoid a possible confrontation.

It was only a minute later that a light skinned coloured woman approached me and asked what she can do for me.

I told her my family was of mixed race and we were planning on spending some time at the beach.

Her answer left me dumbfounded.

She said, "Well sir, if your wife is about my colour, there shouldn't be a problem. Would you say she is about my colour?"

I could feel the anger rising inside of me and said, "You are kidding me, what do you want me to do, bring you some skin samples so you can tell me if my wife and daughter are light enough to lie on your bloody beach?"

She must have felt my hostility and frustration and added, "Sir, if you prefer to avoid any trouble, the Indian and coloured beaches are about 500 meters further down and the Black beach is where the rocks are at the end of the bay."

I didn't know how to express my anger and disgust.

I lost it.

Screaming profanities at her, the hotel and at the whole screwed-up country, I stormed over to the elevator and went back to the room to get the hell out of this godforsaken place.

It took me a while to calm down but this, my worst day in South Africa, had just started.

We drove along the 'Garden Route' famous for its stunning scenery. The vistas soon made me forget the trouble of that morning. Since we had left Port Elizabeth rather early, we figured to be by noon at our next hotel in Plettenberg Bay. We planned on having lunch in one of their restaurants since the restaurants and bars in international hotels were multiracial.

The drive up to the hotel was stunning. It was situated on a rocky headland in one of Africa's most spectacular beach towns overlooking the Indian Ocean.

After we pulled up to the entrance, Jackie asked me to go ahead and make sure we could get a room and there wouldn't be a problem.

Passports in hand, I walked up to the reception desk and asked if they had rooms available. The desk clerk said he had vacancies and asked me for how many nights we intended to stay.

Before booking, I asked him to verify that this was an international hotel.

The clerk looked at me and said, "I'm sorry sir but our international certification will only take place as of January 1st 1978, right now we are a 'Whites Only' facility."

Oh no, not again!

I showed him the list from the South African Embassy in Canada that included Plettenberg Bay as an international hotel.

After looking at it, he pointed out that the list was titled:

'International Hotels in South Africa for 1978'.

He looked at me sheepishly and asked politely if he could book us a room for early January. There was no emotional outburst as I walked back to the car. I was at my wits end and felt like crying.

We stopped at a roadside stand and bought sausages and chips for lunch. We found a rock to sit on overlooking this gorgeous bay. We had to make plans on where to spend the night.

Jackie's best friend Merle had given us the address of her brother Bill Barry who lived in a town called Pacaltsdorp, a coloured township near George the largest city along the Garden Route.

We decided to stop by at his place since Merle had told us we would be welcome to stay with his family and she had mentioned to them that we might be dropping by.

Pacaltsdorp was less than 100 km from Plettenberg Bay and we could be there by late afternoon. I did not know what to expect. I had heard many stories about him and not all were favourable.

Bill was an entrepreneur and had, what one could call a small business empire. He owned a farm, movie houses, grocery stores and even a night club. Many said his success in business was mainly due to the fact that he was co-operating with the whites and taking full advantage of the Apartheid system, using it to build his fortune. He was not very popular with people who actively opposed the system and that included Merle's husband Reg.

We arrived unannounced and were greeted by his three sons, who told us that their parents were away on a business trip and not expected home for a few days. However, they knew about us and welcomed us into their home.

And what a home it was. It was more an estate with a full staff of maids and gardeners. Certainly not something I expected to see in a coloured township.

The brothers insisted on us staying for the night even though the family owned a hotel in town. Staying in their hotel could have been illegal since we would have been subject to the 'Immorality Act'. The hotel was for non-white patrons and my presence could have been problematic.

The oldest son, Roger, was a great host. He asked a lot of questions about life in Canada, his aunt and uncle and his cousins in Toronto.

He told me that he had no illusions about the future. He expected that one day there would an uprising by the oppressed masses and he might have to settle outside of South Africa.

Roger used a phrase I had heard often in South Africa, "We are treating our Blacks very well."

Most people, Whites, Coloureds and Indians alike, knew that the black Africans were the most disenfranchised and most exploited of all the racial groups in their country.

To justify the exploitation and oppression, lessen their own guilt and ultimately leave themselves with a clear conscience, they convinced themselves that patronizing and being nice to Blacks was what they ought to do to improve their lives.

Roger was the first one who told me that coloured people had no future in South Africa. They were too dark to be accepted by the Whites and too white to be accepted by the Blacks.

He recalled a conversation he had with one of his African labourers. He asked him if there was an uprising, would he kill him or would he be safe since he always treated his African workers well?

The answer surprised him and me.

"No Boss," he said, "I know you're a good man, but my brother doesn't. He'll kill you."

It became harder and harder for me to envision a positive future without violence for this country.

The next morning, Roger asked us to stay one more day but we wanted to get to Cape Town and left after breakfast. We thanked them for their hospitality and were on our way.

Jackie had told me not to worry about accommodation. Any of her old friends would be willing to put us up for our stay in Cape Town.

None of her friends had any idea that we were in South Africa.

We showed up unannounced at her friend Pam's house. She was excited to see Jackie again and was delighted to meet her family.

She was a teacher and a widow living in a large house with the youngest of her four children, Michael. She right away offered, no she insisted, that we stay with her for the duration of our visit.

Pam was an unbelievable host. To please me and make me feel welcome she went shopping for German food early the next morning. Rhine wine, Löwenbräu, bratwurst and schnitzel were not exactly what I was looking forward to. I wanted to experience Paarl wines, Castle beer, smoked snoek, a local fish, boerewurst and other South African delicacies, but I appreciated her efforts to make me feel at home.

Pam also called everybody who knew Jackie from her days at university and as a social worker. She planned a great get-together in her honour and to introduce me to her friends.

But before that could happen, I had to be checked-out to see if I was politically and ideologically fit to be trusted and accepted .

Pam and most of her friends and colleagues belonged to an underground group called, 'The Unity Movement'.

They were a multiracial underground organization. Their members, ranging from liberals to Marxists, consisted mainly of teachers, social workers and other educated people. Their leader was Victor Vessels, a former teacher who was jailed, banned and put under house arrest for many years without ever having been convicted of a crime.

He grilled me for two hours before shaking hands with me and announcing that I was okay. I guess my marrying Jackie, my trade union background and history with the Social Democratic Party in Germany and my left leaning liberal views qualified me to be acceptable in their midst.

Many of Jackie's friends had been arrested, imprisoned, put under house arrest and tortured for speaking their mind and opposing Apartheid. I met and talked with many of them.

Although engaging, I found that the Unity Movement was not a militant organization looking to overthrow the government. It was more an elitist group that theorized a lot but had no real plans or the popular support amongst all racial groups to be a factor in the struggle to free their country from Apartheid and be part of a democratic multiracial society. I never saw or met any white or black members of their group. The large majority was coloured with a few Indians making up the balance of their movement.

I questioned what the Unity Group, many of them teachers, was doing the previous year when their students were shot while simply protesting the introduction of Afrikaans as the medium of instruction in their schools. Afrikaans was the language of the white Afrikaner or Boer, and most Coloureds, Indians or Blacks spoke English or an African language like Zulu or Xhosa. Many told me there was nothing they could do. They stood by and watched as over 176 children were killed by South African police throughout the country.

I accused some of them of cowardice and was told I didn't understand. 'The time was not yet ripe for an uprising', was a phrase I heard often in defence of their inaction.

I sensed for the first time that some members of the group mistrusted me. They looked at me as a white man first and as a like-minded individual who shared their beliefs second. To them, I still looked like the enemy. Victor took a liking to me and asked me if I wanted to go into one of the black townships and squatter-camps, normally off-limits to whites. Since he was banned from teaching, he was working as a paralegal for a non-white solicitor who defended black Africans who had gotten into trouble with the law, which was not difficult for them to do.

He picked me up the next morning and we drove into Gugulethu.

Victor told me to keep the heavily tinted windows of his car always closed and only to get out when he told me that it was safe. What I saw shocked me.

There were some modest one or two room brick houses. The majority of dwellings ranged from prefabricated galvanized iron sheds to cardboard boxes covered by plastic garbage bags to protect the families who lived in them from the elements. Few had water or electricity.

We made one brief stop where Victor introduced me to an old African who looked at me suspiciously until Victor told him I was a Canadian who wanted to see what life in an African township was like.

We chatted only for a few minutes before Victor started feeling uneasy and wanted to get back.

I met many interesting, well educated, politically aware and active people in Cape Town but realized they had their democratic rights, from freedom of speech to the right to assemble, revoked. I could not see a peaceful and democratic solution to their plight.

Let me close with an almost humorous example about the beaches of Cape Town, that wasn't funny at the time. There were some moves by Cape Town city council to ease Apartheid. Cape Town was possibly the most progressive and liberal city in this totalitarian country.

They tried to integrate the beaches of Cape Town and frequently took the 'Whites Only' signs down, only to have the Provincial government put them back up the next day.

One beautiful sunny morning, Pam's son Michael said that he just heard the signs were down at Muizenberg beach, one of the more popular beaches around. We decided to pack a picnic and spend the day frolicking in the warm waters of the Indian Ocean.

We were still putting our blankets and picnic baskets down

when police cars and vans loaded with nightstick-wielding cops started chasing everybody who did not look lily white and therefore didn't need to work on their tan, off the beach.

Anybody resisting or pointing out that there were no signs designating this as a 'Whites Only' beach, was beaten up. Mine was the only white face in our group. I quickly grabbed my things and threw them into the trunk of my car.

My already tanned wife, daughter, friends and I sped off in a great hurry to escape a beating. There were twelve of us in four cars and it was a mad scene of cop cars with their sirens blaring chasing us until we had left the beach area. It reminded me of a scene in a Keystone Cops movie but I wasn't laughing at the time.

Nobody got hurt but this was the closest I had come to experience the gentle art of persuasion of the South African police force.

This trip to South Africa, the first of many, left a deep impression on me. It explained why so many South Africans, who lived a large part of their lives under Apartheid, saw everything through racism-coloured glasses. They are also aware, and often offended, by seemingly harmless racial jokes, actions and open or subtle discrimination.

Who can blame them?

Chapter 34

Planning A Career In Sales

It was one of those Saturday evenings at the Lesches' place when we discussed anything and everything.

I had just quit my job and was wondering what to do next. Was it worth to consider getting back into my trade as a brewmaster? The idea didn't excite me in any way. I mentioned my dilemma to Reggie Lesch and Kenneth Cairncross, a good friend of the Lesch family, over a few drinks.

My memory is not clear on who first mentioned that I should consider going into sales, but once it was mentioned, Reggie and Kenneth pointed out the qualities I had that would make me a good salesman.

As the evening went on I was wondering why I hadn't thought of it before. It sounded like I was born to be in sales. I was a good talker and a good listener, was passionate about my beliefs, very convincing in my arguments and very competitive.

Even my less desirable traits like my stubbornness and impatience could be helpful if used in the proper way.

Jackie and I had just moved in together and being employed as a manual labourer was not what I had envisioned for the rest of my life. We discussed me taking a chance at starting a new career and Jackie was very supportive. We combed through the weekend papers to get an idea of what kind of sales positions were available without prior experience.

There were lots of ads that offered full training, rapid advancement and above average income. Many of them did not give details about the product or the company.

We picked out a few for me to call Monday morning to make appointments for interviews. Some of these jobs turned out to be door-to-door positions for encyclopedias, aluminium sidings, vacuum cleaners, cookware and other household items. Not what I had in mind.

I arranged two appointments for Wednesday to give myself some time to prepare a good resume to present myself in a positive light for a future career in sales. The only suit I owned was a heavy, grey wool suit from Germany and was not something one would wear on a warm day at the end of May. I'd gained a couple of pounds since arriving in Canada and the fit was now a bit too tight.

To make me look the part of a young go-getter ready to conquer the business world I had to buy a new wardrobe.

My image of a flashy salesman came from the way they were portrayed on TV and the many used car salespeople I had dealt with in the past. Money was also a problem at that time and a Harry Rosen or an Armani suit were definitely not within my financial means.

I went shopping at Honest Ed's, a low-budget department store in Toronto where you can find almost anything except good quality. At that time in my life neither my fashion sense nor my taste were exquisite or exhibited any sophistication.

The outfit I bought gave Jackie almost a heart attack when I picked her up for lunch before going to my first interview.

I had bought a blue blazer, a red satin shirt, an off-white pair of dress pants, a white tie with red stripes to match my shirt and black patent leather shoes made from high quality plastic.

I don't think I paid more than $49.95 for the whole outfit.

According to Jackie I looked like a used car salesman working for the Mafia. She pleaded with me to go home and at least change the shirt for my interview, but there was no time. My appointment with Don Merriman, the Branch Manager of Commercial Union Assurance Company, was at 2 o'clock.

I could see him looking at me with raised eyebrows when the secretary showed me into his office. After we introduced ourselves, I apologized for my wardrobe and told him I was going to an Italian dinner party after the interview and that I normally don't dress like this.

He bought my explanation and we had a long chat after which he asked me to complete a math and aptitude test.

Don Merriman seemed to like me and told me he would call me after the test results came back. If they were positive, he would schedule a second interview. I had a good feeling about my performance and was confident I would be called back.

The second interview I had arranged for that day was for a retail sales position. They also told me that they would call me back after their screening process was finished. However, I was not interested in their offer since I had no desire to work in a retail store selling appliances.

When I got home, Jackie told me that a Don Merriman from Commercial Union had telephoned and wanted me to call him back in the morning. I called him promptly at 9.00 o'clock and arranged to see him that afternoon.

Dressed in the same blazer with a white shirt and grey slacks, I was hoping to be offered the position with Commercial Union.

Don, as the manager asked me to call him, was very quick in telling me that I had scored 100% on the math test and showed a great aptitude for a career in sales.

After he outlined the three month training program and the remuneration package, he offered me the job. I accepted on the spot and a salesman was born.

Since I had no previous experience, I was handed my training package the same day to give me a head start. When I showed up in the office on June 1st 1970 to begin my official training, a lifelong career in sales was about to begin.

Chapter 35

Commercial Union Assurance Co.

June 1970 - September 1971

I had no Idea how much there was to learn. There was whole life insurance, endowment insurance, full term and decreasing term insurance, participating and non-participating policies, paid up policies, spousal policies, partner insurance and much more.

I had to study legal, tax, inheritance, income, medical and property implications; and also familiarize myself with age and marital considerations, beneficiary selection and estate matters.

I had to learn how to prospect, uncover needs, write proposals, close deals, answer objections and service existing clients by reviewing their ever changing needs and circumstances.

It made my head spin.

I made calls with some of our senior underwriters and was taught how to build a client base.

My boss, Don Merriman, was a firm believer in the power of positive thinking and motivation. All salesmen had to attend seminars by people like Zig Ziglar, Earl Nightingale, Bob Proctor and many other motivational speakers. We had to read self-improvement books by Dr Norman Vincent Peale (*The Power of Positive Thinking*), Napoleon Hill (*Think and Grow Rich*), Dale Carnegie (*How to Win Friends and Influence People*), Dr Maxwell Maltz (*Psycho-Cybernetics*) and others that proclaimed to have found the secrets to growing rich, self-improvement and everlasting happiness.

I was introduced to ideas and values I had never before experienced and almost swallowed the whole thing hook, line and sinker. My values have always been to protect the vulnerable in our society. I was a strong supporter of the labour movement and was a social activist during my youth in Germany.

The social safety net was not as well developed in Canada as it was in Germany and I saw a need for life insurance. I had no qualms about making a living by selling a product that brought stability and security into the lives of families.

Even though I was fairly successful and was making a good living selling insurance, my conscience bothered me.

It didn't take me too long to notice that this was not a social service agency and the idea of securing peoples' futures was not what was motivating most of my colleagues. The goal was to squeeze as much money as possible out of clients by selling them, in my mind, mainly policies that paid high commissions, like whole life and endowment policies. In many cases, policies were sold with high premiums and lucrative commissions rather than term insurance with higher death benefits.

I believed that no family should suffer if a provider dies but I also believed that having a decent standard of living was just as important. Most of my clients were recent immigrants and young families just starting out in life. I knew from my own experience that saving large amounts of money for a rainy day was not on the top of my agenda. I had a tough time selling ideas like sacrificing things that made life worthwhile today for the goal of financial independence in retirement.

My priorities in life and my employer's thoughts of how I should convince other people to think about theirs, were not compatible. I also refused to actively hunt down my friends to sell them life insurance. Don asked me if I would feel guilty if one of them should die without insurance and his family was to end up in financial difficulties. I told him that they knew what I was doing and could approach me. I did not take advantage of my friends and their families.

My friends knew that I was willing to talk to them about their insurance needs or answer any questions. I would ask them for leads of somebody who could use my services but never pushed the issue.

There were many reasons why I left the insurance agency but I can highlight a few.

I think it was a seminar by Earl Nightingale in which he advocated the idea to move out of one's neighbourhood as one becomes financially and professionally more successful. One should acquire new friends and try to surround himself with people more successful, to aspire to even higher goals and riches. Our old and not as prosperous friends will hold us back on our climb up the ladder of social mobility and prosperity. They have outlived their usefulness and are no longer of any use to us. We should be looking for better people to inspire us.

I was appalled and had many discussions with colleagues and friends about that subject. This was not the way I wanted to live my life.

It had to happen that one of the policy holders died and a cheque to the beneficiary had to be delivered.

Tom McCrann was one of our senior underwriters. He was an older chap with a good sense of humour and a droll personality. There was no mistaking him for anything but a lovable Irishman. He was supposed to teach me how to handle the payout of the claim.

He told me that this was a prime selling opportunity and a great way to make a quick buck.

The show he put on was disgusting. He played on the many emotions of the widow. He even cried as they exchanged stories.

She talked about her loving husband and Tom praised him for having had the foresight of caring for them in the case of him prematurely dying. The way Tom took advantage of her emotional state and sold her paid up policies for the children and an endowment policy on her life was loathsome.

"Now is the time to invest and secure the future for you and your loved ones," he told her as he filled out the policy applications.

I can't remember exactly how much the death benefit was, but he bragged about the fact that most of the money went straight back to Commercial Union and most of that premium ended up in his pocket as his commission.

I asked him if he felt bad about what he had just done. He said that most grieving widows end up drinking their insurance money away. He just helped her and her children secure their future and she helped him in getting closer to his retirement plans as well.

I had already made up my mind to look for a different career when the Ontario Government called an election in 1971.

One of our underwriters was the campaign manager for one of the liberal candidates.

Since our office was located in his riding, he thought it would be a good idea to hang up some Liberal posters in the office and asked Don for permission. Don thought that this was a good idea and said that he was a card-carrying Conservative and he too would display a placard or two.

I was working for my local NDP candidate and thought I could also put up a sign in the office to show who I supported.

Well, the proverbial 'you know what' hit the fan.

I was told there would be no support for socialism exhibited in our office and to take my posters down. I objected and said that I had just as much right to campaign for the political party of my choice as anybody else had to campaign for theirs. One filing clerk agreed with me and we stood firm. Don finally decided to remove his election posters and stop the distribution of party literature.

My main reason for leaving however was very personal.

My politics and my philosophy were not that of a life insurance salesman. I had just been married and realized that I would have to work evenings and weekends for a long time. Most of the people

I knew and called my clients were working people who had nine to five jobs and were only able to see me in the evenings or on weekends. My dream was to have a family as a full time husband and a future father.

I was looking for a career were I had customers that were only able to see me during regular working hours, Monday to Friday from nine to five.

That's when I saw the advertisement from Olivetti offering a career in the office equipment industry.

Chapter 36

Olivetti - 1971/1978

Thomas Ugray, the branch manager of Olivetti's west branch, was an odd character.

He was a Hungarian immigrant and according to him, his family was an aristocratic one. He firmly believed in hiring immigrants over Canadian-born applicants. "Canadians," he said, "think they are owed a living and immigrants came to this country to better their life through hard work."

This theory didn't apply to him. He considered himself as an aristocrat and more qualified to delegate and make the hard decisions. He did stress that he too worked his way up from the bottom after arriving penniless in this country at the end of the Hungarian revolution. I liked him, even though most of the people found him a bit conceited and lazy.

I hope I got the job not only because I was an immigrant but because of my potential as a great salesman.

The office was full with people from around the world. My sales manager, Reg Smith, was South African, the other two managers were Italian. The sales people, all of them male, came from all over the world. We had Indians, Pakistanis, Italians, English, Chinese, Turks, Saudis, people from Eastern Europe and the Caribbean Islands and many more of all colours, creeds and religions. It was truly a mini United Nations with a handful of Canadians thrown in. Reg Smith was my boss and mentor. He sent me out on calls with some seasoned reps and taught me as much as possible about the industry and the job in general.

Olivetti was known for their great training program and product knowledge was what I needed most. Typewriters, adding machines, calculators and photocopiers were not things I was familiar with. There were no pocket calculators or computers in those days.

After learning the basics in their local offices, the new salespeople from across the country had to attend a three week training program at the head office in Toronto. Product knowledge of our equipment and that of our competitors, leasing, financial and tax implications and selling skills were part of a packed and intense curriculum.

The training, experience and guidance I received from Olivetti built the foundation for my success as a salesman and manager throughout my career.

Everybody hates rejection and avoids it at any cost. I learned how to handle it, even expect it and invite it. Their sales philosophy helped me overcome rejection. It was a numbers game.

You were supposed to get one trial out of every ten cold calls and one out of four should lead to a sale. If I had a better than ten to one ratio I was winning, if I had less, well, there was always tomorrow. My ratio was almost always better than the expected average.

My job was to call on businesses in my territory, trying to uncover needs or problems that our equipment could address. I offered them our equipment at no charge to convince the decision maker to purchase or lease the equipment after the trial period was over.

It was a tough job. We had to deliver and install our equipment as well as train the employees by stressing the advantages of our machines over their old models.

My first territory was Little Italy along St. Clair Avenue and the garment district around Spadina Avenue. I can truly say the experience I gained there was invaluable. It taught me about negotiating. Dealing with mainly Jewish and Italian clients was an experience.

I cherish the memories and must confess that the stereotypical image of Italians and Jews talking with their hands and trying to 'nickel and dime' you to death is not a myth but something I lived with daily. I learned quickly that I could also take advantage of buying wholesale, or at cost, when wheeling and dealing with my customers. It was great fun.

The importance of relating to my customers on more than just a business level is also something I quickly learned. Selling to Italian business men, and also to many other people 'from the old country' was different than selling to an average Canadian or even second generation immigrant.

'Cash was King' for them. For me, it was a headache. Our order processing didn't accept cash. We had to buy a money order to process the paperwork. Paying cash meant a lot to these people, they didn't believe in banks. No leasing, renting, loans or paying within 90 days of receipt of invoice.

I can still see that typical Italian gesture stretching out both hands towards me with their fingertips touching and in their heavy accent muttering the phrase of almost every Italian businessman, "How a mucha discounte iffe I paya you cash?"

At first, I was sceptical and scared to be given the garment district where most of my clientele was Jewish. Being German was certainly not an asset dealing with that ethnic group, or so I thought. I could not have been more wrong.

Yes, there were Jews who would not deal with me or even talk to me but that was very rare. More often a German calling on them made them curious about many things.

They wanted to know how young Germans felt about what happened during the Third Reich, what my family did during that period, did I ever talk to my parents about the past and do I feel collective guilt or shame. They also told me about their experiences in Europe during that time.

For most of them I was just another salesman and my background didn't bother them, business is business, was their attitude. My career at Olivetti was one big success story and my rise in the organization was almost meteoric. After only 18 months, I was promoted to National Accounts Representative for reprographic products. Olivetti had been dabbling in the photocopy market with some liquid electrostatic copiers for some time and tried to break through in large national companies.

I still remember the first and biggest national deal I was able to sign. It was with CN/CP for hundreds of units to be placed in every train depot across the country.

My commission cheque on that deal was more than I had ever made in any six months period in my life. It was over $4000.00, a fortune back in early 1973. Would they cut me a cheque that size? I had my doubts and didn't tell Jackie that soon we might be rolling in money.

When I saw that big number on my paycheque at the end of the month my heart started racing and I felt like a millionaire. Since I had not told Jackie about this huge deal, I was looking for a way to surprise her.

I went to the bank and asked them to cash the cheque and give me the money in $1.00 bills. The cashier just looked at me and told me she will have to speak to her manager but she didn't believe they had that many single dollar bills. The bank manager chuckled after my explanation but I had to settle for 2000 $1.00 bills and the rest in fives and tens.

After that, I visited a hardware store and bought a few hundred feet of string. I crisscrossed the string through our whole house, every room, kitchen and hallway back and forth. I then hung all the bills on the line. It took me hours to put them all up and the house looked fabulous.

To see Jackie's facial expression when she walked through the front door was priceless. I don't think she had ever seen so much money before and asked me where I got it. She must have thought I robbed a bank. We had a lot of fun throwing money around and being silly before going out to a fancy restaurant and celebrating this windfall. The next morning I took the money back to the bank and deposited it. The teller was not happy to have to count out $4,000.00 in small bills.

It took only four months before I was promoted into a newly created position. My job title did not fit on one line on my business card: *Area Manager for Reprographic Products, Central Canada.*

The job description was to increase Olivetti's market share in copiers by assisting our branches and dealers through continuous training and assisting in special situations. I was also in charge of copier training for new hires from across the country in our national training centre in Toronto. My territory stretched from Sault Ste. Marie to Brockville and North Bay to Windsor.

The first time I travelled I thought it would be fun but soon noticed that spending a night alone in places like Chatham or other small towns was not very exciting.

Teaching at the training centre was what I enjoyed most. When Olivetti decided that copiers were going to be added to the regular duties of area sales managers I was offered two jobs, a position as a sales manager in Toronto or a special six month assignment in the newly created systems and accounting division. Being part of something new excited me.

Olivetti was introducing the first electronic accounting machine in North America and I was supposed to research and develop applications by test marketing the equipment.

I knew nothing about accounting or marketing. A quick course at their North American Trainings Centre in Tarrytown, New York was their solution. For two weeks I had to learn everything there was to know about the subjects with other sales and marketing people from all over the USA.

It was an exciting and rewarding six months in that job. After my contract expired, I was offered a permanent position in marketing. A desk job in Head Office was not what I wanted even though my boss, Paul Manina, urged me to stay.

I accepted the offer for sales manager in the Toronto's West Branch. Tom Ugray had left the company to open his own dealership and Parnell Clark was the new branch manager. We got along fine. He was a fun loving, hardworking and hard drinking kind of a guy. I quickly grew into the job. I had only been with Olivetti for a little over three years and the next two years were going to be two of the most enjoyable years of my professional life.

Olivetti kept up the high standard of training. We had a few week-long training courses during that time, although not everyone was successful.

I remember a seminar at the Horseshoe Valley Resort that went wrong in a lot of ways. The course was given by two psychologists from Guelph University. It dealt with improving communication through openness and trust. They were manipulating our minds and indoctrinating us about the benefits of their teachings for 12 hours a day. They preached to adhere to these principles not only in the workplace but also in our private lives.

One of the attendees had a nervous breakdown and one manager went home and divorced his wife. The concept of total honesty, no secrets and trust were accepted by many but it is useless if only one person practices it. I tried to apply it in my marriage as well but it didn't go over too well. I forgot that Jackie hadn't taken the seminar. It is amazing what two trained psychologists can do to the human mind in just six days. The second seminar for upper management was never booked and the whole program was ultimately cancelled.

Olivetti amalgamated the East and West Branch in the fall of 1977 and reduced the sales teams to just an east and west team. I was chosen to be the manager for western Toronto. A new Branch Manager was shipped in from Calgary and he and I took an instant dislike to each other.

Rumours were flying that Olivetti was going to abandon the direct sales division and sell their branches to the managers as independent dealerships. The company was categorical in its denial.

I was offered to manage the Belleville-Kingston Branch and seriously considered it. Jackie and I even drove down to have a look at the office, homes and job possibilities for Jackie in social services.

We finally turned it down. It wasn't worth uprooting the family to just minimally further my career. It was a good and wise decision. Joe Pascetti, a colleague of mine, accepted the offer, sold his house and six months later Olivetti told him he could purchase the branch as a dealership. They would have assisted him with the financing, but if he refused the offer he would be terminated. No proposition to assist him to relocate back to Toronto was ever given.

By that time I had left Olivetti. My conflict with the new branch manager and a great job offer from Pitney Bowes made my decision fairly easy.

I have fond memories of my time at Olivetti. I made many friends and keep in touch with many of them today. I am grateful for the experience and training they provided.

The DeFilippo Incident

In my 30 years in sales, I had many occasions where I had to deal with crooks and gangsters. Some were co-workers and others were customers.

One of my salesmen was Joseph DeFilippo. He was hired by Thomas Ugray shortly before I arrived on the scene as a manager. Joe was a likeable guy, he seemed to be hardworking but had a bit of a temper. He was successful and it looked like he worked his territory well.

One day the sales rep handling the Ontario Food Terminal told me he found a new Olivetti Typewriter in one of the offices of the terminal. He was sure that he had not sold it to them.

When we checked the serial number we established that it was sold to a company at an Etobicoke address in Joe DeFilippo's territory. I recognized the address since it appeared frequently on the delivery and installation reports.

Assuming that this was a big office building I decided to check it out. To my surprise, the address was a single family home in a residential area with only a single name on the mailbox.

There was no way that it could house eight companies that we had shipped six typewriters, eight calculators and a copier to in the last six months. When a salesman sells into the territory of somebody else it is called poaching and is reason for immediate termination.

I called Joe into my office and asked him if he knew somebody living at that Etobicoke address. He grinned at me and said it was his uncle. He told me that his uncle was an influential man at the Ontario Food Terminal and had brought a lot of business to Olivetti by passing leads on to him.

Joe then pulled out a roll of hundred and fifty dollar bills, looked me straight in the eye and said, "How much does it take for you to forget the whole thing ever happened?"

I just looked at him in disbelief. I made it clear that I didn't want his money and that the ultimate decision of his future with Olivetti was in the hands of the new branch manager Parnell Clark.

His eyes became more piercing as he stared at me and said, "This is not about the money. It is very important to my uncle that I am successful in business and I am not going to disappoint him. Be very careful in what you decide to do." He then moved even closer to my face and very slowly in an icy voice uttered the words that scared me, "You don't want anything to happen to your family now, do you?"

I don't know if he saw that I was shaking but I think I was pretty calm when I asked if he was threatening me. He got up and on his way out he smiled at me as he said he simply wanted me to think about the best way for the two of us to get out of this situation.

Parnell already knew about the situation but asked me not to fire him before he had a chance to talk to him. He thought maybe he would show remorse, pay back the commission and beg for his job. I walked straight into Parnell's office and said, "Fire him, he threatened me and my family."

He was given five minutes to clean out his desk.

The branch secretary told us after he left that she was happy he was gone. He had asked her to lend him the key to the warehouse for just an hour. When she refused he told her that if she changed her mind it could be worth a few hundred dollars to her. Nobody would get hurt and everything was insured anyway.

A few months later, I had almost forgotten about Joe DeFilippo, is when I saw the headline in the newspaper one Saturday morning:

Gangland shooting on St Clair Avenue
Two die in a hail of bullets

Apparently, a gunman had pretended to be a pizza delivery man. Mrs. DeFilippo opened the door, the killer pushed her inside, then killed her and Joe and wounded two others.

It was then that I realized the danger my family and I had been in and that Joe did have the means to go through with his threats. The hit-man was never found and no motive for the killings was ever established.

In early 2000, I heard the DeFilippo name again in connection with the Montreal Bonanno crime family and the New York Mafia arrests and subsequent trials.

Here is an excerpt from *Wikipedia* about the DeFillipo family:

> A longtime member of the Bonanno family, Patrick DeFilippo became a made man sometime in the 1970s, though his involvement with the family dates back much farther. His father Vito was a high-ranking Sicilian-born member of the family and a close associate of Joe Bonanno. During the war of the 1960s, Patty served as a driver and bodyguard to Joe's son, Salvatore Bonanno. During this time, the younger Bonanno was detained in Montreal, Canada along with both Patty and Vito DeFilippo and several other associates. The group was alleged to have met with the family's powerful Canadian faction and attended the wedding of Vito Rizzuto. DeFilippo's early criminal activities included labour and construction racketeering, extortion, loansharking, illegal gambling, and bookmaking.

I have always wondered if Joe DeFilippo was part of that family. My gut feeling tells me he was. I am grateful to have survived this episode without any harm to me and my family.

I guess he didn't make me a deal I couldn't refuse.

Chapter 37

Pitney Bowes - 1978/1983

The Branch Manager's name was Bond, James Bond. The senior salespeople called him Jim, the others addressed him as Mr. Bond. He was seldom at the office as he preferred to spend his days at the Port Credit Yacht Club, where he could enjoy his Martinis without being interrupted by telephone calls and work related matters.

Aside from the name and his love for Martinis and other alcoholic beverages, there were no similarities between him and Ian Fleming's agent 007. He knew how to surround himself with people that would do his job and let him know when his presence at the office was needed.

One of my former salespeople from Olivetti, Ted Tobias, had convinced me to follow him to Pitney Bowes. He told me that PB, as Pitney Bowes is called for short, was a sales person's paradise. Great commissions in an industry where there was almost no competition. He had talked to Mr. Bond about me, had given him my resume and arranged an appointment for an interview.

It was one of the strangest interviews I've ever had.

The average salesman at Pitney Bowes made more money than I had been making as a manager at Olivetti. After the introductions and glancing over my resume, which he must have read before, he looked at me and said, "If you were so successful how come you didn't make any money? Are you not interested in money or too stupid to see that you are being exploited? Maybe you aren't as good as you are trying to make yourself out on your resume? Which one is it?"

It took me a moment to digest the three options he had offered me and come up with an answer that didn't include any of these choices. I said that I had started as a greenhorn in the industry and Olivetti had provided great training and advancement.

I felt ready now to join PB and am sure I would be a great addition to his sales staff. He replied by asking if I was such a slow learner that it took six years to learn how to sell bloody office equipment. Without waiting for an answer he said that nobody would babysit me here and that I had to learn quickly on the job. He then offered me the job and asked when I could start.

Three weeks later I reported to my manager, Boris Chambel, who spent some time with me teaching me about postage meters and mailing machines, gave me a few books and audio tapes, a sales manual and arranged for some training at PB's head office. After that I was on my own.

Selling postage meters and mailing machines was child's play compared to selling Olivetti's line of typewriters and calculators. IBM controlled the typewriter market and the competition in calculators was fierce from companies like Borroughs, Friden and later the Japanese with their first electronic machines sold by Sharp, Eaton's and other vendors.

Pitney Bowes controlled 95% of the market and most people weren't even aware that they had any competition. The selling tactics sometimes bordered on being unethical. There was no comparison shopping or getting competitive quotes. If the serviceman, or sometimes even the salesman, condemned a machine for dubious reasons, namely to sell them a new one, there was nothing a customer could do, unless he complained loudly, which hardly ever happened. Anybody who couldn't sell mailing equipment couldn't give candy to a baby.

Many salespeople exploited their customer base and by the

1980's Pitney Bowes clamped down and established very stringent ethical guidelines. Even with these guidelines in place it was still an easy sell. The only thing that slowed things down was the recession in the late 70's and early 80's. People and companies just couldn't afford new equipment.

My career took off again. Within 14 months I was promoted to National Accounts and shortly after that my good friend Guy Fraser was instrumental in helping me to get the position of Sales Supervisor in the Toronto Central Branch.

Due to the fact that I was one of the top performers in my first full year, I qualified to attend the National Sales Convention in Puerto Rico in 1980 and again in May of 1981 in Hawaii.

These conventions were mostly play and no work. It was time to relax and have some fun with colleagues.

An incident in Hawaii almost ended my career with Pitney Bowes. Five of my salesmen had made the trip and to show my appreciation for the good job they had done for me I invited them for dinner. We were staying at the Ilikai Hotel on Waikiki Beach, one of the better hotels in Honolulu. I made reservations for six at their very popular restaurant.

When the six of us arrived the maitre d' said that the Brinck Party of six had already arrived.

I said that there must be a mistake and asked him to let me talk to the people who had taken our reservation. He showed me to a table and there were the Vice President of Sales Steve Walker, the General Sales Manager Steve McGill and the Branch Manager Noel Gillen from our Toronto East Branch and their wives seated at what was supposed to be my table.

Before I was able to say anything the East Branch Manager, a real arrogant and obnoxious person, said right away, "Hey, we looked at the reservation and it was for a guy who spelled Konrad with a C and Brinck without a C and that's not you. So send somebody over who is the real Conrad Brink and we'll leave."

In my mind I quickly went over my options. Should I just walk away like a coward and lose the respect of my salesmen who were witnessing this scene or stand up for my right and possibly risk my career? As the anger and fury built up inside of me, I decided to choose the second option.

I leaned over and said to them, "Monday to Friday, from nine to five, you can walk and shit over me because you are my superiors, but here I am on my own time and you don't have the right to humiliate or take advantage of me. I want you to get up and leave right away."

Steve McGill got up and pulled me aside and said he would fix it and I should keep my calm. He called the maitre d' over, slipped him a $50.00 bill and told him to solve this little misunderstanding.

A table was quickly put together by the kitchen door and when I said to him that they should be seated there, Steve asked me to let it go and apologized by saying he was sorry and that it wasn't his idea to grab our reservation. Noel Gillen did it without the others' knowledge.

Steve Walker never forgave me for embarrassing him in front of other people.

Shortly after the convention, James Bond was asked to take over the Hamilton branch. He accepted since his health was declining and he was looking forward to cutting down on commuting and his responsibilities. In his place, a protege of Steve Walker's, Tony Nusca, was promoted to Branch Manager. He had it in for me from day one. I don't know if he was told to make my life a living hell or if he instantly disliked me, probably a mixture of both.

A month later, James Bond called me to come and see him in Hamilton. He offered me the sales manager position and was honest in his explanation.

He said, "You know your future with PB is pretty much in doubt. I am offering you a new start. This branch has a poor track record and you can't go anywhere but up. I won't make it much longer, my health is fading and with good results you might be able to revive your career. You might get back into Steve Walker's good books and inherit my job."

Jim, as he asked me to call him now, was only around for another four months. He took ill and never returned. For the next three months I practically ran the branch. Things were improving when Steve Walker turned up one day and announced that the new Branch Manager for Hamilton had been appointed, Tony Nusca. I was in shock. What had happened? Nobody knew why Tony, after such a short time, was demoted to become the new manager of Hamilton.

It didn't matter, I had to get out of there. I asked for a transfer back to Toronto and accepted a demotion to a commercial major accounts salesman. I now started to look for a new start with a competitor.

A former colleague told me Office Equipment Inc, the distributor for Canon Copiers in Canada was establishing a National Accounts Division and the Manager Fred Werner, a Berliner, would love to talk to me.

Chapter 38

OE/Canon - 1983/2001

The early years 1983-1986

I never thought that a job interview in a bar, while having a few drinks and being pursued by a prospective employer, would be a great way to spend an afternoon and could be so much fun..

In 1982, when my problems at Pitney Bowes started, I had applied for a sales position at Office Equipment Inc, commonly referred to as OE Inc. I didn't like the manager who interviewed me at the time. He avoided eye contact and I didn't feel comfortable with him. When he called me back for a second interview, I declined and said that I was not interested. I dismissed OE as a future employer and forgot about them.

A year later Russ McGaw, a former salesman of mine who had joined OE, called me and asked me to meet with Fred Werner, their Major Accounts manager. I was hesitant. Russ told me about Canon's new Major Accounts program and he thought I would like the company and Fred Werner.

I promised Russ that I would call the next day and listen to what he had to offer. I liked his approach on the phone and agreed to meet with him for a chat over drinks later that week.

I will never forget the day that would change the rest of my life. It was early August when we met in a pub in the west-end of Toronto. Fred was a jovial kind of guy and I took an instant liking to him. It didn't take long to get the formalities out of the way and we agreed that I would start on the 6th of September after the Labour Day Weekend.

The rest of that afternoon was spent reminiscing about our childhoods in Berlin and running up a substantial bar bill.

My first impression of Fred was absolutely correct. He was truly one of the best managers I've ever had. He recognized that I knew what I was doing and left me pretty much alone. He was always there for me when I needed him as a non-threatening authority figure a prospective buyer could instantly trust. He was a charmer and what we call a 'schmoozer'.

If clients needed tender loving care or reassurances that their business was appreciated and valued, or if they needed a sympathetic ear to tell their troubles to, he would be there for them. He was a tall, gentle man with a low soothing voice and had the uncanny ability to make anybody feel at ease in his presence.

Freddie is one of the best listeners I have ever met in my career. He loves to play dumb to keep people talking and open up to him. He will not correct or lecture them but will find a way to be agreeable and make them believe that he cares.

I use my listening skills to talk, expand and even be controversial to contribute to a conversation. Freddie sounds agreeable to people and he will ask questions to show his interest and then guide them to his way of thinking. We complemented each other rather well, even though his playing dumb routine drove me up the wall many times.

At that stage in my career, I didn't need any more sales training or motivational support. I only needed somebody to allow me do my thing and be creative. Fred was the man to do just that. He was not the greatest trainer or stickler for details and never pretended to be.

The one thing I needed was product knowledge. I spent hours alone in our demo room practising my presentations and reading up on the features and benefits of our and the competitors' product lines. The copiers Canon produced in the early eighties were state of the art and the Major Accounts Program Canon had designed was brilliant.

It would be pretentious of me to say that my unbelievable success was only based on my supreme selling skills. A great deal had to do with the ageing product line and the outdated sales approach of our biggest competitor Xerox. Canon and OE offered nationwide guarantees for performance, response time and reliability. The flexible purchase, rent and lease options often reduced the operating costs compared to the equipment they were using at that time. This was a combination nobody in our industry could match.

My first big deal involved replacing the whole copier fleet of Great West Life. This was followed by the Toronto Star who was a major advertiser for Xerox. Xerox had hinted to the Star that they might pull their advertising from the paper if they would replace their equipment with that of Canon.

I will never forget when the Director of Purchasing, Maurice Fairweather, told me the reply Beland Honderich, the Star's CEO at the time, gave to Xerox. He said, "Let Xerox know that if they feel that the Toronto Star is not the best vehicle for their advertising needs, they have every right to pull their account from us. We have decided that Canon is the best solution for our copying needs and will do what's best for the Toronto Star."

Maurice told me later that he was praying that the change over to our copiers would be without any problems. Beland Honderich had made it clear to him that the decision was his, but he better make sure he knew what he was doing. I was impressed by the Star and their principled stand not to be bullied by a large multinational corporation like Xerox.

Many other breakthroughs in large major companies followed. My sales quota for the entire year of 1984 was fulfilled by the end of May. I had become a Star at Canon/OE.

With my success came an increase in income. I had only dreamed of making that kind of money before.

The Management Years 1986-1990

After only three years I was offered the position of sales manager for the commercial team of Toronto West. Freddie thought I was making a mistake to accept and told me my potential was much better served in major accounts. I didn't take his advice.

My first year as a commercial sales manager was less than stellar, even though I achieved my assigned quota. I was the manager at the low end of the totem pole for performance.

There were many reasons for it. My selling style differed from what the commercial sales reps were doing. I had to rebuild a team that more or less reflected and responded to my sales philosophy.

In 1988 every salesman on my team overachieved and qualified for the annual incentive trip to Hawaii, something that had never been done before at OE. In 1989 I was named 'Sales Manager of the Year' and received a special plaque of recognition from Canon.

In May of the following year I was expecting a promotion to be the sales manager for a second major account team but instead was asked to accept a demotion back as a major account sales executive.

I was crushed. What had happened?

In 1988 Ted Tobias, a man I had hired and trained at Olivetti, and who later talked me into joining him at Pitney Bowes, was now the branch manager in Calgary and wanted to return to Toronto. He was approached by a headhunter for the position of General Sales Manager of OE Toronto. OE Inc had just been acquired by Canon Canada Inc and was now operating as a wholly owned subsidiary. I liked Ted from our days at Olivetti and Pitney Bowes and urged him to come and join us at OE.

By the end of 1989 Ted wanted to install his own management team. I didn't share his bravado style of leadership. I was not interested in gimmicks and a cheer-leading approach to managing my team. Linda Hellens, the very successful manager of the East Team also didn't conform to his ideal image of a manager in a male dominated industry. He had valid issues with the manager of the central team who later accepted a transfer to a Canon dealership in Calgary. Linda demanded and got her old job back as Canon's legal and accounting representative. It had become available due to the internal shuffling of territories.

I was ready to sue, my ego was hurt and in my eyes there was no reason to demote me. I deserved to be promoted, I felt, because I was still the 'Sales Manager of the Year'.

Ted called me into his office and said to me, "Konrad, I cannot fire you due to your track record and achievements, but let's face it, you don't want to be constantly looking over your shoulder trying to avoid giving me a reason.

"I admire your selling skills and your work ethic and would like to keep you as part of my Major Account team." Then he made me an offer that astounded me. I could create my own list of major accounts that had not been assigned to other sales reps or were not already Canon customers and develop them for six months without any pressure or quotas and he would pay me $10,000.00 per month for six months. We would reevaluate my accounts and agree on a quota on January 1st 1991. I accepted his offer and Freddie became my manager for a second time.

Ted was later transferred to Montreal where he became the director of Sales for Quebec. He had destroyed the creative, vibrant and fun filled company that was OE and turned it into another major corporation where structure and profit ruled every decision-making process. He eventually resigned when he was not offered a position as Vice-President of Sales that he felt he deserved.

The Turbulent Road to Retirement 1990-2001

I took it easy during the summer months enjoying great times with my daughter, playing a lot of golf and doing projects like renovating and gardening.

In September, it was time to take my job seriously and start building my third and final career at Canon.

The following years were enjoyable and I never failed to exceed my annual quotas and was one of the top performers every year. However, in 1995 events took place that almost ended my career and that of many of my colleagues in the National Account Division of Canon.

In 1994 Canon had hired a new Vice President for our division. His name was John Gartland and we hated each other's guts from the get-go.

He was ruthless, dictatorial and brutal in his dealings with employees on all levels, from the most impressionable young sales representative to the most senior manager.

There was no trust, no confidence and no fairness in his decisions and practices. Many senior reps had major run-ins with him and everything came to a head in early 1995.

Every year we had to sign new employment contracts outlining our sales quotas, commissions and bonuses for the following year. That did not happen at the end of 1994. John Gartland told us not to worry. We would have our new plan later in the year and to carry on under the old plan for the time being. When we received our first commission cheques at the end of February for the sales of January, we noticed that there were major changes that we had not been told about and it appeared that a new commission structure had already been implemented.

This had to be a mistake.

We asked John Gartland for a meeting where he presented our new contracts for the first time, retroactively effective to January 1st. We were shocked.

Terry Walsh, one of our senior reps, mentioned that this was illegal. To this, John Gartland replied, "Anybody who challenges my rulings by questioning their legality will be fired on the spot!"

Now we were not only shocked and speechless but very angry and ready to fight knowing full well that this threat was illegal as well.

All the Major and National account executives called a meeting after hours in a nearby pub and came to the conclusion that we needed to organize.

One of our colleagues, Philip Peacock, had a friend who was a labour lawyer at one of Canada's premier law firms, Fraser and Beatty. Phil agreed to call him and ask him to advise us on the possibility of forming a labour union or professional association to protect ourselves and our jobs. He agreed to a meeting the next morning. The initial meeting was free of charge and he offered to help us set up a professional association for a fee of $1,000.00.

Before we could proceed we had to first do our homework. Since labour law is a provincial jurisdiction only our colleagues from offices in Ontario could join the association.

We faxed a questionnaire to all sales people of the major account division and asked if they were in favour of forming the 'Association of Major Account Representatives of Canon Canada Inc.' or AMARC for short.

With their 'yes' vote they had to transfer a $100.00 initiation fee into a bank account that we had opened the same day.

All but two salespeople voted 'yes'. We had the mandate of 94% of our sales force.

We asked for nominations for the election of the executive and I, Terry Walsh and Phil Peacock were acclaimed President, Vice President and Treasurer respectively.

Phil called our lawyer and a meeting was set up for the next morning to finalize the paperwork to make AMARC our legal voice.

The process took less than 48 hours.

The documents were signed, sealed and notarized by 10:00 am. We returned to our office to ask for a meeting with Mr. Jimbo, Canon's Executive Vice President. The purpose of the meeting was to air our grievances and to inform him about AMARC and our intention to sue Canon Canada Inc and launch a complaint with the Ontario Labour Relations Board if our grievances were not addressed.

He was taken aback by our presentation and the existence of our association. He promised another meeting as soon as he had talked to John Gartland and researched our complaints.

The next morning everybody was surprised and pleased to read a memo by Mr. Jimbo announcing that John Gartland 'had resigned to pursue other opportunities'.

The smiles on our faces couldn't have been broader.

Canon's regional sales manager, Mr. Bruce Farrant, was given the responsibility to negotiate. He made it clear that Mr. Jimbo was willing to address our grievances and work on a solution with us. We had to make certain concessions as well.

Mr Jimbo did not want the news of a sales division forming a union-like organization to get back to Japan or his career would have been in jeopardy but he would do everything within reason to rectify the damage caused by his former V.P. of sales.

We could not agree to dissolve our association but promised to be inactive as long as we were treated fairly. We agreed to accept the new commission plan since the CEO and president of Canon Canada Inc had been told by Mr. Gartland that it had been accepted and challenging it legally would have embarrassed Mr. Jimbo and left him vulnerable.

He offered a generous one-time bonus to our sales force and we were told to distribute the funds as we saw fit. We deducted our legal cost, left some money in our bank account to keep the AMARC alive and distributed the balance equally amongst our members to cover some of the losses from their first quarter commission checks. We also issued a refund to everybody for their initiation fee. The two dissenters didn't see a penny of that money.

Mr. Jimbo and Mr. Bruce Farrant both gained a lot of respect from us for the way they handled the crisis and management respected us for the way we conducted ourselves.

In the following years, I set new sales records by breaking new ground. The first ever 'Fleet Asset Management Plan' making Canon the sole supplier of photo copiers, faxes, colour copiers and printers for RBC Dominion Securities was signed the end of 1996 and also secured the business of the Bank of Montreal by negotiating the same kind of agreement in 1998. In 1997 and 1999 I was honoured as 'Salesman of the Year'. I enjoyed an extremely good income and by 1999 my client list had shrunk to only three customers, the Royal Bank and its subsidiaries, the Bank of Montreal with its subsidiaries, including Nesbitt Burns and Harris Bank in the US and the Noranda Inc. group of companies.

When Canon offered me my contract for 2000 they tried to

bring my income in line with most other sales reps. They reduced my commissions, raised my quotas and tried to remove Noranda Inc and the banking arm of the Royal Bank from my account list, leaving me only with RBC Dominion Securities and the Bank of Montreal as clients.

This was unacceptable to me and I refused to sign my contract.

Canon was in a precarious situation. They could not afford to have me quit and join the competition. The contract with RBC had only 18 months to go and my strong personal relationship with the director of purchasing, Mr Art Bowen, and my high profile within RBC meant they could lose millions of dollars in revenue if I joined the competition. The Bank of Montreal had two years to go and that too made them vulnerable for an even greater loss of revenue.

My sales manager Dan Sharp asked me what I wanted and I told him that I could see myself working in my position until age 65 but if I didn't feel that I was seen as a valuable member of the sales team I wouldn't mind retiring early and seeking happiness in what was known as 'Freedom 55' or early retirement.

The truth is that I had become tired of the constant changes and computerization in our industry. There was no more creative selling to my clients. The contracts I had negotiated reduced me to an order taker, which only required the users to choose from a list of our products. There was no more competition and no excitement. I was a victim of my own success. Only the money kept me going.

Dan said he would arrange a meeting with the V.P. of human resources John Needham to discuss my employment contract or a retirement package. When I met John, we ended the meeting by agreeing to meet again in a week. Each of us was supposed to put together a list of things required to reach an agreement. I was to write down what I wanted in a retirement package and John would write down what Canon was willing to offer.

Our next meeting was rather short. I had put down a list with things Canon would surely find too expensive. When we sat down John asked me for my list and I said in a nonchalant way, "Why don't you go first and show me your list?" He agreed.

To my astonishment they offered more than I was asking for on my list.

Canon guaranteed my income for 2000 at the previous year's level and pay commissions and bonuses above that if I should exceed my previous year's achievement. Canon would continue paying me until June 2001 and continue paying my profit sharing, life and health insurance, vacation pay and other fringe benefits and bonuses as well as contributing the maximum amount to my Canon Pension Plan.

I would work in my job until June and on the first of July would be assigned two salespeople to take over my accounts. I would stay on in an advisory and public relations capacity for my clients, be paid commissions and bonuses from business generated by my successors and train them until the end of the year before retiring on December 31st 2000. I would stay on Canon's payroll until June 2001. I would also have to introduce my replacements to our offices across Canada and the regional offices of my clients in Montreal, Calgary and Vancouver.

When John asked to see my list, I simply said that his list was acceptable and that I was ready to sign.

Freedom 55 was now a reality!

My last three months were the most fun I've ever had in my working life. My two replacements, my manager Dan Sharp and I travelled across the country meeting clients and co-workers. Everybody either threw me a little retirement party or a luncheon. My sales team organized a retirement dinner at a lavish restaurant and Canon arranged a retirement dinner with various directors and Vice Presidents attending. I had no idea I was that popular or maybe everybody was just happy to see me go and wanted to make sure I was leaving.

The biggest party was arranged by our office manager Linda Lylyk at the Sheraton Hotel.

It was the official going-away party and many past and present Canon/OE co-workers were invited as well as my best clients. People I had not seen in years showed up. It was truly a humbling experience and an evening I will never forget. It was fitting that Fred Werner, who had hired me and retired a few years before me, made the last speech before I made my parting remarks almost overcome with emotions. We partied until the bar closed and the hotel asked us to leave.

I didn't want it to end.

When I walked out of Canon's front door for the last time late in the evening on December 29th 2000 it was anticlimactic. Nobody walked me out the door, nobody waved, nobody was there to hug me and say goodbye. I had signed off on my last billing sheet and left unnoticed with everybody working late to finish the year. I didn't want to disturb them. My time had passed.

I wasn't part of the Canon family anymore.

Chapter 39

The Penis Trilogy

Most men, when talking about their penises, will talk about their virility, conquests, performance, size and glory.

I believe that there are many more tales to tell about their failures, embarrassments and painful memories.

Here are three of those stories.

1 - The Unwanted Erection

In 1966, I was diagnosed with high blood-pressure and my doctor thought it was necessary to have me checked out at the local hospital. One of the tests was a cystoscopy which, in those days, meant a short stay in the hospital to recover from the procedure.

For those of you who don't know what a cystoscopy is, I will explain.

A cystoscope is a rigid instrument about 30 centimetres long and has the thickness of my little finger. This instrument is inserted into the opening of the penis and shoved through the urethra right up to the bladder.

This description should make you cringe because your assumption that this is painful is absolutely correct.

It is normal for patients to get a local anaesthetic to dull the pain. However, back in Germany I assume that half the doctors believed the pain was bearable and the others must have been trained by Dr Mengele or were disciples of the Marquis de Sade.

No anaesthetic was provided.

When told to disrobe, lie down on the examination table and cover myself with the sheet the good-looking nurse handed me, I did so without hesitation.

I had overlooked the slit strategically located in the centre of the sheet and possibly would not have exposed my genitals anyway even if I would have seen it. When the doctor, also a female, came into the examination room she noticed that I had not laid bare the part of my body that she was most interested in for purely medical reasons.

At the age of nineteen, it didn't take much to get an erection, especially not if a female reaches under a sheet to pull out your manhood and exhibits it to a gorgeous young nurse observing the action with great interest.

It must have taken less than a millisecond for my little soldier to rise to the occasion and stand at full attention.

The doctor looked at my now fully-erect penis. She nonchalantly grabbed it with her left hand, leaving the head exposed, and smacked it with her right hand like the bottom of a ketchup bottle, mumbling, "We can't have that here now, can we?"

I sat straight up emitting a short yelp of pain, knocking my head on the overhead light, and then fell back onto the table wanting to die of shame and embarrassment.

I don't know what hurt more, the physical pain of the smack to my little friend, the insertion of the cystoscope or the humiliation of the whole episode.

2 - No Toy for a Pussy

The party at the Lesch's was over and it was time to go home on a beautiful summer night.

My convertible was parked in their driveway with the roof down and I didn't bother to check the back seat before driving home.

It was only after we got home and when I was closing the roof that Jackie noticed the little kitten snuggled up on my jacket in the back seat. We decided to keep her for the night and call Merle in the morning to let her know that her little kitten had deserted her and we had granted her temporary asylum.

Jackie put a few pillows down for her to sleep but the kitty decided to cuddle up with us on our bed.

At this point, I should maybe mention that I sleep in the nude, especially on hot summer nights. I prefer fresh air caressing my naked body to closed windows and an air-conditioned bedroom.

I assume everybody is aware that men frequently have an involuntary early morning erection, also known as a 'Woody'.

That morning, the sun must have just come up, the cat woke up and found herself in a strange bed without any toys and was probably looking for something to play with.

It must have been precisely at that moment that she noticed something moving lower down on the bed, below my belly and seemingly sprouting out from between my legs.

I can just picture her slowly crawling towards this mysterious mushroom shaped growing object swaying back and forth with every deep, snoring breath I took.

She possibly even interpreted my snoring as growling at this thing and got ready to protect me from a dangerous and threatening situation.

Maybe, she thought it was an inflatable toy or even a scratching post put there for her amusement.

It doesn't matter what she thought, her instincts told her to pounce on it and try to scratch and bite it into submission.

And that is exactly what she did!

The pain was excruciating as I got jolted out of my deep sleep and tried to remove whatever had attacked and was mauling my penis.

Not expecting my violent reaction, the cat sunk her claws even deeper into my rapidly shrinking member but my earth-shattering scream convinced her to let go of my most sensitive body part. She jumped off the bed, partially assisted by my throwing motion, and ran for dear life trying to get away from me.

Jackie snapped out of her deep sleep, saw the cat flying through the room meowing and me holding onto my scrotum and screaming in pain.

After she had examined the damage, she started laughing uncontrollably and making jokes about me having been attacked by a scratching and biting pussy.

I did finally rediscover my sense of humour and told the story to Reggie and Merle upon returning their cat.

Jackie wouldn't have allowed me to keep this little episode a secret from her friends anyway.

Happily, there was no permanent damage to me or my penis but for some reason the cat never trusted me or came close to me ever again.

I wonder why?

3 - The Sperm Test

My penis and I, as well as Jackie, had a fun and exciting time in our many attempts to produce an offspring. However, it became increasingly obvious after many months that our efforts were not producing the wanted results.

Jackie's gynaecologist, wanting to eliminate the obvious reasons first, suggested I should have a sperm test performed at the local hospital. He handed me the requisition and told me that no appointment was necessary.

When I arrived at the reception at Peel Memorial Hospital,

there were a few people in the waiting area. I didn't want anybody to hear me, so I quietly whispered to the receptionist that I was referred by my doctor for some tests.

Bad choice of words.

She looked at the requisition and in a loud, boisterous voice announced for everybody to hear, "Your doctor is a gynaecologist?"

I felt everybody looking at me and before I could correct her, she said in an even louder voice, "I see, you are here for a sperm count."

I could now definitely feel the stares of the people in the waiting area andI also felt myself blushing as I was told to sit down and wait.

A few minutes later she called me to her desk, handed me a sample vial and an instruction sheet on how to proceed. I didn't think I needed instructions on how to clean my penis and then masturbate into a jar.

Her next move stunned me.

She called a young volunteer, a candy striper as they were called in those days, and told her to take me to a washroom and wait there until I was done to take the vial straight to the lab. Apparently, time is of the essence since sperm has a high mortality rate.

Unfortunately, I had not thought of bringing a Playboy or other gentleman's magazine with me to get me aroused and knowing that a teenage female volunteer, who knew what I was doing, was standing in front of the door was not exactly putting me into the right frame of mind to complete the task at hand.

Finally, after some vigorous manual labour, my little Willie started growing in the palm of my hand. Precisely at that moment, I heard footsteps coming my way and a voice saying to the volunteer, "Why are you standing around here, don't you have anything to do?"

"I'm supposed to wait for this guy to finish his sperm test and then take the jar right away to the lab for analysis," she replied. The snickering and snarky remark that followed caused my little friend to deflate and that meant I had to start all over again.

After an assertive effort, when I thought I was close, I heard these footsteps approaching once again.

The voice just said, "You mean to tell me that he's still at it?"

There wasn't another word said, just snickering and giggling as the footsteps were fading away in the distance.

My Willie had again opted for a full retreat and I was ready to concede defeat.

The thought of having to explain to a teenager why the jar was not filled motivated me to make one more final Herculean effort.

Just before my arm fell off and my hand cramped up I reached my goal of releasing millions of little tadpoles into the jar.

After checking in the mirror to see if I had popped a vein during this strenuous exercise, I wiped the perspiration off of my face, opened the door and handed the jar to the young lady, avoiding any eye contact. As I left the hospital, it still felt like everybody was staring at me.

Due to the time I took to complete the test, I'm sure there is a medical note somewhere in my file that states that premature ejaculation is not one of my problems.

Chapter 40

Camping, A Return To Nature

To begin the day by waking up to the smell of bacon drifting into your tent from the campsite next to yours is heaven. It feels so good to stretch your stiff limbs after a night wrapped in a sleeping bag lying on air mattress. Boiling water to enjoy a cup of Nescafe to get the cobwebs out of your head from drinking and smoking whatever was available the night before, is an absolute necessity.

Singing golden oldies while sitting around the campfire and slowly getting wasted was so much fun the previous evening. I take a deep breath of clean fresh air before lighting my first cigarette of the day on a crisp morning in the forest. That smoke will take care of that hacking cough and together with the Nescafe get rid of that fuzzy morning taste in my mouth.

Looking at that morning mist hovering over the lake as the sun slowly rises, I'm thinking, "Isn't nature beautiful?"

•••••

In the early seventies, Jackie and I camped almost every long weekend with the Lesch family and their friends. We had a lot of fun and will always cherish the memories. In the eighties, we camped mainly with the Vander Voet family and their kids but also by ourselves as a family.

Thinking back, it doesn't sound very relaxing to come home from work on a Friday night to pack your camping gear, boxes of food, beer and supplies into the trunk of the car and fight the long weekend traffic to get to the campground.

After a few hours on the road you had to unpack, put up the tent, blow up the air mattresses, get the kitchen tent set up and start making supper on the *hibachi* (a Japanese stove using charcoal) or heat up some stuff on the Coleman stove. While Jackie did the dishes, I went to get some firewood to start the campfire. All that was done before nightfall.

To sit under the starry sky at night roasting marshmallows by the roaring campfire and singing along to the boys plucking away on their guitars was divine. We enjoyed our beer or rye with ginger ale, smoked cigarettes and passed around a joint to be enjoyed by everyone. This was the time to mellow out and relax.

The days were full of fun, swimming in the lake, playing volleyball and badminton on the beach or just lying around reading or sunning ourselves. It didn't matter where we camped, Algonquin Park, Outlet Beach, Long Point or any other place, we enjoyed every minute of it.

There are even fond memories of the bad weather days. Is there anything more relaxing than falling asleep as the rain is making that soothing pitter patter sound on the roof of the tent?

And there was always the excitement of sudden thunderstorms blowing the tents away. The pouring rain soaked most of our possessions including clothes, sleeping bags and matches. Some foods, like bread and cookies, are seldom enjoyed in a wet state and salt and sugar are pretty useless after being drenched.

We shouldn't forget that Mother Nature is trying to teach us that other creatures also inhabit the campgrounds and that everybody has to learn to either coexist or be killed.

The killing is mostly restricted to the insect world, and there are lots of them. There are mosquitoes, flies, black-flies, deer flies, ants, beer bugs, wasps, bees, spiders and many kinds of creepy-crawlies that invade campsites and tent.

The world of mammals is also part of the camping experience

but we are much more willing to accommodate or invite their attention, depending on the species. It is rare that a moose trots through a campsite but if it does, it is not a good idea to try to annoy or approach it; just leave it alone and it will go away. If they feel threatened, they have a tendency to charge. It's best to admire these majestic creatures from a distance.

Skunks invaded our campsite almost daily on Lake Erie. It is fairly nerve-racking having to stay put and not move while a family of them waddles through the campsite searching for food. I guess they are aware of their awesome weapon and show no fear of humans. Unfortunately, many curious cats and aggressive dogs learn too late to avoid skunks.

Kids love the little chipmunks scurrying around and some chipmunks are tame or brave enough to come right up to humans and eat out of their hands.

Raccoons and bears are the ones who are most destructive and aggressive when searching for food.

Most campgrounds advise to put your food into coolers and store them in the car or in your tent. They also advise to burn your garbage or deposit it in the locked and bear-proof garbage cans supplied by the campground.

Two stories involving bears and raccoons are my favourite camping stories.

Sharky and the Bear

In Algonquin Park, it was not unusual to have bears come into the campground at dusk to search for food.

One of the rules was to put your cooler into your car and get rid of the garbage, since bears have a very good sense of smell. They will rummage through garbage to find edible things and will rip up tents if they smell food. If they are successful, they will be back again the next night and could get nasty if they don't find anything.

One evening, our things had been put away and everybody was

getting ready to settle down around the campfire for our nightly social get-together and sing-a-long when a whole family of bears came out of the woods to search the camp for their dinner.

This had happened before but normally they would go away after not finding anything and settle for their traditional meal of berries and leaves in the forest.

We watched them walking through various campsites sniffing around until they came to the site of Sharky Brown, who was sitting with us about 50 yards away.

As they emerged from behind his tent one of the bears was dragging a cooler down the road trying to get it into the forest.

"Shit, I forgot to put my cooler away," Sharky said as he jumped up. Running after the bear, he yelled, "Oh no, you don't! Stop!" but the bear didn't listen and kept on running.

He caught up with him in no time. It was interesting to find out that a man in running shoes can run faster than a bear dragging a cooler. What we didn't know was how a bear would react being chased by a human who is trying to take his family's dinner away.

Nobody knew what Sharky would do after catching up with the bear. As a matter of fact, we were rather stunned that he had the guts to chase a 300 pound bear to get his cooler back.

At first, everybody yelled for him not to be foolish and let the bear have the cooler but it was already too late.

Sharky had caught up with the bear and grabbed the other handle of the cooler and tried to pull it away from him. It was a sight to behold. Here they were, in the middle of the road, engaged in a tug of war with Sharky pulling on one handle on one side and the bear on the handle on the other side.

As comical as the situation was, nobody laughed. What would happen if the bear got tired of this game and attacked Sharky? We had to act.

I think it was Merle who yelled to grab some pots and pans and make a lot of noise and try to chase the bears away. Most of the other bears had stopped running away and were watching this spectacle from the edge of the forest.

Now an army of campers banging on pots and pans approached

the two main combatants in this epic battle over a Coleman cooler between the 300 lb Goliath and the barely 140 lb David. I don't think any of us knew what we would have done if the bears had turned around and started chasing us. Luckily, they recognised that they were outnumbered and fled into the woods.

Goliath must also have been intimidated by the mob of banging and screaming campers. He let go of the handle and scampered off into the safety of the forest.

When we reached Sharky, who was huffing and puffing from exhaustion, somebody asked him if he was crazy to run after a bear and fight him for a cooler, he just looked at him and said, "I won, didn't I?"

The Saga of an Escaped Murderer, a Sick Little Girl, a Bumble Bee, a Kidnapping and a Boy Scout Troop

It was supposed to be a relaxing long weekend on the shores of beautiful Lake Kipawa in northeastern Quebec. Our friend Wolfie had told us about this fantastic campsite/RV Park with a lovely little beach. It was also supposed to be a great spot for fishing. The Swedish owners Erik and Sonja were apparently the nicest, most accommodating people you could ask for.

It was the August long weekend in 1975 and Toni was just a few days away from her first birthday.

Nobody knew the adventure that was awaiting us.

We took off early on the Saturday morning for Lake Kipawa. Five minutes into the trip, Toni wanted her favourite stuffed animal, Freddie the Fox, that her Granny had brought with her from Germany. It would only delay us by 20 minutes to turn around and get him. Toni was inseparable from Freddie the Fox and spending a weekend without him was unthinkable.

It was supposed to be a leisurely five-hour drive to this little piece of paradise. The weather forecast predicted a hot few days. The day before Montreal had set a new temperature record, a fraction of a degree short of 100ºF and Toronto wasn't far below that.

On the outskirts of North Bay, we ran into a traffic jam. It turned out that the police had set up roadblocks and were searching for a convicted murderer who had just escaped from the North Bay Penitentiary. The fugitive was apparently armed and dangerous. His name was Donald Kelly. He was serving a life sentence that began in 1970 for robbery, kidnapping, forcible confinement and two murders.

The police searched every car. Everybody was questioned as to whether they were approached by anybody. Nobody was allowed to leave their cars because Kelly could have hidden anywhere.

We waited over an hour in the boiling heat, running the air conditioning frequently to cool ourselves off. Finally, the police allowed us to carry on but told us not to stop for anybody or anything for the next 50 kilometres.

We arrived at Camp Kipawa in the early afternoon, put up our tent on a large wooden platform with a veranda and were informed that the owners were hosting a fish-fry that night and everybody was welcome.

I rented a boat for the next two days and still went out that evening for a little spin on the lake. I took my fishing pole with me to catch a pickerel or two to contribute to our hosts' fish-fry.

I didn't catch a thing that evening.

After Toni was fed and Jackie put her to bed in her playpen, Jackie and I joined the campers around the fire and enjoyed some delicious fish that Erik was frying up over an open fire in a huge cast iron pan.

Our tent was in full view from the gathering and we kept an eye on it checking on Toni every few minutes. She was fast asleep clutching Freddie in her arms, exhausted after an eventful day.

The next morning I got up early to do some fishing before Jackie and Toni got up.

I didn't catch anything that morning.

However, when I got back, Jackie told me that Toni had thrown up her breakfast and had a bit of a temperature. She must have caught a bug when we were standing at the police blockade with the air conditioning blowing at us and then getting very hot when the engine was switched off to let it cool down. For the rest of the day, it was decided to stay put and take it easy. Toni was very lethargic and slept most of the afternoon. I went fishing for a little while in the early evening and Jackie volunteered to stay with Toni at the campsite.

It was disappointing to return empty-handed, not having caught anything that evening either.

Jackie told me that she was getting worried about Toni. Sonja had loaned her a thermometer and Toni's temperature was over 104 F (39 C). We decided to take her to the small country hospital in Tamiscaming, just 18 kilometres away.

There was only a nurse on duty who did her best to bring Toni's fever down giving her cold baths and told us to come back in the morning if she didn't improve.

We were about to leave when the doctor walked in. He had one look at Toni and said that she was not going anywhere, especially not to a campground. He then admitted her.

There was one room for small children. Jackie put Toni into a crib and tried to calm her down because she screamed her little heart out whenever we attempted to leave. The doctor told us she would calm down if she didn't see us anymore. It was now getting late and the other children in the room were not getting any sleep.

Her crying could still be heard from the open window of her room as we walked back to the car in the still sweltering heat of the night. There was no air-conditioning in the hospital.

We were worried and wondered what else could have been done to prevent her from getting sick. The usual second thoughts entered our minds. Neither Jackie nor I slept very well that night wondering if it was a good idea to take a one-year old camping.

We got up early and were back in the hospital on Monday morning to see if she was getting better.

She squealed with delight when she saw her Mom and Dad walk into her room . She clung to us during our entire visit. The nurse said that she wasn't eating anything except fruit and was only drinking juice. Jackie told her that Toni was a picky eater at the best of times but she loved yoghurt. I went to the convenience store and bought her favourite flavours. She ate every bit of it while we sat with her.

The nurse also told us that Toni was very weak, still had a fever and might have to stay another few days. She again screamed the house down when it was time to leave and in the process broke our hearts and almost made us cry along with her. On our second visit to the hospital in the early evening she seemed a lot better but performed her crying and screaming routine again to break our hearts when it was time to leave.

The nurse asked us to visit our daughter only once the next day since she exhausted herself with her crying and needed all her strength to overcome this nasty virus. Apparently she was happy when we weren't around.

That evening, Jackie joined me for an hour on the lake watching the sunset while I was fishing, but again, I didn't catch a thing.

On Tuesday, Toni was playing and 'baby-talking' with the other little kids as we walked into the room. She ate her lunch and was a happy child playing with us until the early afternoon.

After saying our good-byes, she put on another performance of heart wrenching tears and cries for her Mommy and Daddy.

We stopped by at the doctor's office and asked him when she would be well enough to be discharged. "If she continues to improve I will discharge her tomorrow," he said.

He looked at us as he said, "You will have to promise me to stay at least until Friday before returning to Toronto. Right now, she is not well enough to travel."

He said he would examine her in the morning and would most likely discharge her. That was good news. Toni had stopped screaming as we walked by her open window on our way to the parking lot.

Back at the campground, Jackie said she would spend the rest of the afternoon reading her book and then prepare supper. I went fishing. When I returned I was pissed off because I again didn't catch one lousy fish.

The next day the doctor had already done his rounds when we

arrived. Toni was well enough to be discharged. He told us to come back if she got worse and reiterated that she needed a couple of days' rest at the camp to regain some of her strength. Five or six hours in an air-conditioned car would not be the best for her. I promised not to drive home before Saturday morning.

That afternoon, Toni was a happy little girl. After her dinner, Jackie took off her diaper and went to fetch her pyjamas out of the tent. Toni was standing in her playpen, without a diaper on, when she spotted a bee landing on Freddie. She bent down and grabbed the bee and started screaming immediately. The bee had stung her hand. She stood there in shock, peeing over herself and her beloved stuffed animal.

Erik and Sonja heard her scream and gave us some ointment to keep the swelling down. We were distressed, poor Toni hadn't been out of the hospital for more than a few hours and now this happened. It took a while for her to calm down and for the pain to subside. The biggest problem for her was that she couldn't even hug Freddie for comfort since he was soaked in her pee.

Jackie tried to wash him as well as she could and hung him on our clothesline to dry overnight. We felt sorry for her and stayed with her, singing songs and telling bedtime stories until she faded away into the land of dreams. Hopefully, she had more pleasant adventures in her dreams than the ones she experienced on this trip to Kipawa.

To relax, I went out on the lake to do some fishing before nightfall. I caught nothing. By now, I was convinced even the fish were conspiring against us.

When Toni woke up in the morning, she asked right away for Freddie. I knew she had a rough time so far and got out of my sleeping bag to get Freddie who had to be dry by now.

When I stepped out of the tent and looked at the clothesline my heart stood still.

Freddie was gone!

In a panic, I started looking around. Maybe a gust of wind had dislodged him from the line. No sign of Freddie anywhere.

I ran over to Erik's and Sonja's cabin and asked them if they had seen Freddie, maybe a kid from the campground had taken him. They shook their heads. Freddie was gone.

What were we going to tell Toni? I couldn't just go and get another Freddie, they were only available in Germany. He was irreplaceable. Eric told me that it was possible that he was kidnapped by a raccoon that was attracted to the stuffed animal and the smell of the urine. That made sense.

He mentioned that he had a Boy Scout troop of over thirty kids checking in that afternoon and would organize them to comb the woods to search for Freddie.

I told him that wasn't necessary but he insisted. Everybody in the camp felt sorry for poor little Toni by now and tried to help.

I asked Erik if I could use his phone and make a collect call to Germany to my mother. When she heard the sad stories, she offered right away to send another Freddie by courier. Knowing my mother, she would rush out right away to buy a new Freddie and get him to her heartbroken granddaughter in Canada. It didn't matter what it cost.

Jackie told Toni that Freddie had most likely gone home to Brampton by himself and was waiting for her to come on Saturday. We also promised to look for him in the woods just in case he got lost on the way home. She was happy with that explanation and didn't ask to many questions about him afterwards.

By four o'clock in the afternoon Erik and the boy scouts were ready to comb the woods. Most of the other campers had volunteered as well and there were well over fifty of us ready to search the forest inch by inch.

This resembled almost a professional police action. Erik gave his final instructions to look up every tree, under every bush and behind every rock. Then he spaced us about five yards apart to form a line about 300 yards wide and starting from the shore the search party walked through the campsite into the bush. All this work for a stuffed animal.

I don't know how far we walked, but after half an hour everybody was told to turn around and look even more closely on the way back. No trace of Freddie. I don't know who was more disappointed, Erik or I. He talked about a second search in the morning but enough was enough. Freddie was gone. Toni was relieved when we told her that Freddie did not get lost in the woods and is most likely home already. Who knows how much a one year old would understand but she was content with our explanations.

I just had a drink that night sitting around the campfire. Why bother going fishing, chances were I wouldn't catch anything anyway?

The Friday was uneventful. Toni seemed fully recovered and we got ready to leave early Saturday morning. I gave it one more try to catch at least one fish for Friday night's supper but had to accept defeat. I am most likely the only person ever to go fishing on Lake Kipawa for a whole week and never catch a single fish. Nobody at the campsite had an explanation, they caught lots of fish and used the same kind of bait as I did. I guess it just wasn't one of our better vacations.

When we got home on Saturday afternoon, there was a note in our mailbox from a courier service. Hallelujah! Granny's parcel with Freddie had already arrived. I rushed to their office at the airport to get it.

When I walked back into the house and put Freddie into Toni's arms she had the biggest smile we've ever seen on her face. Happiness was a new Freddie.

My mother never told us how much the courier service charged to get Freddie to Canada in less than 48 hours. I guess we didn't want to know.

To her, the happiness of her only grandchild was priceless.

Donald Kelly, the murdering outlaw who escaped from the North Bay Jail and eluded police for several weeks in 1975, was eventually recaptured and died behind bars in 2009 at the age of 71. Contrary to some rumours, the police never suspected Kelly to be involved in Freddie's kidnapping and he did not die holding him in his arms as he drew his last breath.

Chapter 41

The Blue Monster

I didn't talk much to Harold who lived on the other side of the street. It took me a while to notice the blue school bus parked at the end of his driveway, not visible from our house on Barkwood Court.

Once I became aware of it I wondered why it never moved. It was permanently parked in his driveway. It was my neighbour John who told me what Harold was doing.

He had bought this 21-seater bus from the Seahorse Hotel. They had used it as a courtesy bus for clients and to drive their employees home after they finished the late shift.

Harold was in the process of converting it into a motor home.

He worked hard for a whole year and I watched him tear out the seats, install appliances, build beds and cabinets, as well as putting in a washroom with a chemical toilet.

It was towards the end of summer of 1975 when Harold told me his wife had changed her mind about owning a motor home and wanted a cottage instead.

I had always admired his workmanship and expertise and had expressed some interest in buying a trailer or motor home in the future. Harold offered to sell me his bus because he needed the money as a down payment on the cottage. He wanted $5,500.00 and showed me the receipts from the purchase of the vehicle and the add-ons. They came to almost $5,000.00 and he figured his labour was worth at least another $500.00.

We had been camping for years and enjoyed it. However, the hassle of packing and unpacking was getting to us and we had already talked about buying a camping trailer to add some comfort and luxury to our outdoor adventures.

After talking it over with Jackie and checking our ability to afford this luxury, we decided to make him an offer. Harold was unimpressed when I offered him $4,000.00. He countered with $5000.00 and told me this was as low as he would go. I refused.

It was a few days before he had to come up with the money for the closing costs that he knocked on our door and asked if we were still interested in buying the bus.

He had been unable to sell it for what he wanted and was unable to raise enough money to close the deal on the cottage. We hesitated; the summer was almost over. It was the end of August and there were only a few weekends left to enjoy it. On the other hand we would likely never get an opportunity like this again.

The bus was ours for $4,000.00. We named our bus *'The Blue Monster'* and for the next three years we enjoyed every minute of it.

Although summer was waning during our first trip in 1975, we still experienced enough hot days to suffer in the bus. The following year, I had a room air conditioner installed after removing the rear window. It was a normal 110 volt unit and we could only use it when camping on a serviced site.

The refrigerator functioned with either twelve or 110 volt, but also with propane. The stove and the heating system operated on propane. The first year we used the *Blue Monster* until late fall. When we used the heater on chilly nights and cooked a meal, the gas would run out quickly and more than once I found myself changing the 10 pound propane tank in the middle of a freezing night.

In the spring of the following year, I had a 100-lb propane tank installed underneath the chassis so that one fill-up would last us for most of the season. This decision, as you will read later, had grave consequences but served us well for the next two years.

We had great experiences with the *Blue Monster*. We went to the Montreal Olympics, travelled to Nova Scotia, experienced Quebec and Northern Ontario and camped in many Provincial Parks. But one trip stands out.

Shake, Rattle and Roll That Tire Down The Road!

On the May long weekend we took our first trip of 1976. My mechanic checked out the whole bus to get it ready for a long and adventurous season.

The day before we left, I picked up *The Blue Monster* from the garage to put back the things we had removed for the winter. We packed our clothes, food supplies and Toni's toys for our trip to Lake Nipissing in Northern Ontario.

We left on Friday afternoon and I noticed a slight vibration in the rear end. As soon as we hit the highway and picked up speed it disappeared.

However, as soon as we started crawling in the heavy weekend traffic it started again to vibrate a bit. When we got to Barrie, I stopped to investigate. Everything looked just fine. After Barrie, the traffic lightened and I could keep the speed constant at 100 km/hr. The shaking went away as long as I kept the bus above 80km/hr.

In South River, 300 km into our journey, we stopped for fuel and noticed that the vibrations were now more like a slight shaking as I slowed down.

The attendant at the gas station took a look but couldn't see anything wrong. He suggested a wheel balancing or wheel alignment once we got to North Bay.

I knew it wasn't an unbalanced tire, they shake at high speeds and are not noticeable at low speeds. It baffled me.

We arrived at our campground at the mouth of the Little Sturgeon River with the bus still shaking as we pulled in. Fellow camp-

The Blue Monster - Three years of adventure...

ers suggested everything from a tire bubble to a bent axle when I told them about my problem, but nothing made sense.

We had a great weekend boating, swimming, catching a few fish and watching Toni having fun with the owner's dogs.

I had almost forgotten about the vibrations until we pulled out of the campground on Monday afternoon to start on our journey home. It seemed to have gotten worse and when we hit the open road after going through North Bay the vibrations didn't stop even at higher speeds.

We prayed that we would make it home but our prayers went unanswered. We had just passed South Bay and were going down a small hill when the bus suddenly started to violently shake and rattle. As I pushed on the brake-pedal, fearing to lose control of *The Blue Monster*, I saw one of my left rear tires was passing me and roll down the hill.

I managed to come to a stop and my heart must have also stopped for a moment.

Jackie was scared and screamed in panic. Toni didn't sense the danger and must have thought it fun to be shaken up. After we had calmed down I got out of the bus to find out what had happened.

It became clear that the mechanic, when servicing the bus, had not tightened the nuts on the twin tires on the left rear. Slowly, the rims cut through the bolts until they were completely sheared off and one of the tires flew off. The second tire was hanging on the axle extension and would have come off after the next few revolutions.

We were in the middle of nowhere.

After retrieving my tire from the bottom of the hill, I hitchhiked to South River to get some help. The gas station attendant told me that there was only one man working on this holiday Monday, an independent mechanic and tow truck operator in Sundridge about 10km away. He apparently listened to his CB radio 24 hours a day to help stranded motorists like me. His name was Ivan and he was a Russian loner living in the woods close to the road.

I was a sitting duck for a con artist and it sure sounded like I was going to be ripped off. My concerns couldn't have been more unfounded.

The gas station attendant called Ivan on his CB radio and he said he'd be there in half-an-hour. A motorist, who was filling his tank, offered me a ride back to the bus and I arrived just as Ivan pulled up with his tow truck.

I was surprised as he jumped out of the cab of his truck. I had imagined a big, tough, bearded man with a heavy Russian accent, looking like Rasputin.

He looked nothing like it. Ivan was clean shaven, very short, skinny but did have that heavy Russian accent I suspected. He had a friendly personality and a charming smile and enquired first if everybody was okay. I liked him right away.

I looked at his truck and expressed my doubts that this rather small truck could tow my heavy bus.

Ivan assured me there was no problem as he put the rear end of the bus on the hook and secured it with chains and a rubber holster. He told me that my family had to stay in the bus since there was only room for one passenger in the truck. I didn't feel good about that and asked if that was safe.

Again a reassuring, "There is no problem, everything good, don't worry" reply in his thick Russian accent, accompanied by a broad smile.

Then came the trip from hell!

I made sure Jackie and Toni were in a safe seat in the bus and told them not to get up for any reason. There were no seat-belts in the bus.

I got into the tow truck with Ivan and was absolutely horrified when he got going. The moment he accelerated his front wheels came up. *The Blue Monster* was too heavy.

This did not deter Ivan. With his front wheels up in the air he kept on going. "Are you crazy?" I screamed, "You can't steer, your wheels aren't touching the road."

"No problem," he replied, grinning from ear to ear. "If I need steering me push brake and wheels come down, you see?" To prove his point he stepped on the brake and naturally the front end came down and he adjusted his course down the road.

"Have towed many big trucks before, will be okay, no worry."

He sounded reassuring but I was still in a panic. Jackie and Toni had no idea what was going on up front. Jackie would have been hysterical if she knew.

The traction was fine going downhill and the front wheels kept contact with the road but uphill was a challenge, short spurts of braking and gentle acceleration left Ivan with very little steering control.

Just as I had somewhat calmed down there was a huge thud and a sudden jerk almost throwing me forward in my seat.

"What was that?" I shrieked.

"No worry," Ivan replied in a calm voice, "Rubber holster broke but bus still safe, chains and hooks won't break, we alright."

He didn't even stop to check if everything was safe.

I knew I was in the hands of a suicidal madman.

"We okay," he said as if he was reading my mind, "Will not do dangerous things, have done this lots before." He smiled again and finished by saying, "Almost home, just a few more minutes, no worry."

It was already dark when we arrived at Ivan's place.

He lived in a house trailer that was standing next to a large shed that he used as his garage and workshop.

He asked us if we would be alright to sleep in the bus because his own trailer would be too small to accommodate us. We told him we would be okay for the night.

Ivan said he would call the local dealerships in the morning to get a rim and new bolts and hoped to have us on the road by the afternoon.

He also mentioned that he would be up early in the morning to feed the animals and asked if we would like to watch. He said he was friendly with all the animals in the forest and talked to them, called them by name and that Toni could pet them since they trusted him and his visitors.

Even though I thought he was a bit nuts, I told him we'd love to see it.

The number of animals that showed up that morning was astounding. Chipmunks, deer and hares came out of the forest to be fed and Ivan had something for all of them.

It was like a scene out of Dr. Doolittle as he talked to them and they did seem to respond appropriately. In a calm voice, he introduced us to them and we did end up feeding them. Toni was thrilled to feed the little chipmunks and Jackie and I couldn't believe that the deer were eating out of our hands.

What a unique experience!

We got more and more endeared with Ivan, what a likeable and caring character. He told us that he spent a lot of money on the animals, especially on hay feeding them in the winter.

After breakfast, he started calling around for the parts to fix our bus but it soon became apparent that they had to be ordered from Toronto. It would take three to four days to get them to Sundridge and Ivan said he could have the repairs done by the weekend.

Jackie and I had to get back to work and decided to take the train from Sundridge to Toronto's Union Station later in the afternoon.

This was going to be another adventure.

Ivan dropped us off at the station in Sundridge. It was deserted, no stationmaster, no ticket seller, not a living soul in sight.

"Where do we buy tickets?" I asked Ivan.

"You buy tickets on train," he said and continued to tell us what to do to get on the train.

He explained that this was an unmanned station and the train would only stop if there were passengers either getting on or off. He pointed to a red flag at the end of the platform and told me that when I saw the train coming, I should grab it, stand on the middle of the track and wave it and the train would stop to let us on.

Jackie and I looked at each other thinking that this would be the way things were done in the Wild West and not in Canada in the 1970s.

Welcome to rural life in Canada.

My heart was racing as I heard the train whistle and then spotted it in the distance. As instructed, I grabbed the flag and jumped on the track waving it vigorously.

I heard the squealing brakes and saw it slowing down as it approached the station. I quickly jumped back onto the platform, put the flag back into the holster and walked back to my family to board the train after the conductor opened the door to let us board.

There was no first class, no dining car, no upholstered seats and no sleeper cars even though this so called milk run took a full day to journey from Cochrane to Toronto. There were only wooden benches to sit on and the only things available were some packaged snacks, candies and cans of soda you could purchase from the conductor that he sold out of a small cubbyhole in one of the cars.

Toni didn't fall asleep even though we didn't get to Toronto until 11 o'clock that night after a seven hour snail-paced journey. Jackie's attempts to sing her to sleep only encouraged her to sing along at full volume. Fellow passengers were amused at her repertoire of songs and started applauding her.

Noticing that she had an audience she certainly wasn't going to sleep but instead started walking up and down the compartment singing her heart out and entertaining everybody on board.

The following Thursday I phoned Ivan and he told me the parts had arrived and I could pick the bus up whenever I wanted.

I told him I would be there on Saturday.

Eric Fikri, a colleague of mine, volunteered to drive me to Sundridge on Saturday morning and drive back by himself.

Ivan had told me on the phone how much the parts were but hesitated to tell me how much he would charge me for labour.

I thought, 'Here we go, I am getting taken to the cleaners.'

He then handed me the bills from the supplier and asked me if $50.00 for towing and his labour was too much to ask.

"$50.00," I asked in amazement, "That's all?"

"I just put tires on rim, put tires on bus and tow was only 10km, nothing else," he said and then added, "If fifty dollars too much, how much you think is fair?"

I gave him $75.00 thinking that at that price I was the one ripping him off.

Ivan didn't want to take the extra money at first, telling me he didn't need much money living up north and since I was young and had a family, I probably needed money more than he did. He only accepted my $75.00 after I told him to use it to feed the animals and look after them.

We drove through Sundridge a few years later and the trailer and the shed were gone.

The local gas station attendant told us Ivan had died the year before. I wondered if the animals survived the following winter without him as I wiped a tear from my eye.

The Death of the Blue Monster

It was in October of 1977 that my insurance agent Doug Williams called and told me he wanted to talk about my bus. It was covered by a rider on my regular car insurance policy since I used it only occasionally a few weeks a year. The insurance company wanted to discontinue the rider at expiry and issue a separate policy for the bus at a considerably higher premium.

I told him I was planning on selling it and had already put an advertisement in the weekend's Toronto Star asking $4,500.00 or best offer and was prepared to let it go for as low as $4.000.00.

Doug told me that it would be no problem as long as it was gone before my present policy expired in June. I mentioned that we were thinking of buying a trailer and asked if that would qualify for a rider. That, he said, would be no problem.

A few days later John Polan, my neighbour across the street, asked me if he could borrow *The Blue Monster* for a two-week vacation to Disney World in late November. In return, he would paint and decorate our house. John, a painter and decorator running a small company, was a trustworthy and reliable neighbour and I accepted his offer.

John, his wife and two young daughters left on a Thursday in November. His oldest son Rick stayed behind in order not to get behind in his studies in college.

The following Sunday morning the doorbell rang. It was Rick telling me that his father called and he wanted to talk to me at noon. He wanted to make sure I'd be home.

I assured Rick I'd be home and asked if he had any idea what it was all about?

"Well," he said rather hesitantly, "my dad said your bus blew up."

"What?" I replied rather confused, "You mean the engine blew up."

"No, no, the whole bus blew up," he said. "That's all I know, my father will tell you the whole story at noon." With that, he turned around and walked away.

I was stunned. Jackie heard the whole conversation and we both speculated as to what could have happened? Was everybody okay? We waited eagerly for John's call.

As the National Research Council Time Signal on CBC radio beeped to let us know it was noon, the phone rang.

It was John.

He didn't know how to start telling me what happened but finally told us the story with Jackie listening in on an extension phone. They had just arrived at the campground at Disney World on Saturday night, settled in and finished their supper when they heard a hissing sound. First they thought it was a snake but upon inspecting the cause of the sound behind the stove John noticed that there was a gas leak at the mainline where it splits and leads to the furnace, the refrigerator and the stove.

He told his family to grab what they could and leave the bus immediately. John then turned every electric and gas appliance off and left the bus to get to a telephone booth about 60 yards away to call the fire department.

He was still talking to the dispatcher as the bus exploded in a big fireball and burned out. When the fire trucks arrived there was not much left to be rescued. The windshield landed fully intact forty yards down the road.

How could *The Blue Monster* explode with all electrical devices turned off and no open flame around?

The answer is simple. The bus was equipped with a Colour TV and even though John had switched it off there was a little glow wire constantly on as long as it was plugged in. When the propane level reached that wire the bus exploded and burned out.

Luckily, nobody was injured but their clothes and personal belongings were gone, including their passports. John did grab his wallet before leaving the bus and his wife Eva had travellers' cheques in her purse. The fire marshal helped by arranging accommodation at a nearby motel and supplied the basic necessities to get them through the night.

There was some good news for me. The preliminary report of the insurance adjuster stated that my bus was valued between six and eight thousand US Dollars.

John told me they would stay and visit Disney World anyway, especially since the Disney people were kind enough to give them free entrance passes to the park for the next four days and a few other perks to help them get over the traumatic experience.

He then gave me the relevant information to contact my insurance company.

I called them on Monday morning and I was told they had received a call from their office in Orlando and would get in touch with me as soon as they had all the documents, which they expected within a day or two. I called them back on Friday to enquire if they received everything and find out when I could expect a settlement. The adjuster told me that they were still trying to establish the value of the bus and they expect to be ready to settle within a few days.

I told them that I knew about the appraisal of the bus which had come in at $7,000.00 US and I would accept a check for $7,700.00 CDN since the exchange rate at the time was $1US = $1.1 CDN.

He told me he'd make a note of it and they'd call me the following week. The insurance adjuster called me at the office on Tuesday morning and asked me to come to his office to settle my claim and sign a few papers. When I asked him if that afternoon was okay, he said any time before 4:00 pm would be fine.

When I arrived, the receptionist took me to a big boardroom where three people were seated with notepads in front of them. One of them also had a file folder. We introduced each other and the man with the folder turned out to be the adjuster, the woman was a secretary and the third person was from their accounting department.

The adjuster opened the conversation very bluntly,

"Mr. Brinck, I have these forms for you to sign stating that you have no further claims against our company after cashing this settlement cheque for $4,280.00."

"What?" I said in disbelief, "$4280.00? What happened to the appraisal of $7,000.00 US from your adjuster in Orlando?"

"Mr. Brinck," the adjuster replied calmly as he pushed a small piece of paper towards me, "Is this your ad in the Toronto Star asking for $4,500.00 to sell the bus?"

"Yes it is," I stuttered, "but it was appraised much higher by your own people in the US."

He just dismissed my reply by gently shaking his head and waving his hand and said, "And didn't you tell your agent Mr. Williams that you were willing to let it go for as little as $4,000.00?"

"But, but, but..." I stammered as this calm and collected penny pincher and destroyer of dreams of riches continued by saying,

"I am sorry Mr. Brinck, you set the value of your vehicle yourself and we are paying you every penny of your evaluation plus the applicable amount of sales tax for a total of $4,280.00."

He made it sound like I should be thankful that they had lived up to my expectations.

I was speechless and getting extremely upset knowing that there was probably nothing I could do. Just as he was pushing the cheque and the papers towards me to finalize my claim I said, "What about the things that I wouldn't have sold with the bus? The linens, my stereo, the air conditioner, the TV, the pots and pans, blankets and the other things I would have taken out?"

He sat back down again and explained that anything attached as a permanent fixture, like the stereo and the air conditioner are part of the bus and included in this settlement. However, other things like audio tapes, the TV, linens, blankets and household items could be claimed from my home insurance and, since their company also handled that policy, I should submit a list of these items and he would personally pass it on to an adjuster from that department.

Jackie and I had no idea how valuable the contents of *The Blue Monster* were. We worked hard on that list not forgetting even the extra rolls of toilet paper and the Bic pen in the glove compartment.

We were mad and we wanted revenge. We got it!

The home insurance combined with the cheque from the bus was over $6,000.00. That was a lot more than selling it through the newspaper would have gotten me, nobody ever answered that advertisement anyway.

Doug Williams deservedly lost me as a client after snitching on me about my conversation with him. We even saved a few dollars by switching insurance companies.

So thanks to *The Blue Monster*'s untimely demise, we ended up a happy family with some unexpected, but very welcome, extra dollars in the bank.

Chapter 42

The In-Laws Are Coming! The In-Laws Are Coming!

January 6, 1972.

I am standing with Jackie at the arrival gate of Toronto International Airport. We are both excited to welcome her parents. I am a bit more nervous than Jackie.

What will they be like? Will they accept me as their son-in-law? Will they like me? Will I like them? Jackie had told me a lot about her parents, their past, their beliefs and values and their struggle living in South Africa under the apartheid regime.

Will they be able to adapt to Canadian life? After all, they were coming with an open return ticket and wanted to stay with us for at least six months.

All my worries were for naught.

When the gate opened and we greeted them, there was an instant connection between us. I had no problem in calling them Mom and Dad from the first moment we met.

Even though Jackie's mom Ivy seemed a bit shy, I felt a warm and loving feeling towards me.

Jackie's dad Walter took to me right away and called me 'Kon' from the first time we spoke. He had a broad smile on his face when he greeted me and I knew I didn't just get a father-in-law but a friend, drinking buddy and somebody with whom I would have a lot of fun.

He was not very outgoing or gregarious. However, there was a bit of mischievousness about him and an admiration for decisiveness and spunk. He was not the greatest leader but a great guy to depend on and he would be there for you when you needed him.

My In-Laws, Walter and Ivy

Ivy was a bit more reserved, conservative and religious, but definitely more decisive than Walter. Only later did I understand that she was the person in charge in their relationship. I would say that Walter was a lot more dependant on Ivy than the other way around.

We had moved into a two bed-room apartment to accommodate Jackie's parents.

Since I had never been to South Africa, I had no idea if there would be an adjustment to Canadian life and to a lifestyle with no obvious racism in a relatively classless society. The biggest adjustment was definitely the weather. Even though they had experienced snow before, the bitter cold temperatures in the middle of winter were a big challenge.

I will never forget our first trip with them to Niagara Falls in February. The falls were partially frozen and the steady mist coming off of them had coated everything with a thick layer of ice. It was a most impressive, surreal sight of a white, wintery wonderland. The cold and damp air made it almost unbearable for them to enjoy it but we persuaded them to return after dinner and experience the lights that illuminated the falls at night. The reflections, the glare and the glitter of the icicles made for a beautiful and unforgettable spectacle.

They were most fascinated by television, which had not yet been introduced in South Africa.

Since we had to work during their stay with us, TV became their prime source of entertainment. It was also a tool to adjust and get acquainted with racism and prejudice in North American society during that time. Shows like *All in the Family*, *Sanford and Son*, *The Flip Wilson Show* and many crime shows introduced them to a world they had never experienced back home and left a deep impression on them.

During their first few days with us, I remember vividly the two of them watching *The Newlywed Game* one afternoon, a popular game show in the 70's, and the contestants were three white couples and one black couple.

At the end of the show, the black couple had won. The host showed the prizes they would receive and they were celebrating their win by embracing each other while the other three couples looked very disappointed but applauded them none the less.

That is when Walter turned to Ivy and said in disbelief, "Do you mean to tell me the black couple gets everything and the whites get nothing?"

Ivy didn't take her eyes off the TV and said, "I guess so, that's what the man said."

Walter just shook his head and said, "Things are sure different over here." Jackie's parents had suffered greatly under apartheid, both financially and emotionally. All the years of classifying people by race and being told where they could live to where they could work and even who they can love and marry based on the colour of their skin, had taken its toll.

Walter, a stone mason by trade, had built a beautiful house. He built it in his spare time and his wife helped whenever she could while looking after two young daughters.

Their neighbourhood in Kimberley, where Jackie grew up, was one of the better ones in town. When the government decided to declare the area they were living in as a 'white' area they had to move and start all over again. They were not even allowed to sell their house at fair market value but were told what the selling price was going to be. If they were to be offered any more by a white couple, they would only be entitled to 50% of anything over the preset price. They were forced to move to the outskirts of town and lived there until Walter was let go from his job before his 63rd birthday.

Walter had worked for 24 years for the City of Kimberley as a maintenance worker and was laid off four weeks before he qualified for a pension at the age of 64. His wife had always looked after the family and worked out of her home as a seamstress and in later years as a factory worker after the children had grown up.

With Walter out of a job and hardly any prospects of finding new employment at his age and no other income, they decided to sell their house in 1971 and come for an extended visit to Canada. They planned on moving in temporarily with their oldest daughter in Petermaritzburg upon their return and applying for a council house.

They had worked hard their whole life, brought up two beautiful children and supported Jackie emotionally and financially to fulfil her dream to go to university. They assisted their older daughter Ally and her husband financially when times were tough, while bringing up four children.

With that kind of a past, I found it amazing how quickly they adapted and felt right at home and enjoying the life we were living in Canada. I don't know whose idea it was, most likely mine, for Walter and me to go to a strip club. We went to 'Starvin' Marvin's Burlesque Show', a popular strip club on Yonge Street. I made sure we sat in the front row, so Walter could enjoy the show.

I'm not sure if Walter had ever seen his wife in the nude. With their very puritanical and Victorian attitudes towards sex, they most likely disrobed in the dark every night.

So here he was at the age of 64, having a whole slew of beautiful women of all races taking their clothes off right in front of him and parading all their naughty bits in front of his face.

I spent most of my time watching Walter. He did not move. He was glued to his chair, perspiration running down his face. His hands were visibly shaking as he wiped the sweat off his forehead. His mouth was open and I could almost see him drool but then he swallowed hard as each dancer came to the end of her performance. After the first performer, I asked him if he felt uncomfortable and maybe wanted to leave. "No, no, no" he replied firmly, "I'm fine, I'm fine!"

After an hour, the show repeated itself and the same girls appeared for a second time. I suggested again that we leave but he asked me to just wait for one more dancer, a buxom blonde he must have found most arousing the first time around.

On the way home, he made me promise not to tell Ivy what we had just seen. I promised and she never found out about her husband enjoying the sight of naked women. She may not have forgiven me, or Walter, for visiting such a 'place of sin and immorality'.

I also had to promise to come back for one more show before he would leave for South Africa. I did, but we never returned.

Even though they adapted well to our attitudes, many prejudices remained.

I still remember going shopping one day at our local mall.

Ivy adored a coat that she wanted to buy for her youngest granddaughter. She wanted to send a parcel with things she had bought over time, to her daughter and her family in South Africa.

The coat was white patent leather with a white fur collar and detachable hood. It looked adorable. She finally decided that she wouldn't buy it because the coat wouldn't suit her granddaughter. I asked her why not and her explanation shocked me.

"You see Konrad," she said, "this white coat would make her look darker. Back home, you want to wear clothes that make you look light skinned."

We just looked at each other, there was no sense in arguing with mother, after all, she would eventually go back to the reality and absurdity of what was life in South Africa.

Jackie and I had decided before her parents' arrival to sponsor them as immigrants to Canada and started the process in the first week of their visit.

We wanted them to have the option to stay for as long as possible and, if they decided to stay permanently, we would have gladly let them live with us.

It was surprising how quickly they were accepted. By April, they were landed immigrants and were now covered by OHIP, the provincial medical insurance.

OHIP came as a blessing. We had bought visitors' medical insurance for them but it did not cover pre-existing conditions and Walter had suffered from stomach ulcers for many years.

He had many reasons for not having them operated on while he was back home, a lack of sick leave, prohibitive costs and a distrust of South African hospitals for coloured people might well have been some contributing factors.

His ulcers started to get worse and his doctor, an acquaintance he knew from back home, recommended an operation as soon as possible. Within days of being eligible for OHIP coverage, he was admitted to North York Hospital in Toronto. He had been hesitant to have the operation done, but we told him that there were no better doctors or hospitals than here in Canada.

The operation was a great success, not only from a medical point of view but also as an experience to mingle with Canadians of all creeds and colours for the eight days he was in hospital.

Even though he was not supposed to smoke, it was still allowed in hospital rooms in those days, he had his fellow roommates smuggle cigarettes in for him. I can still see the expression of surprise and horror on his face when we walked in one day and he was desperately trying to hide a lit cigarette under the covers.

I think he was more afraid of Ivy's wrath than that of the doctors for violating the 'no smoking' orders.

The smoke, not only from the cigarette but also the smouldering blanket that had caught fire, gave him no choice but to admit he was disobeying orders. We extinguished the fire and the cigarette with the water on his lunch tray and asked the nurses to replace the now burned sheet and blanket. Ivy didn't crack a smile, but Jackie and I couldn't suppress our laughter.

Walter had made many friends in the hospital and still visited one roommate at his home after he was released.

Even though they started feeling at home in Canada they could not overcome the longing for their grandchildren and friends back home.

We had bought a house during this time and said they could stay with us. However, by the end of August, they decided it was time to return to an unsettled future in South Africa. We booked a flight for them and, on a rainy fall day in September, it was a tearful goodbye for all of us as they boarded the airplane for their long journey home.

We promised them that we would come and visit them in a few years' time, as soon as we were successful in making them proud grandparents one more time.

When we finally did make it to South Africa, with their now three year old granddaughter in December of 1977, it was for Ivy's funeral.

Chapter 43

What The Heck, Let's Buy That House!

We had driven to Brampton many times to look at houses. Brampton was a growing, well-established city within easy commuting distance to Toronto.

We had settled into our careers, felt a bit more secure and believed that buying a house would soon be something we could afford. We had no debts, other than a car loan, but had not saved much either.

What did attract us to Brampton was a government program called Home Ownership Made Easy or HOME for short. Under this program you could buy the house with a nominal down payment and lease the land from the province at a low fixed rate for 55 years with an option to purchase after 5 years at a set price. What a deal!

It was a sunny Sunday afternoon in May when we decided to go for a drive to Brampton and have another look at the various model homes. We asked Mom and Dad what they thought of the different houses. The selection was overwhelming, there were bungalows, back-splits, side-splits, two storey, detached and semi-detached. The Madoc subdivision, as it was called, was in its last stage and almost completed.

I drove up to the house we liked and showed it to Mom and Dad. The salesman recognized me from previous visits and mentioned that he had only three houses left and only one was the model that we liked, a detached three bedroom bungalow.

We went over the financial arrangements one more time and said that we still hadn't made up our mind and would give it some more thought. "Suit yourself," he said, "this is the last phase in this subdivision, there will be no more homes build around here. Nobody knows if the government will renew the HOME program and build more houses somewhere else." He then walked away.

What to do?

Jackie and I discussed it one more time on our drive back home. The total price of $28,995.00 just looked like such a big commitment.

We could handle the down payment, it was only $795.00. The monthly payment, including the mortgage, land lease and taxes, would be around $350.00 plus our utilities. It was a rather large increase from what we were paying for our apartment, but affordable. There were also the other up front expenses like closing costs, appliances, a lawn mower, garden utensils, landscaping, drapes... the list was endless.

We had talked, debated, weighed the pros and cons and discussed the sacrifices necessary to manage this financial burden.

It was time to come to a decision and act on it. It was quiet in the car. Jackie and I were mulling everything over in our minds.

That's when I finally made up my mind. I don't know what gave me that final push to jump into the financial abyss. I stepped on the brake and said, "What the heck, let's go back and buy that house!"

Jackie agreed with me right away. It was as if a weight was lifted off our shoulders.

I turned the car around and went back to the sales office.

After an hour of filling out forms we drove home with our heads spinning and wondering if we did the right thing.

Dad was chuckling in the backseat, constantly repeating the phrase "What the heck, let's buy the house" and saying "Way to go Kon, way to go." Dad must have thought that this was a spontaneous decision . He had no idea how long we had been brooding over it.

Now it was a question of getting approved for a mortgage, finding a lawyer and set a closing date. Everything was done by the next day. I had befriended a young lawyer to whom I was selling some office equipment and he agreed to handle the legal stuff for us. Our bank manager called me on Monday afternoon to tell us that our mortgage application had been approved.

The builder had pushed for an early closing date and we agreed on June 30th, 1972. We had less than eight weeks to get ready for the big move.

Moving Day

Saturday July 1st 1972, Canada Day. We now owned a piece of Canada and were ready to move into our first house.

We woke up early and got started after a healthy breakfast. Our moving volunteers showed up and they were assigned to different duties. We had lots of help; an upstairs crew, an elevator operator and a downstairs crew.

The Lesches were there in full force. Horst came with his brother Erno, who was here on a visit from Germany and had sacrificed a day of his vacation to help us move.

Closing was, in reality, the day before. Since the 1st of July is a statutory holiday we had to plan ahead. All shops and businesses would be closed on the day of our move.

We had picked up the rental truck, went to our new house to make sure that all the utilities had been hooked up and stayed around to accept the delivery of our appliances that Friday afternoon.

Everything went over pretty smooth on closing and on moving day. We were surprisingly organized for first time home buyers.

Mom and Dad had helped us for days to pack up everything and get us ready for the big move.

It took us the entire morning to get the furniture from our 18th floor apartment into the truck together with the boxes, bags, clothes and odds and ends.

Our cars and another belonging to one of our helpers were loaded as well. By noon, the apartment was empty.

It was a beautiful, warm and sunny day that Saturday. The bad weather with torrential rains had come the day before, which turned out to be a big problem.

Even though the building of the house was finished, the landscaping had not even started. The house was surrounded by muddy clay. Narrow planks served as a walkway across a sea of mud leading from the sidewalk up to our front door. No gravel had been put down on the driveway. The truck had to be unloaded from the sidewalk to avoid getting it stuck in the muck.

Losing your balance while carrying things into the house and stepping off the wobbly boardwalk meant sinking knee deep into the soggy mess and probably losing a shoe trying to get your foot back out.

The move itself was done in no time. By the afternoon, everything had been brought into the house and most of our helpers relaxed with a few beers and lots of pizza. After assembling some furniture and putting stuff where it belonged, most of them left.

Mom, Dad, Jackie and I continued unpacking and sorting things out until late in the evening.

So many things still had to be done in the days and weeks to come. Jackie's parents had bought us a dishwasher as a housewarming gift and it was only going to be delivered the following week.

We also found a few things the builder had to rectify. There was a crooked wall, a terrible paint job in one of the bedrooms and nobody knew when the landscaping would be done.

By ten o'clock that night, we were exhausted and ready to go to bed.

I was surprisingly fresh and still wound up. When everybody

had retired for the night I made myself a nice drink and sat down on the front steps to relax. It was a warm and clear night.

That is when it hit me. I don't know how to describe this feeling of pride and satisfaction, this feeling of happiness and accomplishment. Gone were the worries about money and the doubts about doing the right thing.

I owned something nobody in my family had ever owned before, my own home.

I looked up into the night sky and hoped that my father would be looking down upon me right then and I knew he would have been proud of Jackie and me.

A tear rolled down my cheek as I thought that he should have been there to share this moment with me. I raised my glass towards the sky and, for some unknown reason, started to cry.

Chapter 44

Joy And Happiness

The big day had arrived!

After years of trying to become parents, after being told that the chances of Jackie becoming pregnant were remote and after 9 months of waiting for the Children's Aid Society to find a newborn baby for us, the day had finally arrived.

It was two months earlier that our social worker called us and told us that there was a young girl in Nova Scotia who was pregnant and had decided to give up her baby for adoption. She was only 17 years old and felt it was best to find good parents for her baby and give her or him a chance at a bright and promising future.

The father of the baby was a schoolmate of hers and had agreed with her decision.

Now our waiting game started.

We used the time to get the nursery ready. Everything was decorated in yellow. We didn't know if we would have a boy or a girl. The basement was filled with boxes of diapers of every size. The closet was filled with baby clothes, towels, sheets, wipes, wraps, bottles and everything a baby could need. There were stuffed animals and baby toys everywhere.

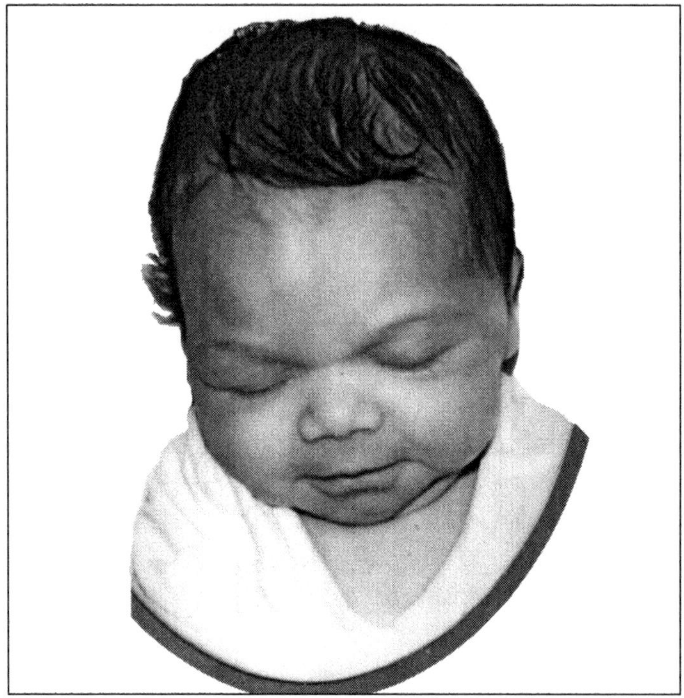

Toni - Day 1

We were ready! We had agreed to adopt the baby no matter what, boy or girl, poor health, birth defect or any other handicap. We wanted it to be as realistic a parenting experience as possible and with that there are no guarantees or choices. You take what fate will give you.

We were not going to turn another child away. It broke our hearts when we had to do it the first time. Even though we had specified that we wanted a newborn, no other conditions attached, Children's Aid contacted us after 3 months to tell us that they might have a child for us.

When the social worker came to our home she told us that this child was not exactly what we wanted but she was going to let us decide. She showed us a picture of Elizabeth, an eighteen month old toddler. She already talked, walked and was long past the infant stage Jackie and I wanted to be part of.

We gave it a lot of thought and felt like lesser human beings for rejecting Elizabeth. Children's Aid assured us that there was no problem placing her with another family but that feeling of having to deny a young child your love and willingness to give her a home was one of the toughest decisions we have ever made and we were never going to face that choice again.

We were going to accept a newborn without any conditions.

August 12th: The long awaited call from the social worker came: "It's a healthy baby girl!"

Our excitement and anxiety grew. The only thing in our way now was the legal 30-day waiting period after the date of birth during which the mother could still change her mind about giving her baby up for adoption. That 30 days of nail-biting was filled with frequent reports from the social worker on how our little girl was progressing.

September12th: Our little baby had officially become a ward of the crown and we were now able to go and get her.

September 13th: We purchased our return tickets to Halifax to pick up our daughter the next day. Our anxiety and anticipation was torturing us. We had a sleepless night.

September 14th: We arrived in Halifax on the first plane from Toronto. It was a bright and sunny morning. The social worker was waiting at the airport to take us to her office to have the papers signed. On the short drive to her office she talked about the background of the parents and how difficult it was for the mother to make the right decision. She also told us that our baby was the cutest baby she had ever seen.

At the Children's Aid offices we completed the necessary paperwork and noticed that the birth mother had named the baby Tasha Joy. We were both upset. We had already decided to name her Toni Belinda and asked if we could rename her. We were assured that there was no problem and the final adoption papers and her birth certificate would read Toni Belinda Brinck.

What a relief!

After the formalities were completed we had to wait for the foster mother to arrive with our little girl. We were told that there would be a slight delay and we should go for lunch and return in an hour. We had no appetite and a short walk around downtown Halifax was not very relaxing.

Time was just crawling along. Why was there a delay? We were getting more anxious by the minute. We returned early and were told it would be another 30 minutes. The explanation was that the doctor, who was to perform a last check-up to make sure our little girl was in good health, was delayed. It was Saturday and his practice was closed and he had to be called in from his home and visit the foster mother's home to do the examination.

I kept looking at my watch nervously. It felt like time was standing still. Was it hot or did my nerves make me perspire? Both of us paced back and forth in this rather large boardroom we were in. It had a large table and comfortable looking leather armchairs, but who could sit still at a time like this? Once in a while we stopped our pacing and looked out the window. The windows were wide open on this warm September day. The street was deserted.

Finally, we saw a taxi pulling up to the front door and a woman holding a baby wrapped in a blanket emerged.

Our hearts were beating so hard that I thought they could be heard echoing through the hallways of the building.

The door opened and the foster mother entered the room and put the little bundle into my wife's arms and said, "Here is your new baby daughter."

Jackie and I looked at this cute little baby. She was fast asleep. Suddenly, both of us started crying uncontrollably, tears of joy running down our cheeks. We smiled at each other, not being able to say a word.

Jackie kissed our daughter lovingly on the forehead, while I was wiping the tears off of our faces. We looked at this little girl. She was totally unaware that she had just been put into the arms of her new parents. She looked like an angel dressed in a lacy white dress with a matching cap. A lock of her hair peeked out from under her cap and curled across her forehead.

One of our tears fell on her cheek and woke her up. When she looked at us she started crying along with us. Here we were, together as a family for the first time, crying away.

I could not remember a time in my life when I was laughing and crying at the same time. Nothing could have prepared me for this moment. The emotions I felt when I laid eyes on her for the first time and when I held her in my arms cannot be expressed in words. Tears still well up inside of me today when I talk about that moment. I was emotionally drained, exhausted, but filled with an extreme feeling of bliss when I finally calmed down.

The social worker gave us half an hour together before she poked her head into the room and asked if we were ready to go to the airport. We had regained our composure and were anxious to get home.

Once at home, Toni was not a happy baby. She wouldn't stop crying for the next three weeks unless she had a soother in her mouth, was eating or was asleep. We never found out why she cried so much during that time. Jackie and I were desperately looking for answers. Was she aware that her life was in turmoil for the first four weeks and had trouble settling down? Or was she just testing us?

If it was a test we must have passed it because after the crying stopped, we became a loving, caring and happy family.

Chapter 45

Mom Versus Granny

When we adopted Toni, the law was not on our side. It was not only the difficulty of adopting a baby but the way Canadian law looked upon adopting parents.

There was no maternity leave for adoptive parents in 1974, it was reserved for women that had given birth and was viewed more as a recovery period for a nursing mother.

Even though Toni was not yet four weeks old when we brought her home in September of that year, there was not one day of maternity leave given. Jackie had to take her two weeks' annual vacation and her employer granted her two weeks of unpaid leave.

It was daycare after that.

Our neighbour, Bernice Wheaten, an excellent mother of three young children, was delighted to look after Toni until my mother was able to come to Canada to be our live-in nanny in early November.

During the time that Bernice was babysitting Toni, Jackie would rush home after work and spend every waking hour with her daughter. She was devastated by the fact that she had to go back to work after only four weeks and was afraid of not bonding with her like a birth-mother would be by staying home. She felt cheated and wanted her baby all to herself whenever possible. She played, fed, bathed, cuddled her and sang her to sleep every night. The only other person she allowed to spend some time with Toni was me.

Everything changed when my mother arrived.

My mother came on an open ticket and was willing to stay for up to six months.

It seemed like, and was, a good arrangement. Jackie and I were happy to have her with us.

My mother, or Oma, as we called her and is German for Granny, was even happier to again have a little soul to smother with her love. She was fulfilling her lifelong dream of being a grandmother.

Jackie understood the benefits of having my mother here but a feeling of jealousy and possessiveness soon overcame her. She wanted Toni to herself the moment she came home and didn't want Oma touching her. Any offer to feed her or change her diapers was rejected.

There was almost a touch of hostility in the air whenever Oma was around during Toni's waking hours. Jackie sometimes looked like she was ready to pick a fight with anybody who interfered with her mothering. Oma wisely retreated into a neutral corner when Jackie was home.

This situation was also tough for me to handle, I too stayed out of her way. At least there was one bonus for me, I didn't need to change diapers or get up during the night when Toni cried. Mom was on the job at all hours.

I saw how much my mother wanted to be part of our family only to be rebuffed. I also understood Jackie, wanting to be a loving mother, giving all her time and attention to her daughter while holding down a full time job.

My mother stayed the full six months as planned. She cherished her time with Toni during the day and knitting baby things at night. She hardly ever stayed up much past nine o'clock, so Jackie and I still had some private time together.

She never complained during that time, but stayed away from

Jackie as much as possible. Since Oma cooked and did most of the housework, Jackie did have a lot of spare time to spend with Toni.

It got tougher for us after my mother left and we both realized what a great help she had been.

To leave Toni with a private babysitter was even more difficult for Jackie. I could tell she was not happy. I know that, in retrospect, she wouldn't have minded having Oma around for a while longer.

My mother came back for extended stays in subsequent years to play granny and enjoy life with her granddaughter. Jackie felt she had bonded and Oma was no longer a threat to her.

The tensions were gone and we became a happy, sharing and well-adjusted family after those crazy first six months.

Chapter 46

Toni's Big Adventure

Oma came to visit us for Christmas in 1982 and stayed well into the new year. She was the grandmother that every child dreams about. Toni was her one and everything.

We enjoyed having her around. Oma had brought her dog with her. I am usually not fond of poodles but Rollie, a Harlequin Poodle, was different from the usual hyper, yapping variety of annoying poodles. Rollie bonded with Toni and the two enjoyed the Canadian winter together.

We saw each other fairly regularly, alternating every year with Oma either coming to Canada or us visiting Germany. She taught Toni German and they communicated fairly well with each other.

During her visit she asked Toni if she would want to visit her the coming summer and Toni thought that was a great idea. Oma painted it as a great adventure.

Our reaction was to play along knowing full well that once Oma had gone back to Berlin this subject would die. We couldn't have been more wrong.

Toni, just seven years old, never forgot or recanted her willingness to fly by herself to Germany to visit Oma.

By May it became obvious that withdrawing our agreement to

let Toni travel by herself would be seen as a major betrayal by both. Citing financial difficulties did not work either since Oma had promised to pay for her trip.

Jackie and I were in a pickle. We did not feel good about letting her travel alone, but Oma had done her research with Lufthansa. They had been accommodating single children for some time and we were assured they had never lost one yet. They were confident we had nothing to worry about.

We finally agreed under one condition. We would purchase a refundable open ticket in case Toni changed her mind or showed any signs of homesickness. The airfare was horrendously expensive but Oma contributed her share as promised.

When we booked the flight we had butterflies in our stomachs and hoped that Toni would have second thoughts when the day arrived. We didn't sleep the night before her departure although Toni was excited during packing and never showed any anxiety.

We will never forget the 'What have we done?' refrain playing again and again in our heads as Toni checked in at the Lufthansa desk. Our hearts started racing as the agent told us to go with Toni to the passport control and a flight attendant would come and take her to the plane.

On our walk to the passport control, Toni finally started to show some nerves. I can't remember who started crying first, but there we were crying our hearts out. We told Toni that it wasn't too late to change her mind and if she didn't want to go she could cancel and maybe do the trip the following year.

In a sobbing voice with tears running down her face she stammered, "This-is-my-big-ad-venture-and-I-want-to-go."

When the stewardess arrived she assured us and Toni that everything would be alright.

There was one last big kiss and a long hug for both of us and then we watched Toni walking off holding hands with the stewardess.

Our hearts were ready to break as we watched them walking down the long aisle of the terminal.

Toni never turned around to wave.

Jackie and I had another sleepless night.

We knew she was in good hands, but doubts remained. She had to change planes in Frankfurt. What if the airline lost her? What if Oma was delayed getting to the airport?

She was to arrive at 11:00 am local time in Berlin, 5:00 am our time. The airport was just around the corner from Oma's building, a ten minute cab ride. We expected a call no later than 6:30 am our time, to tell us Toni had arrived safe and sound.

By 7:00 am, the phone had not rung. We started to panic.

I called Berlin.

A cheery Oma answered the phone.

"Oh yes, she arrived alright," she said, "She arrived an hour and a half early. They put her on an earlier flight. I was still at home when Lufthansa called."

"What?" we screamed.

"No problem," Oma said. "They kept her entertained until I got there."

"If she arrived so early, why didn't you call us?" I asked.

"I didn't want to wake you up that early. I know you like to sleep in on weekends. We already took a walk to the ice cream parlour and were just about to call you," she replied.

"You've got to be kidding," I said. "We haven't slept all night worrying."

We were annoyed, but also immensely relieved to hear that Toni was safe. When we finally talked to her she sounded very excited. She couldn't wait to tell us how nice everybody was and how much fun she was having.

Well, no homesickness so far. That was still to come.

Jackie and I were finally overtaken by extreme emotional exhaustion and slept for most of the day.

There was no Internet in 1983 and making a call to Germany was expensive.

Oma promised to let us know if Toni was longing to go home or if anything unexpected happened.

We called after the second day but everything was still okay.

It must have been after that call that Toni started feeling homesick. All the trips to the playground, the ice cream parlours and playing with Rollie didn't make up for not having her friends or Mom and Dad around.

She told Oma she was homesick. She didn't know the German word for 'homesick' and translated it to 'hause-krank' which translated back would be 'house-sick'.

My mother understood but before booking her a flight back home she would give it one more try to make her feel at home.

She took her by the hand and introduced her to the children playing in the street, telling them Toni was her granddaughter from Canada and asking if they wanted to play with her.

It worked!

Toni became the centre of attention in the neighbourhood and made instant friends. She also formed a lifelong friendship with one girl that has lasted until today.

Toni picked up a lot of German and still speaks with a Berlin accent. She also taught the children in the neighbourhood a lot of English. She was popular because she would translate American songs for them. She still recalls the story of how everybody wanted her to teach them the words to *'Electric Avenue'*, the hit by Eddie Grant, that was a big hit in Germany that summer.

The term 'house-sick' didn't come up anymore. Toni had made Berlin her home away from home and was as happy as can be.

When we picked her up at the airport after her four week long big adventure, she had matured and looked rather sophisticated and happy.

She was bubbling over with stories about her friends Kay and Putte, the adventures with my schoolfriend Horst and his family and Rollie and last, but not least, Oma.

There was however one moment and one feeling Jackie and I will never forget. The moment we hugged and kissed holding her safe and sound in our arms again.

Chapter 47

Memories Of A European Family Vacation

In 1980, we planned our first grand European trip. Jackie and I had managed to get four weeks of vacation and we were ready to explore Europe. My mother had not travelled much in her life and we decided to take her with us. We had Paris, a week's stay in Provence, the French and Italian Riviera, Monte Carlo, Rome and other exciting places on our itinerary. A family re-union with my relatives in East Germany was also planned.

The trip was a great success. We loved the sights and Jackie and I were able to enjoy the nightlife, while Grandma was happy looking after our five-year-old daughter Toni.

Everybody was happy and relaxed, well almost everybody.

Linguistic Adventures

We did have a bit of a language problem and sometimes it drove me absolutely crazy. My mother didn't speak English, Jackie didn't speak German. At least Toni had learned enough German to communicate with my mother.

Things got more difficult when we got to France.

With my almost forgotten three years of school French I was now the translator for the family.

It was especially difficult in restaurants. I had to translate the menu into English and German and translate from German to English, English to French and French to German and so on...

I got so confused that I often ended up speaking German to Jackie, French to my mother and English to the waiter. It drove me nuts. It got worse when we got to Italy.

We had a hectic day, driving from Nice to Marina Di Massa on the Italian Riviera, while stopping frequently to visit various tourist sites, including the Leaning Tower of Pisa. That evening we checked into the rather posh, but somewhat faded Grand Excelsior Hotel. I was exhausted by the time we made it to dinner.

The maitre d' seated us and handed us the menus. I was busy translating for Jackie, my mother and Toni as the waiter appeared to take our orders.

He heard me speaking German to my mother when he looked at me and said *'Guten Abend'*.

I was rather perplexed because I expected him to speak Italian and the words that just came out of his mouth did not sound Italian to me. I looked at Jackie and stammered, "What did he say? What did he say?"

Jackie impatiently said, "He said *Guten Abend*," and gestured for me to return his German greeting.

As I turned back he had heard me speaking English and said, "Good Evening."

Expecting him to continue speaking German, I was totally flabbergasted and turned back to Jackie saying, "What did he say now?"

With a clenched jaw and tight lips Jackie hissed at me, "He said 'Good Evening!' What's wrong with you?"

As I looked back at him he sighed, staring at the ceiling with an expression of resignation and shaking his head in disbelief. When my brain started working again I apologized profusely and we proceeded to order. After the meal, I walked over to talk to him.

The answers to my questions, "Do you speak English?" and "Sprechen Sie Deutsch" were, "Nossignore."

I found out that he only knew greetings and the menu in German and English but was not able to speak either language.

He asked me, "Parlez-vous français?" I just nodded and, in my broken French, apologized again for my inexplicable brain-freeze.

The next night, we were seated at the same table. As our waiter came over he bowed his head towards Toni, my mother and Jackie. He then looked out the window and said, very slowly and pronouncing every syllable, "I think I'll try English tonight!"

Then, sounding like Alfred Hitchcock, he turned to me and said, "Good Evening."

Guess Who Was Watching Us?

One part of our lovely vacation came back to haunt me and forced me to remember details of our trip under unexpected circumstances.

We had returned from Germany three weeks earlier and were back into our daily routine. One day, after returning from lunch, I spotted a message from a Sergeant Edwards of the RCMP in my in-box. I returned his call right away to tell him that the RCMP was not my account but I would gladly connect him to the representative who handled it.

To my surprise, he said his call was concerning police business and asked if I wanted to be interviewed at my office or if I preferred to come to the RCMP offices on Jarvis Street.

My curiosity was piqued.

"What is this about?" I asked.

"Oh," he said nonchalantly, "We would like to talk to you about your recent visit to the German Democratic Republic."

We had visited East Germany on our trip. I had applied for visas to spend some time with my cousin Ilse and her family and for them to meet and get to know mine. I was now a Canadian citizen and able to get a visa from the East German Government for myself and my family, which was refused to me as a West German citizen. I was granted permission to stay for four days.

This was my first visit to the GDR since the wall went up in 1961.

So why would the RCMP want to talk to me about it? I was intrigued and told him I would come to their offices the next day but could he please give me a hint as to what this was about.

"We'll talk tomorrow," he said. "Don't worry, it's just a formality."

The next day I asked for Sergeant Edwards in the lobby of the Ontario Head Office of the RCMP in Toronto.

He arrived with a large file folder under his arm and asked the receptionist to assign him an interrogation room. She told him room B was available. The Sergeant asked me to follow him. When we arrived at room B he asked me to sit down.

I felt like I was in a 1950's spy movie. The room was furnished with a small desk, two chairs and a small table. On the desk was a lamp, an ink-blotter and a telephone. The small window was barred, letting just enough light into the room to make it unnecessary to switch on the big overhead neon fixture. He however switched on the desk lamp that created an eerie kind of atmosphere, reminiscent of a setting in a Mickey Spillane novel.

I was getting a little intimidated.

There was no small talk between us. He confirmed my place of birth, address and other personal items in a business like tone of voice. There was an uncomfortable 30 second silence. Then came his first question.

"What was the purpose of your visit to the GDR?"

I told him I was visiting my cousin in Neu Fahrland, a village on the outskirts of Potsdam.

"What's your cousin's name?" he asked next.

I have no idea why I said Hans, we don't have any relatives named Hans. The Sergeant just looked at me, "Hans?" he said in an enquiring tone of voice. I corrected myself right away stammering, "Sorry, sorry, I meant to say Wernie."

"Then, who is Hans?" he asked.

"Nobody, I don't know why that name popped into my head," I said in a nervous, agitated way.

"Okay," he continued, "What were you doing on July 7th at number 7 Jäger Allee in Potsdam?"

"I don't know Potsdam that well," I said. "Is there a bank, store or a tourist site close by?"

In a slow and deliberate voice he said, "Not really, it's the Officers' residence of the Soviet Red Army." Potsdam was a garrison town since the glory days of Prussia and was now the home of the Red Army in East Germany.

I jumped up and objected vehemently about his questioning and asked him what this was leading up to.

He told me to calm down and just answer his questions. He made a point of mentioning that he wasn't accusing me of any wrongdoing.

I said I don't remember being there nor what the street looked like.

He opened his folder and pulled out a 10 x 8 black and white photo of me getting out of my rented car with the number 7 clearly visible on a large doorway of a big mansion.

"Maybe this will jog your memory," he said, placing the picture in front of me.

I started to sweat and confirmed that the man in the picture was me but I still didn't remember what I was doing there.

I took a sip of water from the glass he had put in front of me before we started our friendly talk.

He then said, "By the way, how come you were driving a car with German Customs licence plates, registered to the Canadian Embassy in Frankfurt?"

I was baffled again. I had no idea the car was registered to the Canadian Embassy.

At the time Renault was offering short term leases to foreign nationals with a guaranteed buy-back. That way Renault could show the car as an export and bring it back to France as a used car and avoid paying high domestic taxes. This was very advantageous to anybody who stayed in Europe for at least one month. The cost was less than half of a comparable rental car from Hertz or Avis.

I explained that to Sergeant Edwards and he said that's what they had found out as well. He just wanted to confirm it with me.

He then asked me about the rest of my vacation and had pictures for every day of my stay. They even followed us to Wittenberg and asked what we were doing there. I told him we wanted to see where Martin Luther had nailed the ninety-five theses to the door of the All Saints Church.

He had pictures of every stop we made. It was unsettling that we were followed for four days, but never noticed anything.

However, Sergeant Edwards kept the most unnerving pictures to the end of the interview.

He pulled a picture out of his folder and said,

"Just one more thing, this is a picture of you, isn't it?"

It most certainly was. I had no idea where the RCMP got it from, likely from German passport authorities or possibly my immigration application. It showed me at about eighteen or twenty years of age.

"It sure is," I said.

The Sergeant then put another photo right next to mine and said, "Now I want you to look at the man in this picture and I want you to tell me if it could be the same man approximately fifteen or twenty years older?"

I was again startled. There was a resemblance, but the second picture wasn't me.

"That's not me," I declared. "And I can prove it. I've had this beard since 1969. I can bring in hundreds of people that can swear to the fact that my face has not been clean shaven for all these years."

"But you have to admit he looks a lot like you," he insisted.

"No," I said, "he doesn't have a beard and, therefore, he doesn't look like me."

He saw me getting extremely frustrated and annoyed and said, "Calm down, we know it's not you but we had to make sure. That's why you are here. The man in the picture is the one we are looking for."

He now smiled and started to be a bit friendlier. I asked him who the man was but he said he couldn't say and was not going to comment any further.

I asked him if it was the CIA who followed me and took those lovely pictures. He again said he didn't know the whole story but he didn't say no.

When we said goodbye, I asked him to let me know if the CIA intended to follow me on my next vacation. If that was the case I wouldn't bother taking my camera with me since they take better pictures than I do.

"I'll tell them to give you a call," he said, smiled and walked away.

Epilogue

It was a few years later, on a subsequent visit to East Germany, that I told my cousin about being followed by the CIA the whole time I was there.

He just smiled and said that now everything was falling into place.

Wernie said he had noticed strange cars and people watching his farmhouse round the clock during my last visit and assumed it was the STASI, the East German secret police. He didn't say anything so I wouldn't worry and feel uncomfortable during my visit.

My story made him realize what happened.

He told me that the US Military Liaison Mission (USMLM) was attached as a military unit to the Soviet Army and was located less than a mile from his farm in Neu Fahrland. It had a staff of up to 65 people, some military, some civilian and some CIA.

The Allies established these Military Liaison Missions in 1947, attached to each military headquarter of the occupying forces in Germany. As such, they enjoyed full rights of extra-territoriality.

The HQ of the Soviets was in Potsdam with the American Mission located next to their barracks in Neu Fahrland, a suburb of Potsdam.

The Soviets had their Mission in Frankfurt next to the main

base of the US Army in West Germany. These bases were created to oversee each other's military activities. Their existence was also conveniently used to spy on Germans and on each other.

I chuckled when I realized that the guy in the raincoat stalking tourists in East Germany was most likely not KGB or STASI but a CIA agent of the local espionage office in Neu Fahrland.

Wasn't the Cold War beautiful? Everybody had a reason to be paranoid.

Chapter 48

Death And Dying In Berlin

If the phone rings at 4 o'clock in the morning, it's never good news. The best you can hope for is that it is a wrong number.

The persistent ringing in the early morning hours of February 19, 1986 woke us up. It was Annemarie calling me from Berlin. She told me that my mother had suffered a massive heart attack and was in hospital. The doctors were not optimistic and she thought I should catch the first available flight to Berlin.

She called me back 30 minutes later to let me know that I could take my time, my mother had died just a few minutes earlier.

We had visited her for Christmas and New Year just two months ago and found that she was frail but still full of life.

I have written about my close relationship with my mother before and expressed my feelings on them. This story is not about grief and sadness but about the experience of handling the estate, German bureaucracy and dying in a divided city.

I was able to book a flight and arrived in Berlin on Thursday, the 20th of February.

My friend Horst Grudde and his wife Annemarie picked me up at the airport. We drove first to my mother's apartment where Margot, my cousin who lived next door, met me. She had the key to my mother's apartment. I wanted to start getting myself organized.

It felt strange to walk into the apartment without my mother being there. I felt like an intruder rummaging through my mother's belongings to find the documents I would need. We found the wooden box where she kept her papers, her bank book and the book for her postal savings account. It also contained the addresses of most of the contacts I needed.

The bank book showed a balance of less than 4,000.00 D-Mark and in the postal savings account she had just over 2,000.00 DM. I was shocked about the low balances. My mother had a good pension from my father but also supported us with generous gifts whenever she could and spent a lot of money travelling back and forth to Canada.

There was more than enough to pay for my plane ticket, my car rental and my personal expenses for the three weeks I had planned on spending in Berlin but I had to get an idea if there was enough money to pay for her funeral and any outstanding debts.

Margot and Annemarie were a big help in assisting me and pointing me in the right direction.

Annemarie offered me a place to stay at their house if I felt uncomfortable sleeping in my mother's apartment. I accepted her offer right away.

I was exhausted from the flight and asked if we could go to her place. I needed some rest and be refreshed for the next day. I had a lot of places to go and people to see.

Margot and I arranged to meet early the next morning at her office. She was the administrator of the local cemetery and had already contacted the funeral home and arranged for a burial plot.

We went to see the funeral director. He handed me my mother's death certificate and told me I needed it and a certificate of inheritance to deal with most institutions, the government and debtors. He also informed me that my mother had a small insurance policy through my father's former employer and that, with the death benefit from the government, would cover funeral costs. I told him my mother wanted to be cremated and I would arrange for the church service and a reception at a local restaurant. The job ahead of me was trickier than I anticipated. I was no longer a German citizen, had no German residence and needed the proper papers to fulfil my role as an executor and be able to inherit.

I had no idea how to close her accounts, pay her back taxes and utilities, cancel the lease on her apartment, how to sell or get rid of her possessions and get some of the things of personal interest back to Canada.

Next, I went to see the bank manager. He was a friendly man but told me right from the get-go that without the certificate of inheritance he was not even allowed to confirm that my mother was a customer or if the balance in her bank book was up to date. He played a childish game of 'If you ask the right question I'll give you an answer that might give you a good idea of what you want to know.'

He told me to ask him when my mother was last seen by any of his employees and since there was no Internet or telephone banking in those days that would have been the last time she could have deposited or withdrawn any money. He told me he saw her last on a date that corresponded with the last date in her bank book. With a wink and a nudge, he basically confirmed that the balance was current.

He also told me that even if I had the certificate of inheritance, he wouldn't be able to release the money right away since he would have to first notify the finance department to arrange to have her back taxes paid and also notify the utilities in case there were any outstanding bills. He was, however, able to start the process by copying the death certificate so that my wait wouldn't be too long.

The next stop was City Hall to apply for my certificate of inheritance, where the real fun was about to begin.

In the old days in Germany, when a couple got married they received a book called a Family Register. It would be the record book for the whole family, containing one marriage certificate, followed by pages of blank birth certificates, which would be filled out as the couple had children and the last section was pages of death certificates to be used as members of the family passed away.

To apply for my certificate I needed my passport, my mother's death certificate and the family register. I was in for a shock when I heard what the civil servant, who took my application, said to me, "I can't issue you a certificate of inheritance unless you produce a will or testament from your mother or a death certificate for your sister."

"What sister?" I replied.

"In your Family Registry is a birth certificate for a Harry Brinck in 1932 and the corresponding death certificate in the appropriate section. Then comes a blank birth certificate where somebody pencilled in 'female stillborn' without a date.

"Next is your birth certificate from 1946. If you claim to be the only living offspring of Kurt and Hedwig Brinck I need proof that your sister was stillborn, like records from a hospital or a doctor. Otherwise, I will deem her to still be alive," he explained.

I told him that everybody in my family knew that my mother had a stillborn baby in or around 1936 and that she was heartbroken about it.

"I believe you," he replied, "but in the dirty thirties there was an active market in unwanted babies and black market adoptions due to the poor economic and political conditions in Germany."

He continued by saying that since my parents had the baby before the division of Germany in 1947, I would have to produce a letter from Berlin's pre-war city hall, which was now in East Berlin, stating that my parents had not registered a will or testament before 1947. He would also require a letter from City Hall in West Berlin confirming that no will was ever registered by Hedwig Brinck. He pointed out that any will, regardless where it was registered, would be considered legal.

I told him that the hospital was still there today and I would enquire about their records and I would travel to East Berlin to apply for a search of their records.

I asked him what would happen if the hospital had no records of a stillbirth that happened more than fifty years ago. "You better produce a good witness to verify your story and find a sympathetic judge to give you a death certificate for your sister," he answered. It was surreal. Suddenly, I had a sister that according to the bureaucrats was still alive but, as I knew, had never lived.

I had a lot of work to do. That evening, I sat down and drew up a plan and a timetable of the things I had to do.

It had been a long and stressful day and I went to bed before 10:00 am to catch up my sleep.

It was the weekend and hardly anything was open on weekends in Germany. Shops closed at 1:00 pm on Saturdays and nothing would open again until Monday morning. Only pubs, bars, gas stations and places of entertainment were allowed to operate.

On Saturday morning, I went to the hospital where my mother had her stillborn baby. I was hoping the administration office was open. I was in luck and the administrator was on duty. I asked her if she could search her records for a file of a Mrs. Brinck who had a miscarriage in or around 1936. She asked me if I was kidding. There were no pre-war records or anything older than 10 years. Patient's records were passed on to their physicians and I should try to get in touch with him if he was still alive.

It was my first official dead end in the search for my missing sister. After this little disappointment I went to the apartment to seriously start sorting out things.

Margot was waiting for me and before we got started I told her about the problem with my suddenly living and missing sister. I had no idea who would be able to testify that my mother had a stillbirth. All her siblings and close relatives were dead by now.

"I remember," Margot said, "I was only thirteen or fourteen years old but I recall my father consoling her and everybody was talking about your mother's misfortune."

"I wonder if they would accept you as a witness since you were so young at the time, but it's worth a try. Let's go to City Hall together this week and see if we can straighten the whole thing out," I said, hoping that this could end the whole affair.

We now got started on organizing and cataloguing what was in the apartment. Margot told me that some neighbours and friends of my mother had asked her if I was interested in selling her belongings. “Of course,” I said, “we'll see what we can get rid of.”

I went to talk to the neighbours who had expressed interest. I also visited my mother's best friend, an older woman everybody endearingly called ‘Cookie Lady’ because she owned the biggest, fattest beagle in the neighbourhood and his name was Cookie.

My mother always said that she would like to help Cookie Lady, who was not very well off. I asked her what she wanted and told her I didn't want any money from her. I just wanted her to have some memories of my mother. She still had an old black and white television set and asked if she could have my mother's colour TV.

“Just arrange to have it picked up and it's yours,” I said.

Margot and her husband Ferri were also interested in a few things and I certainly didn't want any money from them.

Over the weekend, we got rid of a lot of stuff and I collected a few hundred D-Mark for things like the refrigerator, washing machine, some furniture and a few knick-knacks. Nobody wanted the big wall unit, beds and other bulky furniture. There was still a lot left. I wanted to take some items back to Canada. There were some books, photo albums and mementos from my childhood that I wanted to keep.

We decided that Margot could sell whatever was left or donate them to a charity. I was done selling things. I also decided to take my mother's bedding and linens to my cousin in East Germany. Good quality was not readily available in the East. I would call them when I went to East Berlin for the search of the will and arrange to meet. It was easier to call them from there since there was no direct telephone link from West Berlin to the East.

On Sunday afternoon, we were going to sort out my mother's clothes and stuff she kept in drawers and cabinets. The basement also needed some attention since a lot of my father's tools and other forgotten things were still stored there.

I was busy checking the pockets of my mother's dresses, coats and gowns when I felt a bundle of something in one of her dressing gowns. I couldn't believe what I pulled out. A big roll of German banknotes. I yelled to Margot, “Look what I found!”

We looked at each other in wonder and started counting. There was a total of 12,000.00 D-Mark in 100 and 500 Mark bills. "Unbelievable," I stammered. "So that's where she kept most of her money."

Then a horrible thought occurred to me. "Just imagine if we would have just grabbed the clothes and donated or sold them without checking."

Margot shook her head in disbelief. I told her to call Ferri, Horst and Annemarie. We were going out to dinner that night. My treat! It ended up being a great weekend.

I was not looking forward to the coming week. It was going to be hell.

Monday morning, after a delicious breakfast, I was off to East Berlin. I decided to leave the car behind. It was easier to take the subway and enter East Berlin at the only stop that served as a border crossing, Alexanderplatz.

After obtaining my 'Day Visa' for East Berlin and exchanging 25.00 DM into worthless 25.00 East-Mark, which was mandatory and non refundable upon leaving East Berlin, I was off to City Hall.

I was pleasantly surprised with the prompt and friendly service. I was told that the fee for the record search would be 20.00 DM.

When I tried to pay with the East German Marks I had been forced to exchange, they informed me that as a Canadian I had to pay in US or West German Currency.

"What am I supposed to do with the East German money I just had exchanged?" I asked him.

"I don't care," He said with a smile. "Have a nice lunch and donate the rest to a good socialist cause. There are donation boxes on your way out."

He then asked me to what address they can mail the search results. "I thought I could wait for the results. I need them right away," I told him.

"If you want us to put a rush on it we can have it ready in three days and you can pick it up yourself. But there is a surcharge of 25.00 DM," he proclaimed.

"West Marks of course," I said, sarcastically.

"Naturally," he laughed. "That's the only currency we accept from foreigners." He assured me that the letter would be ready for me to pick up by Thursday morning.

At least I had a firm return date. I then went to the post-office to make a call to my cousin Ilse and her husband Wernie. We agreed to meet on Thursday at the famous world clock on Alexanderplatz and have lunch at a restaurant nearby.

That call, a sausage on a bun from a street vendor and my subway ticket back to West Berlin cost me less than 5.00 East-Marks. Since it was illegal to take East Marks out of the country and they didn't refund your western currency I tipped the sausage vendor the 20.00 DM had left.

He was so thankful, I thought he was going to kiss me.

After going through the strict border control I was on the train to West Berlin by noon. I thought I better stop at the West Berlin city hall to make an appointment for Friday morning with the civil servant who was working on my case.

I told him I would have the search report from East Berlin and that although I was unable to find any records about my mother's stillbirth, I could produce a credible witness who would verify my story.

"I am not in a position to take a sworn affidavit and frankly, I don't know how to handle the situation. If she was stillborn, I can't issue a death certificate, only a judge can deal with that situation. I will try to book a judge for you. Just show up on Friday and we will take it from there."

Tuesday morning I went to the post-office to see how to get the money out of my mother's postal savings account. I showed the clerk the savings book and told her that my mother had died. I asked if I would be able to withdraw the funds without too much of a problem.

She took the book and asked if I had my mother's postal identification card as well. I showed her the card that was stored inside the plastic cover where my mother kept the book.

"Is this it?" I asked.

She leaned forward and said, "I shouldn't be telling you this, but if you have the card and the book you can draw up to 500 DM per day without any questions asked. It would only take you four days to get the money out. Leave a few pennies in the account and forget it."

I could have kissed her.

I knew where my first stop would be in the morning for the next four days. I was in an up-beat mood when I went to see Margot in her office at the cemetery.

She greeted me with, "Look who just arrived," pointing to a corner in the office. I turned around and didn't see anybody. "Where?" I asked.

"There, on the floor in that urn, that's your mother," she said.

Looking at the tiny vase I swallowed hard. It was unexpected and I was not prepared for it. I really don't recall the emotions that ran through my body and the thoughts that went through my head. I just stared at the urn shuddering at the thought that it contained all that was left of my mother.

Margot saw that I was a little shaken and apologized right away for her tasteless attempt at humour to lessen the impact she suspected it would have on me.

I went over to pick it up and it was lighter than I expected. The urn looked like metal or ceramic but was much too light to be of either material. Margot explained that it was a biodegradable compound that would eventually dissolve and when the twenty year lease on her plot expired there would be nothing left but dust.

The finality of it struck me and I said I would have to go outside to gather my thoughts for a couple of minutes.

When I came back into the office after a short walk Margot announced that she now had a date for the burial. It would be on the 4th of March at 1:00 pm. She had already booked the chapel and told me I should get in touch with an organist and arrange a minister to deliver the sermon and an organist.

I went to have a chat with the pastor of the local Lutheran Church. I knew Pastor Berndt and he remembered me, my mother and Toni's baptism.

He sat down with me, checked his calendar and agreed to conduct the service and bring the church organist along. He asked me many questions about my mother and our family to write a proper sermon for the service.

Then he asked me what my mother's favourite hymn or song was. I thought for a moment and said it was '*Mamatschi*'.

I am sure he expected a hymn or classical religious piece of music and not a sentimental tearjerker of a pop song from the 1950's about a boy seeing his mother being hauled away in a hearse pulled by four majestic horses.

Pastor Berndt just looked at me and before he could say anything I said, "Look, you asked the question. I know it's not the answer you wanted to hear but it was my mother's favourite song. That's the kind of music she loved."

He agreed to work it into the service somehow and I indicated that I would make a generous donation to the church in return. I asked him how much of a gratuity was customary for the organist. Margot had already given me an idea and I was going to be a bit more generous. I knew the pastor from my daughter's baptism. He was a modern, progressive Lutheran whose style I liked.

After some small talk, I said good-bye and headed back to Annemarie's place. She had told me to be home by 6:00 pm for dinner. We had a nice evening together and Horst and I drank a few good German beers and sampled drinks from his collection of exotic spirits.

I could hardly find the way to my guest room in the basement after sipping my way through every bottle on the shelf. I fell asleep the moment my head hit the pillow.

I woke up feeling like somebody with a sledgehammer was trying to break through my skull from the inside. Annemarie made me a strong coffee and asked me to look out the window.

It had been snowing most of the night so I decided to spend the morning on the telephone.

I wanted to call the airline and book my flight home for the 5th of March, the day after the funeral. I was told I still had to go to the local British Airways office or a local travel agency to get my tickets. No booking on line or by phone in 1986. Annemarie said she would take care of my booking with her travel agent.

I also asked the airline how much they'd charge for overweight luggage since I had decided to take some things home with me.

In those days the weight allowances for intercontinental flights were still generous. Two bags weighing 25 kilos each was the norm. Excess weight, however, was expensive. The British Airways agent told me the price per kilo would be 50.00 DM.

I had one big suitcase and now had to buy an extra one to pack the things I wanted to take with me.

Annemarie drove me to the subway. I didn't want to drive my rental car and risk getting stuck in side streets that hadn't been ploughed yet. It was just a short walk from the subway to the apartment. I decided to sort out what I wanted to take with me to buy the right suitcase.

But first I stopped by at the office of the cemetery to talk to Margot who had called me that morning to tell me she had received the bill from the undertaker. The funeral director hadn't mentioned if expenses were covered with the insurance money and the death benefits from the government.

Margot told me that she had spoken with him and that everything was paid for. In fact, I had a refund of 135.00 DM coming after all funds had been received. I called him and he mentioned that it might still take a while until the insurance claim was processed and asked where I wanted the cheque to be sent to. I told him to make it out to Margot and she would settle up with me. I felt that Margot had to be reimbursed for the help she had given me.

She also called the restaurant next door to tell the owner I was coming to see him to book his banquet hall for a reception. She had dealt with him before and he promised her that he would look after me.

It took me only a couple of minutes to agree to his plan and the price. I had no idea how many people would attend my mother's funeral since I had not kept up with her social life. I figured there would be between 30 and 40 people.

He suggested that he would serve coffee and cake, which is the traditional German afternoon snack served between 3:00 pm and

4:00 pm and if more than 40 people showed up he could always get another cake from the pastry shop next door.

I got to the apartment in the early afternoon. I was amazed how much of my mother's stuff I wanted to take home with me.

My mother had some very delicate plates, dishes and glasses that Jackie had admired. There was also some new cookware and my mother's collection of cups and saucers.

I wanted some memories of my youth. My old Teddy bear, a doll my mother had bought me once and some childhood books. The most important things were the two toys I remembered most and was very fond of. The first was a toy stagecoach from my old Cowboys and Indians set and the second was a big wooden fire engine I had ridden on as a two year old and played with until I was five.

And of course there were all kinds of papers, photo albums and knick-knacks.

When Margot came home we weighed everything and were shocked when the total weight came to 39 kilos. The trunk we had to buy would have to be a large steamer trunk weighing at least five or six kilos for a total of about 45 kilos. After deducting my allowed 25 kilos that would mean at least 20 kilos of excess luggage costing 1,000.00 DM or $600.00 CDN.

I swallowed hard but knew I wanted all of it. I planned to buy a trunk on Saturday morning. I also packed two suitcases of towels, bedding, linens and some dishes to take with me to East Berlin to give to my cousin and her family. Good quality textiles were hard to get in the East, so Ilse and Wernie were happy when I offered to bring two suitcases of my mother's stuff along with me to our lunch the next day. That way I cleared out not only a big part of her closet but was also able to give them two good suitcases. The ones available in East Germany were mainly made of paper-mâché or heavy cardboard.

I joined Margot and Ferri for dinner and then took the subway back to my temporary home at Horst and Annemarie's house.

The next morning I left early. I first drove to the apartment and picked up the suitcases and proceeded to Checkpoint Charlie to cross into East Berlin.

The Crossing went rather quickly. I went into the Barrack to get my 24 hour visa, for a fee of 20.00DM and exchanged my mandatory 25.00 East-Mark spending money.

The border guard inspected my car to see if I was importing contraband. He asked me what was in the suitcases. I told him they were clothes and personal belongings. He made a remark about my Canadian passport and then waved me through.

As promised, my letter was ready when I got to City Hall. It stated that no last will and testament was on record for either Mr. or Mrs. Brinck.

The famous world clock, which is really an astronomical clock, is in the centre of Alexanderplatz and the preferred meeting place for people. It was only a five-minute walk but I drove closer to avoid having to carry the suitcases through the snow and there was no shortage of parking spots in East Berlin. Traffic was light since a car was the ultimate luxury for East Germans and not many could afford one. There was a seven year waiting period to buy a car and no credit or financing was available.

I was early. I had assumed I would be at least an hour at City Hall and now I had an hour to kill. I walked into the Communist book store to waste some time where I had a clear view of the world clock. I leafed through some books when I saw Wernie and Ilse walking towards our meeting point.

Thank heavens they were early as well.

We kissed and hugged and walked to an old historical restaurant to spend a couple of hours together.

We had a great time together. Wernie insisted on paying the bill but I told him that I would pay the first 25.00 East-Mark with my forced exchange, otherwise I would again have to donate it to some good socialist cause upon leaving.

We walked to my car, hugged and kissed, I handed them the cases and drove back to Checkpoint Charlie.

As I wrote before, the inspection by the border guards to leave the East was painstakingly thorough. They checked every cubic inch of the car to make sure nobody was hiding in the car, under the car, in the gas tank, in the upholstery or in the trunk.

The guard who inspected me was the same one who checked my papers on the way in. He remembered me, which was not good.

When he checked my trunk he asked me, "Where are the two suitcases you had in your trunk and what was in them?"

I knew I was in trouble!

"Oh," I said innocently, "just a few things, like towels and bedding, I brought as a gift for my cousin."

"Don't you know that you need an import permit to bring goods into the German Democratic Republic? Did you get a permit?" he asked.

"Look," I said trying to defuse the situation, "they were used things from my mother, who died last week, and I thought it would be nice to give some things to my cousin as a memento."

The guard was not impressed or didn't express any sympathy for my loss. "So what you are telling me is that they were used goods. Are you aware that used clothes and textiles imported into the GDR need a dry cleaning certificate from your health authorities? Do you have that certificate?" he asked.

As I shook my head, he pointed to a spot close to the barracks, told me to pull over and he would call his superior officer to handle this highly illegal situation.

I pulled over and was asked to go inside the barrack and wait.

After 15 minutes, an important looking officer approached and summoned me to his office.

Surprisingly, he never asked me who I gave the suitcases to. I had been trying to come up with an excuse why I couldn't remember my cousin's address to prevent getting him into trouble for accepting illegal goods.

The officer told me that what I did was a chargeable offence under East German law and punishable of up to 3 years in jail.

"But," he added, "if you have a clean record I will talk to my superior and see if we can let you off with a fine."

'Aha,' I thought 'they want money.'

His next question was, "How much money do you have on you?"

Like every morning, I had gone to the post-office to cash another 500.00 DM from my mother's account. "About 550.00 DM", I said after counting the bills in my wallet.

"Let me make a phone call and I'll see if that is enough to cover your fine and keep you out of jail." He got up and left me alone in his office.

It was one of the longest 45 minutes I have ever spent by myself. I wondered if I would get back to the West and if not, how would I let the people in the West know that I had been arrested? I was sweating in spite of the freezing temperature in the poorly heated office.

"Sorry it took me so long," the officer said as he walked back in. "It is your lucky day today. My commanding officer agreed to only fine you 300.00 DM for the importation of illegal goods."

I was never so happy to be bilked out of 300.00 DM as I was at that moment.

" After you pay your fine and an additional 100.00 DM in processing and administration fees you are free to go," he added.

'You bastard,' I thought, 'You just screwed me out of 400.00 DM.'

I smirked at him and thanked him for letting me off so easily.

He must have known what I was thinking. "You are lucky," he said condescendingly, "you could have gone to jail for this crime."

After paying my fine, I got back into the car and drove off mumbling obscenities under my breath while smiling and nodding at the guards who waved me through the raised barrier.

When I got back to Annemarie and Horst I had to have a drink to calm down and relax. I wondered what the police officer would have done if I hadn't had any money. I'd possibly still be there.

It took me a while to fall asleep that night. I was reliving my adventure in the East and mentally getting ready for Friday's day in court where I most likely had to try to kill off my dead sister to finally get that inheritance certificate.

The sun was just coming up on a clear but bitterly cold morning. I left at 7:30 am to pick up Margot to be at City Hall for our 9:00 am appointment.

The civil servant told us we could go for a coffee since the judge could see us only at 10 o'clock and we should go straight to his courtroom where he would meet us.

It was a small and unimpressive room where we gathered. The judge was a middle-aged woman who had a warm and friendly smile. After listening to the facts and looking at the birth register she asked me if I had any proof or witnesses that this was a stillborn child.

I told her about my visit to the hospital and that the only living relative of mine, who is old enough to remember the incident, was my cousin, who was willing to swear an affidavit.

She pointed to Margot and asked if that was my cousin.

She asked her to verify my version of the events and she had to swear that my mother did have a stillborn child around that time. Margot then had to sign a sworn statement, prepared by the clerk. The judge then asked to be excused for a minute to deliberate her verdict.

When she came back she said, "I've never had a case like this before and had to look up the law. I do believe that Mr. Brinck and his cousin are telling the truth. There is no evidence to the contrary. But since this child was stillborn and never lived, I cannot issue a death certificate. I can, however, order that an inheritance certificate be issued and declare Mr. Brinck as the sole heir to the estate of his mother Mrs. Hedwig Brinck."

Case closed.

I thanked her profusely and asked how long it would take to have the certificate issued.

She said that I should follow the civil servant back to his office and he can issue it right away. She understood my time limitations and knew that I wanted to return to Canada as soon as possible.

When I went to pick up the inheritance certificate I had another little surprise. Besides the 20.00DM fee for the certificate there were additional court costs of 189.00DM to get my dead sister out of the way. I didn't know that killing your already dead sister would be that expensive.

Margot and I were back in her office before noon.

We went for a quick bite to eat at the restaurant next door after calling the bank manager and telling him I had the inheritance certificate and wanted an appointment to see him right after lunch. He checked his calender and agreed.

When I walked into the bank he smiled and said the timing couldn't have been any better. The letter from the finance department had come in that morning and there were no outstanding taxes. I could close the account right now. I asked him to convert the funds into Canadian Dollars and give me a money order.

It was still early in the afternoon and I thought I have enough time to go and buy the trunk.

'Koffer Panneck' was the largest luggage store in Berlin and had a large selection of travel trunks. The cheapest one was 69.00 DM, but this iron monstrosity weighed at least 15 kilograms. At 50.00 DM per kilo it would cost me 750.00 DM to get it home.

I explained my predicament to the saleslady and she pointed out that the trunks get more expensive the lighter they get. I picked the lightest one. A beautifully crafted, shiny aluminium trunk that barely weighed four kilos.

At 400.00 DM I would save money. Eleven kilos less weight would mean a saving of 550.00DM and it was only 331.00 DM more expensive, a saving of 219.00 DM. We could use it as a decorative corner or coffee table when I got home, it was that beautiful to look at. The cheaper one would possibly end up rusting away in the garage. I dropped it off at my mother's apartment before going back to Horst and Annemarie's.

On Saturday morning Horst and I went back to the apartment to start packing my trunk. Horst stopped to buy Styrofoam peanuts to fill empty space to prevent breakage and shifting.

When we were finished, we put the trunk on the scale. It weighed exactly 45 kilos, almost 100 pounds.

My flight on Thursday was early in the morning and to avoid any problems with an oversized trunk, I called the airport and asked if I could check in the trunk on Monday and pay whatever charges there were. The answer was no. But the woman on the other end then suggested I don't send it airfreight if I can drop it off on Monday. It would be in Toronto by Thursday when I arrive.

"And," she said, "you could save some money doing it that way. Airfreight is a lot cheaper than excess luggage."

"How much cheaper?" I asked

"I don't know how much excess luggage is per kilo to Toronto on British Airways," she said.

"50.00 DM per kilo," I interjected.

"Well, you see, airfreight is only 3.90 DM per kilo," she said.

"What?" I said, "45 kilos then would cost me less than 200.00 DM."

"Oh no," she further explained, "there is a minimum charge of 100 kilos."

Now I was getting extremely agitated.

I realized that if I would have bought the iron clunker of a trunk at 69.00 DM, I would still be under-weight and saved 311.00 DM.

This was getting ridiculous.

I was blowing money left, right and centre based on not knowing what to do and nobody explaining the rules of the game to me. Did anybody know the rules or was everybody trying to drive me to the brink of a nervous breakdown with fees, fines, costly misinformation and bureaucratic insanities?

I just had it.

I thanked the lady and asked where I had to go on Monday to send my trunk and if there were any more little details I should be aware of.

She rattled off some directions, rules and regulations. I thanked her and hung up.

We now repacked the trunk and put in a few more things that we had decided not to include because of the cost. They still didn't bring the weight up to 100 kilos.

Horst arranged for me to have a nice relaxing Sunday. We went to his parents' house and he, his father, my friend Kalle and I played cards the full day. On Monday morning, I went to pick up the trunk and Horst and I dropped it off at the Cargo building.

After handing over the shipping manifest, signing some papers and paying the 390.00 DM freight charges, Horst drove me back to see Margot. There were still a lot of loose ends to tie up.

I signed a power of attorney for Margot to act on my behalf.

She was to sell everything that was left and keep the money. She told me later she made well over a thousand D-Mark selling Mother's furniture and other things of value.

She also handled cancelling the lease and other odds and ends. We had everything notarized and I went home to Horst and Annemarie's to get ready for the next day's funeral service.

I got to the cemetery early and talked to the pastor and some other early guests. The church was decorated with more flowers than I had expected. My mother's urn was prominently displayed on a bed of roses on a pedestal in front of the altar.

A big lump started to form in my throat and I had to fight back tears.

I went outside to greet people that came to pay their last respects to my mother.

More people than I expected showed up. Neighbours, friends and people my mother had cared for, volunteering for a non-profit social agency, came and expressed their sympathies.

Many of my friends and their families attended.

Margot and her family were the only relatives I had expected to be there. None of my relatives in East Germany received permission from their government to attend. To my surprise, the widow of my father's brother, Tante Elfriede and her daughter Inge, came as well. Apparently Elfriede read the obituary in the local paper. I had had no contact with them for almost 20 years and would never see them again after the funeral.

I had no idea that my mother still had so many friends that cared enough to be there for her final farewell.

The church was almost full. Pastor Berndt read out a beautiful eulogy and I said my final farewell. It was a short but memorable service. I had problems holding myself together but managed rather well. That is, until the single pallbearer picked up my mother's urn to lead us to the graveside.

At that moment the organist started playing '*Mamatschi*' and I lost it. I cried uncontrollably as I followed him to the graveside, being consoled by Pastor Berndt the whole way. That, for the first time, was the moment where the term 'broken heart' made sense to me.

The pain in my chest was indescribable and I felt like I was being stabbed with every sobbing breath I took.

Yes, I was a Mama's boy.

After a few last words by the pastor and the usual graveside rituals, it was finally over.

I needed a few minutes to collect myself.

Margot and Annemarie asked everybody to join us for a reception at the restaurant. It was the last thing I felt like doing.

I realized later that it was the best thing that I could have done. The mood was upbeat and ended up being a celebration of my mother's life and a tribute to her unselfish willingness to give to others.

She would have loved it.

The next morning, emotionally drained, I boarded a plane to Toronto.

Chapter 49

A Perfect Neighbourhood

I never believed that a house was primarily an investment. To me a house is a home in a neighbourhood where one puts down roots and becomes part of a community.

1978 was the perfect time to make that move. We were looking for a house that would be our home until we were too old to take care of it and had to move into a seniors' residence. We hope that day is far off.

This was also the year in which Toni was enrolled in a kindergarten program at her daycare centre. We wanted her to be settled before she started school. This way she had two more years to be with her friends from her old neighbourhood and also got to play with the children from her new one. We felt that providing a stable environment in her early years was very important.

Jackie and I felt financially secure enough to commit to a larger house with a larger mortgage. It was time to go house-hunting.

We were driving around Brampton in March of that year, when we found a new development with uniquely designed houses. All models had won various architectural awards. We fell in love with a 2,100 square-foot three bedroom double storey house with a double garage on a ravine lot. The backyard backed onto a conservation area with a creek running through it. It was perfect, suburbia in the front yard and country living in the back of the property.

There was only one house of the model we wanted on the ravine side of the street. It was the model home and sales office. We asked when it would be available since the builder had just started construction in the development. We were told that he planned on selling all his units no later than July. That suited us fine and we put in an offer with a July 10th closing date.

Our neighbour was a realtor and we signed a conditional listing with him the same day. Our offer on the new property was accepted the next day and we had three offers for our house.

This was all going too fast. At least we didn't have to worry about many things other people had to go through when moving into a brand new home. This house was a professionally decorated model home with many upgrades. The rooms were wallpapered, the light fixtures and carpeting were upgraded and every room had curtains and shears. All we had to do was put down our furniture on moving day.

Buying the house on Parkside Drive was one of the best decisions Jackie and I have ever made. Not only because it's a beautifully designed home on a ravine lot with all amenities close by but also because we were only the second couple to move onto the street.

I literally became Mr. Welcome Wagon.

Whenever I saw a moving truck pull into one of the driveways close to us I went up to greet the new arrivals and offered them help if they needed it. I knew things didn't always run smoothly on moving day, from utilities not getting hooked up in time, a lack of tools to quickly fix things, to appliances that do not work. A helping hand was always appreciated. This way I got to know all the new people on our street and laid the foundation of having the best group of neighbours anybody could wish for.

Over the following years we became a close knit community. We formed many friendships that continue up to today, even though many families have moved away over the years.

We were not a clique of gossiping busybodies nor did we hang out constantly in each other's houses, but we were a group of helpful neighbours that got along with one another and knew how to party.

We had parties for any reason, New Years Eve, Halloween, birthdays and sometimes for no reason at all. The pool parties in the heat of the summer were spontaneous, but big events, like the annual 'Lobster Cook Out', were planned and everybody looked forward to them.

Our children had a great time playing by the creek, catching frogs and little fish or playing the usual games in the street.

It was, and still is, a great neighbourhood in which to live.

•••••

Here are a few stories highlighting stories what life on Parkside Drive was like.

Child's Play

Growing up with a creek in the backyard, lots of other children her own age to play with and neighbours with swimming pools was a great way to enjoy her childhood.

Toni's friend and favourite playmate was Aaron DeLeskie. For a while they were inseparable. Aaron's father, the principal of a Toronto high school, took great interest in teaching his and other children all kinds of interesting things and making it fun.

There were always projects involving building or fixing things in his garage. He even served his special pancakes with coins hidden inside when children came over to join them for breakfast.

His wife Mybritt, a nurse, served as the local medic to mend the scrapes and bruises children suffered during their activities.

One of the more memorable stories involving a parent was **'The Soccer Game'.**

Bill Campbell had two children, Andrew and Shannon. Andrew was Toni's age and he and Toni both played soccer. Bill, the assistant coach for his boys' soccer team and I, coach of Toni's team, the Brampton All-Stars, thought it might be a good idea to let the girls play a pre-season game against the boys.

When the teams arrived at the field there was a noticeable

difference in attitude. The boys were giggly and very cocky and felt insulted to have to play girls. Their confidence and smugness knew no boundaries. The girls took a more cautious approach but were ready to accept the challenge.

Maybe I should mention that, at the age of twelve, girls are physically slightly more developed than boys and some of our girls were definitely bigger than their male counterparts.

The boys were in for a surprise. It was no contest.

I don't know if it was a sign of chivalry, trying to be gentlemen and not hurt the girls but the boys' aggressiveness disappeared when they fought for the ball. There was no hesitation or any kind of holding back in the girls' approach to the game. They didn't act like ladies to live up to the chauvinistic expectations of their opponents. They were taking no prisoners and were there to win a soccer game.

The girls tackled and the boys went down like dominoes. We had to carry some of them off the field. I don't know if the injury to their limbs or the injury to their pride hurt more.

Looking back, the line 'There is no crying in baseball' from the movie *A League Of Their Own* came to mind when I think of the tears of injured boys on the sidelines. That day there was crying in soccer and it wasn't the girls that cried.

The final score was 4-0 for the girls. It could have been worse except for an outstanding goalie on the boy's team.

Bill approached me later and told me that the boys were embarrassed and mad. They wanted a re-match. The second match was a lot closer but the girls still won 3-2.

Travel

Whether it was camping at Darien Lake NY or Long Point Beach on Lake Erie, going skiing in Quebec, New York or Vermont, driving to Florida for the March Break or spending a weekend at Bill and Christine's cottage, we did it all.

We even travelled to Montreal for the Hockey Soviet Super-Series in 1983 to watch the USSR beat the Canadiens 5-0. A few years ago we went on a Baltic cruise and travelled through Germany together with the DeLeskies and we have spent lots of time with them and others in Mexico in recent years. All these memories could fill a book. We travelled as a group, just with another couple, with and without children, it didn't matter, we always had fun.

Parties

The parties we had were legendary. Our circle of friends grew as people from other areas in Brampton were being added.

As mentioned earlier, we never missed a good opportunity to have a party. However, two parties are worthy of mention.

The New Year's party of 1983 was at our house. Ed Blackbeard and I had talked about the fact that Sue and Colin Church, even though they had been to every party in our neighbourhood and participated in many of our activities, had never invited any of us to their house, not even for a cup of coffee. They were friends of the Baldwins, who lived on our street. Their house was located in a different section of Brampton but they became part of our group and never missed a single invitation.

Ed and I decided it was time for them to throw a big party and we were going to arrange it for them.

We designed a beautiful invitation that we planned to hand to every guest at our New Years Eve party just after midnight. We announced that Ed and I had started an entertainment venture, called Ko-Ed Productions, and everybody present was invited to our inaugural function. We then asked Sue and Colin to help us hand out the invitations. We asked that no one open the envelopes until everybody had one in their hand. We asked Colin to open his envelope first and read the invitation out aloud. It read:

Page 1 -

KO-ED PARTY PRODUCTIONS

A Member of the Parkside Family Of Fine Entertainment

is proud to announce **The Social Event of The Decade**

• • •

Page 2 -

You are cordially invited to attend

'A CHURCHES VALENTINE'

With your Hosts Sue and Colin Church
On February 11th 1984
At 30 Madeline Court, Brampton, On.
From 8.00 pm to ????

Admission: Your choice of alcoholic beverages
'Exotic Delicacies' to please your palate
will be served by your hosts.

DON'T MISS THIS UNIQUE OPPORTUNITY
IT MIGHT NEVER BE OFFERED AGAIN!

When Colin started reading the second page he just stuttered, blushed and half way through he muttered, "I thought something like this was coming."

Both of them were good sports and said the invitation would stand and they would do their best to get their rec-room finished and throw a party we'd never forget. What else could they have done? They were the ones who handed out the invitations.

Colin finished his rec-room the morning of the party.

We had a little special surprise for him to make it a party he'd never forget.

Ed and I collected a few dollars from all the invitees and bought a big 30" trophy with a wooden base and a Victory Goddess on top. At 11:00 pm I asked for everybody's attention and presented Sue and Colin with the trophy by telling them that they were the proud recipients of the ***'Party Avoidance Award'.***

The inscription on the main plaque read

THE PARKSIDE GROUP
presents the
Party Avoidance Award
to Sue and Colin Church

Each of the six plaques on the base of the trophy were inscribed with the words: ' No party in' and underneath the years 1978, 1979, 1980, 1981, 1982 and 1983.

Colin's acceptance speech was full of humour and he thanked us for giving him a reason and an incentive to finally finish his basement. He placed the trophy proudly on a shelf behind the bar.

We did see the trophy every time he gave a party, so no further plaques had to be added to the base in the following years.

The Neighbourhood's First Farewell

Everybody knew that, as time went by, our neighbourhood would lose a few families.

Ed and Izy Blackbeard were the first to sell their house and move away.

Izy was, what some people call a bit flaky but fun-loving and Ed was an entrepreneurial high stakes roller and, at times, bordering on being a lovable con-artist. They were a couple from South Africa and were a bit different from the rest of us. Both of them loved to have a good time. With them it was always party-time!

Ed had many reasons for immigrating to Canada. He said you couldn't run a good business in a country were the government told you who not to hire based on the colour of their skin. He told me that he had to leave South Africa because, at the young age of 26, he owed the government and private investors millions of rand, the currency of South Africa, at that point still at par with the US dollar.

He and Izy had owned and sometimes operated businesses like gold mines, flying schools, bridal stores and a multitude of other companies. When the highly leveraged empire he built started to fall apart he decided to come to Canada leaving his main debtor, the South African Government, high and dry.

He figured that they were the main reason for his business failures due to their many restrictions and they deserved to take the loss. He bought and ran a lot of companies in Canada as well. Businesses close to bankruptcy were bought, made profitable and then sold.

In between ventures he found random sales jobs while looking for another opportunity to strike it rich.

When Ed had money, everybody had money; his generosity had

no boundaries. Izy used to say that she wished he'd settle down because she was getting tired of their roller coaster life, going from rags to riches and vice versa.

Everybody on our street was upset when we heard he had listed his house and was moving to the country.

We decided to give them a send-off they'd never forget.

The decision was made to make it a surprise party with a wake and fake funeral theme.

Jackie and I were going to invite them for dinner and all the neighbours were going to convert his front yard into a cemetery while we ate. Gerry and the children had worked hard the week before to make little white crosses and we also acquired one big headboard shaped like a tombstone and wrote on it:

Edward and Isabel Blackbeard
1979 - 1988
Leave in Peace
You'll be Missed but never Forgotten

While we were having dinner our co-conspirators set up the cemetery scene on their front yard. The children placed rows and rows of white crosses on their lawn together with the 'tombstone'. We also placed an altar/ podium on their front stoop to read a eulogy and testaments to them being great neighbours.

Earlier in the day we installed floodlights on the roofs of the houses around them to illuminate the whole scene when they arrived after dinner.

We had agreed to leave our backdoor open and at exactly nine o'clock that evening the whole neighbourhood, dressed in black, marched through our house pretending they were in a funeral procession.

Bill Campbell, dressed as a priest, was leading the way carrying a boom box playing *The Funeral March* by Frederick Chopin while he was reciting prayers. The women were wailing and crying, 'Why, oh why do you have to leave us?'

Ed and Izy looked at this scene in amazement but slowly had an idea of what was to follow. I then asked them to follow the procession out the front door. They laughed uncontrollably when they saw their yard brightly illuminated and looking like Arlington Cemetery.

The people on our street that had not been invited came out of their houses wondering what this spectacle was all about. Bill then gave a short sermon followed by some eulogies and we proceeded to Gary and Lena Baldwin's house to have one of the wildest parties we've ever had.

There is a footnote to this story.

A couple of years later we were sitting at Bill and Christine's pool with a young black couple from down the street whom we had not met before.

We started discussing parties from the past and told them the story of Ed's and Izy's farewell.

When they heard the story they just looked at each other and said in unison, "So that is what that was all about!"

They proceeded to tell us that it was their first weekend in their house after they had moved in.

They came home from a movie with their young children when they turned the corner and saw the white crosses, the bright lights, people hiding their faces behind veils and a man in a white robe walking up the Blackbeard's driveway.

Their first thought was: 'What have we done? This is a Ku Klux Klan community!'

They kept their children inside for weeks and locked their doors at all times until people at their end of the street reassured them that this was not a racist neighbourhood.

It was only then that they felt totally safe living amongst 'The Crazies' on Parkside Drive.

Chapter 50

The VV's

Sometimes it's hard to understand what makes a good friendship.

In the case of the Vander Voet Family, there are many reasons why a long-term friendship seemed rather implausible.

Our daughter Toni was enrolled in the 'Happy Life Daycare Centre' in Brampton and befriended a little girl by the name of Andrea Vander Voet.

The two became inseparable. Toni and Andrea were both adopted and that must have been the catalyst for their almost instant bond.

Just like us, the Vander Voets made no secret of the adoption and explained, as we did, that they were special, a pretty standard explanation given to children at their age.

The teacher told us about the two of them strutting through the centre and singing in unison, "We are special, we are special!"

It wasn't long before Tony and Susan Vander Voet invited us to their home. We returned the invitation and a casual friendship started.

The VV's, as we called them, were interesting people with an exciting past. They had worked for several years in Colombia with

CUSO, the Canadian University Service Overseas. Their son, David, was born in Bogota while they were posted there.

In 1973, they lived in Chile where Tony taught as a professor of chemistry at the State Technical University under a CIDA contract. CIDA, the Canadian International Development Agency, was an organization that administered Canadian aid programs in developing countries. While the VV's were there, Chile underwent a bloody military coup that toppled Salvador Allende. During this violent and dangerous time, they adopted a little Chilean baby girl and named her Andrea.

Many CIDA workers opted to leave the country in opposition to the inhumane treatment of its own citizens by the Junta.

It was fascinating to listen to their stories of living through the brutality and turmoil of the Pinochet regime.

When we moved away and Toni started school we lost contact.

A couple of years later, shopping in a lumber store, of all places, we ran into them again. Toni and Andrea acted like they had each rediscovered a long lost twin sister.

We've never lost contact again, even though it appeared that we did not have much in common. I love sports, Rock & Roll and had a career in the business world. Tony is more the 'artsy' type; he is an accomplished painter, piano player and good at anything that requires the touch of an artist, with a career in academia and the civil service. We have never been bored with each other or ran out of subjects to discuss. As a matter of fact, we complemented each other very well.

With both Toni and Andrea being gifted soccer players and playing first for Brampton and later for Mississauga rep teams, we spent a lot of time travelling together to tournaments across Ontario. Our friendship deepened.

In 1986 Tony, a geoanalytical expert, was engaged as a consultant under a CIDA contract to assess and provide training and technical support to a geological laboratory for the Government of Thailand. This meant he had to uproot his family and live in Bangkok for six months.

It didn't take him long to accept the assignment and embark on this adventure of a lifetime. The Vander Voets asked me to look after their affairs while they were gone.

I was honoured to be asked and accepted the challenge to keep their affairs in order while they were gone. This was before the Internet made life a lot easier. I was given power of attorney to do their banking, handle any legal and monetary issues and be the landlord to the tenants of their house that they had rented out for the time they were away.

They decided to make this a trip around the world, going westward to Thailand and continuing westward on their way back home, making stops in China, India, the USSR and many places in Europe.

Susan and the children came home after five months and started their regular life in Brampton.

Tony stayed for the full term of his contract and on his way back I had promised to show him Germany. We met up in Frankfurt and started our whirlwind tour of Germany and Austria.

I took him to the places he was eager to see and the ones I felt were important for him to explore. We went on a day-cruise down the Rhine, visited Heidelberg Castle where Tony relived his favourite movie *'The Student Prince'* with Mario Lanza and he was fascinated by Neuschwanstein Castle that was the inspiration for Disneyland's Sleeping Beauty Castle.

In Salzburg, we spent half a day at the Mozart House and in Bayreuth we visited Wagner's house, now a museum, his grave and the Festival Hall. Tony loves Wagner's operas and he studied every exhibit and artifact on display. My love for Wagner was almost nonexistent and I decided half way through the museum that I would explore the pub next door where Wagner might have had a beer or two, but I rather doubted it.

We stayed in an Austrian castle where the rich and famous enjoy being treated like royalty and visited the Dachau Concentration Camp to be reminded of the darker side of German history. We were overwhelmed by the German State Opera's performance of Nabucco and lived it up at the 'Six Day Bicycle Races' in Berlin.

We enjoyed the nightlife of West Berlin and visited the stark contrast of life on the other side of the Wall in East Berlin.

I loved the experience and enjoyed Tony's eagerness to soak up the cultural treasures of Europe as well as experiencing the reality of a divided Germany with its checkered past.

We had the time of our lives.

My friends in Berlin treated Tony like he was one of them.

I will never forget our last night in Berlin.

We had dinner with my friends and relatives in the dungeon of Berlin's centuries old fortress 'The Citadel'. The theme was, of course, medieval, from the food to the costumes of the staff.

What robbed Tony of large stretches of his memory on how he got home and back into his bed that night was the way they served one of the medieval specialty drinks, mead.

One of the wenches walked around with a bucket of this fermented honey beverage and you were given a large ladle and served yourself right out of the bucket, no glass or chalice was needed.

Tony and some others had no idea how powerful mead is. Tony found out the next morning when Annemarie, our hostess, woke him up so he wouldn't miss his flight to London. I had left earlier that morning for my flight back to Canada and was not able to say good-bye to him. The mead was still keeping him in the medieval dreamland of Germany when I left.

Susan and the children moved in with us for a short time until their renters had vacated their house. When Tony returned from Europe, he had travelled on to explore England for a few days, his family had just moved back into their house and started to fix it up to put it on the market. It sold fairly quickly and they bought a house in our neighbourhood just one street away from where we are living.

We are still the best of friends, Tony and Susan still won't watch Monday Night Football and I still can't stand Richard Wagner but I could write a book about the things we have done together and possibly will still do in the future.

What is remarkable is the fact that Tony and I have never fought in all the years we've known each other. We have had many disagreements but never had an altercation. I assume that is mainly due to Tony's congenial, non-combative personality.

His wife Susan and I have found lots of ways to annoy and needle each other over the years, but we have never fallen out to a point where our friendship was threatened. Both of us have a stubborn and 'know it all' streak in us that invites some heated discussions with unsatisfactory endings. Funnily, she and I get along great when there are just the two of us but I guess sometimes we want to score points in front of others. Luckily, neither one of us knows how to carry a grudge.

I have always admired Susan for sticking to her principles. She is a fierce fighter for women's rights and social justice and has dedicated much of her life to work for the less fortunate, especially disadvantaged minorities and women.

She possibly sacrificed a lucrative and successful career in the private sector to improve the world we live in. She is one of the most generous and selfless people I know and both of us are willing to try new and exciting things. Susan, as well as I, have tried more than one scheme to make some money but have both been failures in ventures we've tried. Well, I guess you can't be good at everything.

I know that if we are ever in need, the VV's will be there for us.

Chapter 51

Toni's Big Announcement

The road of life does not run in a straight line and sometimes there are bends that take you into unfamiliar territory or places you don't expect.

As a child, Toni was always the daughter I wanted and the son I never had.

She was the prettiest, cutest girl I had ever laid eyes on, but also a rough and tumble tomboy who loved all kinds of sports. Jackie would dress her up and she would look and act like a perfect little princess but on the playground she would be the daring little rascal on the swings and monkey bars. She preferred playing baseball with the boys to playing hopscotch with the girls.

In high school, Toni excelled not only in her academic endeavours, but became also a star athlete. She participated in almost all team sports the school offered and was voted MVP for soccer, field hockey, skiing and honoured as the 'Athlete of the Year' in her senior year.

We noticed she didn't show much interest in boys, but wrote it off to the fact that her busy schedule didn't leave her much time for dating. One evening, when Toni was in her first year at university, Jackie asked her about a boyfriend and was told that she hadn't met anybody interesting yet. Jackie then asked her point blank if she was gay and I remember Toni's firm and decisive answer, "Mom, I'm not gay!" That was good enough for me.

Later that year, she confided in her mother that she had met a boy but he had broken up with her, leaving her heartbroken. Only once during her time at university did Toni have a serious enough relationship with a boy she felt comfortable enough to introduce to us.

It was a sunny summer day when she introduced us to Jason and had him join us for a BBQ. He was a country boy from St. Thomas, Ontario, and the middle linebacker of the Guelph Gryphons, the university's football team. He was a mountain of a man and dwarfed Toni. Jason was rather quiet and shy but I liked him. Toni ended up breaking up with him when he became too serious and it was obvious that her ambitions and interests did not match his.

It was late in 2000 and I was getting ready to retire. Jackie and I had made plans for our lives together after retirement and hoped a wedding and grandchildren would be part of our future. Toni was settled now and could concentrate on more than just her career.

I will never forget the night I came home from my weekly card games at the German club. Jackie greeted me with the words, "Welcome home, you won't believe the news I have for you. Our daughter is gay."

I was stunned. Toni had visited earlier and during the course of the evening told her mother that she had known for a long time about her sexual orientation but had never found the right opportunity to break the news to us.

My reaction went from disbelief to a totally mixed bag of emotions.

I harboured no homophobic prejudices and did not ask why and what did I do wrong for her to be gay. However, I do have to admit that I was hurt. My first reaction was, 'Why didn't she tell me herself? Why did I have to get the news second hand? Did she not trust me to be a loving father who is understanding and supportive?' I also realized that my future expectations of one day

Our Happy Family

walking her down the aisle or becoming a grandfather were shattered. I was also concerned for Toni, knowing full well that a life as a lesbian was not going to be easy in a society that still, to a large extent, discriminated and condemned homosexuality.

Jackie and I had a sleepless night. We talked and felt sorry for ourselves and for Toni's future. The first thing I did in the morning was to call Toni to ask her to have lunch with me. She agreed and we met at the Sutton Place Hotel. We were both very emotional and it was a tearful afternoon. We parted, knowing that nothing had changed between us as a family. I assured her that our love for her was truly unconditional and Jackie and I would adjust to our new reality and future expectations.

Our fears and disappointments turned out to be baseless.

Toni did end up getting married to Tonya, a beautiful young woman. I was able to play my part as father of the bride in a memorable ceremony and felt like a proud father when I made my speech. I gave my blessings to the happy couple, just as I had hoped for when I planned my life.

Today, Jackie and I are the happy grandparents of two beautiful girls, Ivy and Kenley, who fulfil our lives and make it fun.

It certainly is remarkable when I look back on the fears, doubts and worries Jackie and I had about our and Toni's future. We are one big happy family, part of a changed, more open and tolerant society, having overcome many prejudices and misconceptions of the past.

The road of life may not always run in a straight line but when one masters the detours and avoids the potholes, it will inevitably lead to happiness.

Chapter 52

Journey Into The Unknown

The idea of retirement scared the bejeebers out of me.

It wasn't the thought of being afraid of boredom or a feeling of having outlived my usefulness in society. I had enough projects planned to keep me busy for years.

I worried about my marriage.

I was scared of spending 24 hours a day with Jackie and upsetting her routine and the lifestyle she had already established in her six years of retirement.

How could we get used to living together 24 hours a day, seven days a week, 52 weeks a year till death do us part? Would we drive each other crazy or would there be a way to ease us into the world of constant togetherness?

A trip around the world lasting four months could be the answer. I began planning our adventure the moment my effective date of retirement was negotiated and agreed upon with my employer, Canon Canada Inc.

Jackie always had a mild fear of flying and our itinerary with its 19 flights looked daunting. She was also sceptical about living out of a suitcase for four months but got more and more excited about the trip as time went on.

Our first stop couldn't have been more appropriate to rekindle our romance, Tahiti and the Bali Hai Resort on the island of Moorea. Our bungalow overlooked the blue waters of the Pacific Ocean and the setting of the resort was spectacular.

There is nothing more romantic than having dinner by the light of the *tiki* torches and listening to the tropical sounds of the *ukulele.* The rhythm of the drums, the melodious voices of the native singers and a starry sky added to the enchantment.

In the Cook Islands, we stayed at a youth hostel on the slopes of a mountain overlooking the ocean. Surrounded by young people, we felt vibrant and rejuvenated. We rented a moped to explore the island's cultural and natural treasures. Joining the church service of the Cook Island Christian Church on a Sunday morning and experiencing their unique music and choir was inspirational and uplifting.

Fiji was our introduction to two different cultures, the unhurried life of the natives and the industrious culture of the Indians, brought there by the British in colonial times. They still don't mix but coexist as two different societies. We enjoyed *Kava*, a local drug widely used in Fiji. The effect of the *Kava* was relaxing, but the taste was vile.

New Zealand was a world in one country. We were overwhelmed by the diversity and stunning beauty of New Zealand. From tropical beaches to majestic mountains, from jungles to glaciers and from fjords to forests, it's all there to be explored and enjoyed. We visited pristine towns and villages with people of many backgrounds living in harmony with the native Maori population. New Zealand taught us what tolerance and acceptance can do for mankind.

Australia was the fun place everybody said it would be. From Sydney to Cairns we had a great time with a fun-loving and sociable people. Snorkeling in the Barrier Reef was even more spectacular than we expected.

Bali delivered what the travel posters promised. The beauty of the land and the people was unbelievable. We travelled from the hustle and bustle of the beach resorts of Sanur to the spiritual centre of Ubud and the tranquil beaches of Lovina and experienced a people rich in culture and modest in lifestyle rooted in deep religious beliefs. We witnessed great pride alongside oppressive poverty and felt both inspired and depressed at different times.

There is no poverty in Singapore. Singapore was nice but sterile and had the trappings of a police state. Even though the accomplishments of the Government were impressive, the city state lacked the warmth of other societies we had experienced and we were not upset to leave the small nation.

South Africa was mostly about Jackie's family and friends but we also enjoyed a safari in Kruger National Park that was unforgettable. Seeing the 'Big Five' (lions, leopards, rhinoceros, elephants and water buffalo) in their natural environment was an adventure of a lifetime.

We went on day and night safaris and experienced nature at its grandest. We travelled by train from Cape Town to Johannesburg and got to see the splendour of South Africa as well as the squalor of the remnants of Apartheid. South Africa is a country of extreme contrasts.

Our trip around the Iberian Peninsula started in the impressive city of Lisbon and took us to the breathtaking beauty of the Algarve, where tourism has not yet destroyed the traditional life of the people. We enjoyed the little villages and quaint restaurants by the sea. We travelled on to Gibraltar, the fascinating British enclave on Spanish soil.

We ventured on a short side trip across the Straits of Gibraltar to Morocco where we were mesmerized by the bustling bazaars and the mysterious *kasbahs* of Tangiers. We felt as though we were transplanted into the movie set of Casablanca. We stuck close to our guide because we were not sure if we would be able to find our way out of the labyrinth they call the *kasbah.*

Our travel through Spain was disappointing. The resorts and highrise apartment buildings along the coast catered to British and German tourists.

The traditional and historic Spain, with its quaint fishing villages, had vanished along the Mediterranean shoreline to make room for tourism. Our disappointment grew when we were unable to get tickets to visit the Alhambra. We had no idea that reservations had to be made weeks in advance to visit this marvellous palace.

All that we remember about Madrid is its rather cold and not very hospitable people, the Prado Museum with its great collection of art treasures and the bullfight at the Plaza Del Toros. We also couldn't understand the paradox that a civilized people could produce and enjoy the greatest art and at the same time take pleasure in the torture and slaughter of beautiful animals for entertainment.

Our next stop was Berlin where we devoted most of our time to our friends and relatives and the exciting nightlife of the now unified world-class city.

Our last stop was England. Friends had invited us to experience the life and luxury of the British upper class in a villa formerly owned by a Chancellor of the Exchequer, now an upscale B&B in the Cheshire countryside.

What a way to end a great trip!

We were glad to get home after four months, having achieved what we set out to do. We had rekindled our romance, learned to tolerate each other and to enjoy life to the fullest.

We seldom argued during our travels. In fact, I can only remember one minor fight between us.

We learned to respect the world we live in, experienced many cultures and appreciated the grandeur and beauty of nature along with its fragile ecosystem.

The greatest thing we acquired on this journey was a lifetime of memories that nobody will ever be able to take away from us.

The beginning of our retirement was exhilarating and we were now ready to ease into the routine of everyday life. I knew now that we would be able to enjoy each other's company in our retirement years.

Chapter 53

The Final Chapter?

There are stepping stones along the way that let you know if you have succeeded in reaching your goals in life. Mine were to be a good husband, a good father and be content with my achievements.

I understand that the quest for total happiness and making this a better world is a lifelong journey and one that can never be completed. However, I have met all the traditional obligations, set by the values I grew up with, and have also reached the milestones I set for myself.

Getting married and making my marriage work was the first and most important one. Jackie and I, probably, have a reasonably ideal marriage. We don't agree on everything, but have many shared opinions, beliefs and have the occasional quarrels.

If we had fewer disagreements, we would be bored and more would be unacceptable. We have learned to compromise, shut up or ignore minor issues between us.

Buying a house of my own had always been a dream of mine.

Making the last payment on the mortgage and knowing that the house was ours was a major dream fulfilled and the feeling of achievement was a remarkable one.

With Jackie at an anniversary party.

Having a child and being the best father I could be was a part of life I didn't want to miss out on.

To witness Toni grow up and seeing her ready to be independent and face her life as a proud and successful member of society has been most rewarding.

I will never forget the feeling of pride and accomplishment when she walked up onto the stage of War Memorial Hall at the University of Guelph to receive her Bachelor's Degree from the former Lieutenant Governor of Ontario, the Honourable Lincoln Alexander. She later studied for her Master's Degree at the University of Toronto and received it in a moving ceremony at Convocation Hall.

On both occasions, Jackie and I had tears in our eyes. We knew that we had succeeded in guiding a beautiful and remarkable child as far as we could.

Toni made it very easy for us. We certainly contributed to her education but she worked hard not to be a financial burden on us and made her years at Guelph University and at the University of Toronto a fun time to remember for the rest of her life.

There was no doubt in our minds that she would not only master life but also be a strong, independent and successful woman.

Jackie and I have achieved something that most people are only able to manage much later in life, financial independence. At the age of 54, I retired to start enjoying life without any pressure. We knew we would never be rich but were fairly certain that we could afford a lifestyle with some travel and enjoyment of other modest pleasures.

However, we still expect to get much more out of our lives.

To enjoy our grandchildren, getting involved in the community, volunteering our free time for a good cause as well as discovering new interests, hobbies and activities is our plan to keep life interesting. We did not have the time to do what we really wanted during our working years.

We'll see how well these ideas sort themselves out in Part 2 of my memoirs, if I ever get to write them.

I might be too busy enjoying retirement!

CPSIA information can be obtained at www.ICGtesting.com
Printed in the USA
LVOW06s0744230315

431624LV00002B/10/P